PERVERSE SUBSIDIES

Tax $s Undercutting Our Economies and Environments Alike

Norman Myers
Consultant in Environment and Development,
and Honorary Visiting Fellow of Green College, Oxford University, U.K.

with

Jennifer Kent
Research Associate

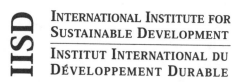

INTERNATIONAL INSTITUTE FOR
SUSTAINABLE DEVELOPMENT

INSTITUT INTERNATIONAL DU
DÉVELOPPEMENT DURABLE

Copyright © Norman Myers 1998
Published by The International Institute for Sustainable
Development

All rights reserved

Printed in Canada

Canadian Cataloguing in Publication Data

Myers, Norman.

Perverse subsidies

Includes bibliographical references.
ISBN 1-895536-09-x

1. Subsidies. 2. Environmental economies.
3. Environmental degradation.
I. Kent, Jennifer. II. International Institute for Sustainable
Development. III. Title.

HD 3641.M9 1998   333.7   C98-920062-0

This publication is printed on recycled paper.

International Institute for Sustainable Development
161 Portage Avenue East - 6th Floor
Winnipeg, Manitoba
R3B 0Y4

Tel: (204) 958-7700
Fax: (204) 958-7710
Email: info@iisd.ca

CONTENTS

Appendices

Tables

Boxes

PREFACE

Subsidies are a frequent feature of our daily lives. Some are okay, others less so. Yet these latter—especially those that are adverse to our economies and environments alike—are little known. Precisely because we are generally unaware of them, they are free to work away cancer-like in our body politic. They may total in the region of a cool $1.5 trillion a year worldwide.

This book lays out the scale and scope of these perverse subsidies. It not only looks at them as problems, it sees them as opportunities. At a time when there is a global shift in favour of the open marketplace, certain of these subsidies are being phased out, and by countries as disparate as Canada, the United States, Britain, Poland, Russia, China, Indonesia, India, Brazil and New Zealand. This is a fine start—but no more than a start, eliminating only about 5% of all such subsidies/absurdities. Governments of the world: go for it!

By definition, perverse subsidies are funds going into unsustainable development. Thus the book falls squarely into the IISD's interest in dealing with such fiscal initiatives as green taxes, budgetary reform and other incentives in support of sustainable development. As with all IISD's publications since the Institute's start-up in 1990, there is a strong message for decision-makers. In this case, that the time and circumstances are right to eliminate harmful subsidies.

May 1998

Arthur J. Hanson, President and CEO of IISD
and Norman Myers, Oxford University

ACKNOWLEDGEMENTS

This has been the most complex and challenging of all 15 "big picture" assessments I have undertaken during the past quarter century. The issues are manifold, the sectors are wide ranging, and the information base is extraordinarily deficient. So I have been far more dependent than usual on support from a host of friends and colleagues around the world. Many have sent me papers and reports, 1600 in all—a total so large that I cannot thank all these helpful individuals by name here. Certain others have supplied analytic insights, and anyone who has tackled an intractable research issue such as this one will understand that "ideas people" contribute much more than they are often aware. In the front rank of these are Stephen Barg, Jane Corbett, André de Moor, Peter Gleick, Arthur Hanson, Rick Heede, Douglas Koplow, Jim MacNeill, Mara Myers, David Pimentel, Sandra Postel, David Roodman and Ronald Steenblik.

In particular, I want to express hefty thanks to those people who have taken great amounts of time to read chapters and send back detailed critiques: Dennis Anderson (all), Stephen Barg (all), John Browder, Tom Burke (several), Peter Dauvergne, Tom Downing, Malin Falkenmark, Chris Flavin, Peter Gleick, David Hall, Arthur Hanson (all), Rick Heede (several), William Hyde, Douglas Koplow (several), Ann Platt McGinn, David Pimentel (several), Sandra Postel, Andrew Rajkumar, David Roodman (several), Carl Safina, Douglas Southgate, Ronald Steenblik (all), Michael Strauss, Michael Sutton, Michael Weber and Peter Weber.

Of course the project would not even have got onto the start line if it were not for the generous financial support of the MacArthur Foundation in Chicago. Thanks to Dan Martin, Director of the World Environment Program and Dr. Priya Shyamsundar, Program Officer, World Environment Program both of the MacArthur Foundation. I warmly welcome Dan's gesture of believing in my seemingly way-out idea in the first place; and Priya's patience and forebearance as the project dragged on far beyond its intended finish date.

Thanks too, to Arthur J. Hanson, President and CEO and Stephen Barg, Associate and Senior Program Advisor, of the IISD, who reviewed my work, and certainly helped to make this book the substantial product it has finally become. Further thanks to Julie Wagemakers for publishing this book in as little as ten weeks.

Finally and foremostly, I have conducted the project from start to finish with the unfailing support of my Research Associate, Jennifer Kent; and who researched, reference checked, and spent tireless hours on clarifying the entire manuscript. I can best express my thanks to Jennie by saying it long since became plain that her name certainly belongs on the title page.

May, 1998   Norman Myers

EXECUTIVE SUMMARY

A typical American taxpayer forks out at least $2000 a year to fund perverse subsidies, and then pays another $2000 through increased prices for consumer goods and services or through environmental degradation.

Subsidies are a prime feature of our economic landscape. That much is well understood. Not so widely recognized are "perverse" subsidies, definable here as exerting adverse effects on both the economy and the environment in the long run. This report documents the problem of perverse subsidies in five main subsidy sectors: agriculture, fossil fuels/nuclear energy, road transportation, water and fisheries. Total subsidies in these sectors, plus a few others, have long been thought to be around $1 trillion worldwide per year, which means that subsidies play a prime role in the functioning of the global economy. If perverse subsidies amount to a sizeable proportion of subsidies overall, they exert a significantly distortive impact on the global economy.

It has long been recognized that certain subsidies are detrimental to the economy. Not so well known is that many of these same subsidies are harmful to the environment as well. Subsidies for agriculture foster over-loading of croplands, leading to erosion of topsoil, pollution from synthetic fertilizers and pesticides, and release of greenhouse gases among other adverse effects. Subsidies for fossil fuels aggravate pollution effects such as acid rain, urban smog and global warming. Subsidies for road transportation promote some of the worst forms of pollution, plus excessive road building with loss of landscape amenity and other environmental ills. Subsidies for water encourage mis-use and over-use of supplies that are increasingly scarce in many lands. Subsidies for fisheries foster over-harvesting of depleted fish stocks.

This is not to say that subsidies cannot serve many useful purposes. They can overcome deficiencies of the marketplace, they can support disadvantaged segments of society, and they can promote environmentally friendly technologies. Despite their distortionary effects in many instances, then, there is nothing necessarily bad about subsidies. Sometimes we need a bit of positive distortion, otherwise we might never get as much as we want of e.g., non-polluting and renewable sources of energy with their many benefits—economic, environmental, political, social and even security benefits. True, these energy sources should be able to make their way in the marketplace when once they become established. But without help in their opening phase, they might never become established at all because of competition from entrenched energy sources. The same applies to recycling, dematerialization, agricultural set-asides, and a host of other subsidies beneficial to both the economy and the environment.

The key question is: which subsidies, of what sorts, of what scope and with what impacts, can be viewed as "perverse", i.e., adverse to society's overall interests? What is their total scale worldwide? This is a question of major importance, yet it has only recently been addressed as a salient issue of our times, let alone documented and analyzed.

Types of Subsidies

Subsidies come in many shapes and sizes. They range from financial transfers to opportunity costs, and they can be both direct and indirect. In addition to subsidies of conventional and formal type, there is a host of implicit subsidies, especially in the form of environmental externalities. Car drivers pollute everyone's atmosphere without compensating everyone, so they effectively gain a benefit at everyone's expense. Much the same applies when farmers spray pesticides which then extend their toxic effects into everyone's ecosystems; when industrialists fail to clean up and recycle water taken from everyone's water supplies, which are becoming increasingly scarce in many lands; and when loggers over-exploit forests and deplete the habitats of everyone's wildlife and biodiversity. However little it is acknowledged, these activities amount to uncompensated services from society to individuals. They should count as implicit subsidies in both spirit and substance, even though they are not dispensed by a government department through actual financial transfer. They are just as economically distorting and socially unfair, as well as environmentally damaging, as are many financial subsidies.

Environmental externalities are widespread and significant, and growing fast. The current level of environmental injury is ample evidence that they should be included in a comprehensive assessment of subsidies. While it may be unusual to include them, it is realistic. In Costa Rica, for instance, the depletion of soils, forests and fisheries results in a 25-30 percent reduction in potential economic growth. Soil erosion worldwide levies unintended costs on society of around $150 billion per year, while pesticides harm society's interests to the extent of $100 billion per year—and these two items alone mean that such hidden subsidies are almost as large as the formal subsidies in agriculture. The report's sectoral chapters document a host of similar externalities. They are environmentally adverse by definition, and their societal costs make them economically adverse too. They are subsidies in and of themselves, i.e., they are not dependent on the "up front" subsidies in the form of financial and other transfers from governments. We need not ask what proportion of the annual $150 billion "subsidy" from soil erosion is due to conventional subsidy payments to farmers. Such a subsidy is 100 percent perverse.

The Deficient Database

Despite their importance and the huge amount of literature on them, even overt subsidies, let alone implicit ones, are often difficult to document and the database is incomplete, imprecise and inconsistent. Trying to pin down the essential information is like putting one's foot on a dozen jellyfishes. Understandably perhaps, governments are reluctant to admit that they hand out subsidies of myriad sorts in munificent amounts. Still less do they want to concede that some of these subsidies could be ill conceived, out of date, politically dubious, or otherwise off target. In many instances, moreover, governments simply do not compile consistent and comprehensive records on an issue as contentious as subsidies. As a result, this report's statistics and other data are sometimes patchy, though they still tell a distinctive tale.

If it has been hard to assess subsidies overall, it has been much more difficult to come up with comprehensive estimates for perverse subsidies. Hardly any of the 1600 papers consulted tackles this question directly. In face of the virtual wall-to-wall lack of data and analysis in this respect, the author has generally had to depend on his own best-judgement assessments, based on such information and illumination as are available. He has estimated that in most instances, the proportion of all subsidies that is made up of perverse subsidies ranges from half to three quarters. When he has run the sectoral chapters past several dozen established experts in the five areas, most have proposed that the proportion should be 100 percent.

To this considerable extent, the findings are to be viewed as conservative and cautious. The holes in the database mean that many subsidies are only partially assessed or overlooked altogether, which means in turn that many estimates are surely under-estimates, possibly severe underestimates. At the same time, the author has decided to side-step the problem often associated with complex topics, that of analysis paralysis. He has chosen to go with the limited information to hand, and derive such findings as appropriate for an issue of exceptional significance. It is worthwhile to come up with an exploratory estimate of perverse subsidies (set around with numerous qualifications) on the grounds that political leaders, policy makers and the general public should be appraised of the overall scale of these subsidies—and hence of their adverse impact on both our economies and our environments.

The conclusions may still seem rough and ready to many readers, and unduly rough and ready by comparison with the precise findings presented in most reports reviewing major sectors of public policy, whether as concerns the economy or the environment. To some readers, the figures may even appear arbitrary. The author considers the exercise has been worth doing, however approximate and exploratory the outcome. He takes this stance because of (a) the size of the problem, and (b) the asymmetry of evaluation. Perverse subsidies total in

---

The United States accounts for 21 percent of perverse subsidies.

---

the rough order of $1.5 trillion, this is larger than the economies of all but five countries in the world (using purchasing power parity for the GNPs of China and India). It is a powerfully distortive factor at the heart of most governments' economic activities. Were perverse subsidies to be reduced or phased out, that would correct a factor that grossly depletes economies and environments alike, and would release enormous funds for more productive forms of fiscal management. The measure would also open up the six sectors to marketplace discipline, hopefully making them more productive and efficient.

On the grounds of their sheer scale, then, perverse subsidies need to be documented and appraised as far as possible. This leads on to the second reason for tackling an unusually "mushy" issue. As long as it remains untackled for the most part, there tends to be an implicit presumption that the perverse subsidies total must effectively be zero: there is the asymmetry of evaluation at distortive work. Of course, this is not what is intended. But as long as a problem is not accorded adequate attention, it is implicitly viewed as if it is not a problem at all. It becomes obfuscated by institutional inertia and relegated to the remotest of back burners.

Chief Findings

The principal findings are set out in Table ES.1. Total subsidies are estimated at around $1,900 billion per year, and perverse subsidies $1,450 billion. Plainly, then, perverse subsidies have the capacity to (a) exert a highly distortive impact on the global economy of $28 trillion, and (b) inflict grandscale injuries on our environments. On both counts, they foster unsustainable development. Ironically the total of almost $1.5 trillion is two and a half times larger than the Rio Earth Summit's budget for sustainable development—a sum that governments dismissed as unthinkable.

Note that:

- The OECD countries account for two thirds of all subsidies and an even larger share of perverse subsidies.

- The United States accounts for 21 percent of perverse subsidies.

- The single sector of road transportation accounts for 48 percent of all subsidies and 44 percent of perverse subsidies.

While the two totals—overall subsidies of almost $1.9 trillion per year, and perverse subsidies, approaching $1.5 trillion per year—may seem large to some observers, one should bear in mind that the documentation and calculations are often cautious and conservative to an exceptional degree. Moreover, many environmental externalities (including what could prove to be as big as the rest put together, viz. global warming) are either underestimated or omitted from the final results through sheer lack of documentation of economic costs entailed. In fact, the total for perverse subsidies, approaching $1.5 trillion per year, is surely on the low side. In the road transportation sector alone, total costs worldwide are roughly estimated at around $2 trillion per year, possibly more *(Delucci, 1997; Litman, 1996)*, of which environmental externalities could account for $1 trillion *(von Weizsacker, et al., 1997)*.

Table ES.1

SUBSIDIES: OVERALL TOTALS (billion $ per year)

Sector	Conventional Subsidies*	Environmental Externalities documented/ quantified	Total Subsidies (range)**	Perverse Subsidies (range)**
Agriculture	325	250	575	460 (390-520)
Fossil Fuels/Nuclear Energy	145	***	145	110
Road Transportation	558	359	917 (798-1041)	639
Water	60	175	235	220
Fisheries	22		22	22
Totals (rounded)	1,110	785	1,895	1,450

* *Subsidies of established and readily recognized sorts, including both direct financial transfers and indirect supports such as tax credits.*

** *Ranges: some of these estimates are supported by ranges: for details, see text. In some instances, estimates are not inserted because there is simply too little agreement even about ranges.*

*** *Regrettably it has not been possible to come up with even a reasonably agreed estimate for this value: the data are too patchy and disparate.*

Leading instances of perverse subsidies include:

1. German coal is subsidized to the tune of $6.7 billion per year. It would be economically efficient—and would reduce coal pollution such as acid rain and global warming—for the government to close down all the mines and send the workers home on full pay for the rest of their lives.

2. The annual global ocean fisheries catch—well above sustainable yield—costs around $100 billion to bring it to dockside, where it is sold for some $80 billion, the shortfall being made up with government subsidies. The result is depletion of many major fisheries to commercial extinction, plus bankruptcy of fishing businesses and sizeable unemployment.

3. The European Union has subsidized excess food production until there have been milk and wine lakes and butter and beef mountains (not to mention a manure mountain in the Netherlands). In early 1993 cereal surpluses of 30 million tonnes would have been enough to provide a more-than-sufficient diet to 75 million people for one year. Taxpayers footed the bill to supply the subsidies that boosted these crops in the first place, then they paid again to store the excess stockpiles.

4. In the United States, one government agency heavily subsidizes irrigation for crops that another agency has paid farmers not to grow. To cite the comment of an economist critic, Paul Hawken *(1997)*: "The government subsidizes energy costs so that farmers can deplete aquifers to grow alfalfa to feed cows that make milk that is stored in warehouses as surplus cheese that does not feed the hungry."

5. Also in the United States, gasoline is now cheaper than bottled water, thanks in major measure to subsidies of many sorts. Despite the view of many Americans that gasoline is expensive, it now costs less in real terms than 60 years ago. The same applies to many other aspects of United States road transportation, thanks to extensive subsidies. It may be said that Detroit and oil companies are on a kind of welfare—the unpaid costs of road transportation amount to $464 billion per year, which is equivalent to $1700 per American. Hidden subsidies for oil serve to create an energy policy by default—a policy that is actually the reverse of the government's stated priorities. Oil subsidies prolong the country's risky dependence on foreign supplies, especially from the Persian Gulf. Moreover, this de facto energy policy discourages private investments in new, cleaner technologies such as hyper-cars and other revolutionary forms of energy efficiency *(Heede, 1997; Lovins, 1996)*.

All in all, a typical American taxpayer is paying at least $2000 per year in perverse subsidies, and paying almost another $2000 more for consumer goods and services with their increased prices, or through environmental degradation.

Despite their general irrationality (though they often have a political rationale), perverse subsidies persist virtually untouched. This is because subsidies tend to create special-interest groups and political lobbies, leaving the subsidies hard to remove long after they have served their original purpose. In all major capitals, there are swarms of lobbyists, sometimes a hundred or more for each legislator. By definition, these lobbyists are bent on advancing narrow sectoral interests rather than the public good. For instance, the American Petroleum Institute spends for public relations and other forms of lobbying almost as much as the total budget of the top five United States environmental groups *(Gelbspan, 1997)*. In the face of subsidy support of this scale and leverage, most efforts to cut back on even the most perverse subsidies amount to spectacular failure. In late 1997 during the run-up to the Kyoto Conference on Climate Change, a coalition of fossil-fuel interests in the United States mounted the Global Climate Information Project, being a $13 million ad campaign pushing a do-nothing agenda.

The perverse subsidies total approaching $1.5 trillion is larger than all but the five largest national economies in the world. It is twice as large as global military spending per year, and almost twice as large as the annual growth in the world's economy. It is larger than the top 12 corporations' annual sales. It is three times as much as the annual cash incomes of the 1.3 billion poorest people, and three times as much as the international narcotics industry. Were just half of these perverse subsidies to be phased out, just half of the funds released would enable most governments to abolish their budget deficits at a stroke, to reorder their fiscal priorities in fundamental fashion, and to restore our environments more vigorously than through any other single measure.

Policy Options and Recommendations

We may have reached a propitious time to tackle perverse subsidies. Many governments are espousing the marketplace economy with its reduced scope for government intervention. Many governments also face fiscal constraints that give them further incentive to reduce activist roles in their economies. So the political climate for radical reform of subsidies is probably better than it has been for decades. The transition economies in particular face an admirable opportunity thanks to their political and economic liberalization. At the same time, the OECD countries have a special responsibility to set the pace in that they account for roughly two thirds of all subsidies and an even larger share of all perverse subsidies.

In addition, there is now a solid track record of countries that have greatly reduced or even abolished some of their subsidies. This should serve as a helpful precedent for other countries.

We may have reached a propitious time to tackle perverse subsidies. Many governments are espousing the marketplace economy with its reduced scope for government intervention. Many governments also face fiscal constraints that give them further incentive to reduce activist roles in their economies.

- New Zealand has eliminated virtually all its agricultural subsidies since the early 1980s, even though—or perhaps because—its economy is more dependent on agriculture than most OECD countries. Today there are more farmers in New Zealand than when the subsidy phase-out began. Several Latin American countries, notably Chile and Argentina, have recently taken to slashing their agricultural subsidies.

- Russia has reduced its fossil fuel subsidies from $29 billion in 1990-91 to $9 billion in 1995-96. China has slashed its subsidies from $25 to $10 billion.

- Brazil has gone far to cut back its subsidies for cattle ranching in Amazonia, thus reducing deforestation.

- Since the mid-1980s, Bangladesh and several other Asian countries have recognized that excessive applications of nitrogenous fertilizers, stimulated by extravagant subsidies, are wasteful in economic terms and highly polluting in environmental terms (eutrophication of waterways, threats to drinking water supplies). Indonesia has reduced its fertilizer subsidies from $732 to $96 million per year; Pakistan from $178 to $2 million; Bangladesh from $56 million to zero; and Philippines from $48 million to zero *(World Bank, 1997a)*.

How shall we set about the challenge of reducing perverse subsidies within the body politic? There are various policy openings available. One generalized option is to be opportunistic and to seize on emergent "windows" such as the recent strong political shift in favor of marketplace-ism. The credo of the marketplace stands opposed to subsidies, let alone perverse subsidies, as a form of government intervention that ipso facto must be distortive and counter-productive (this applies especially to the economies in transition with their switch to market liberalism). Resistance to subsidies in general also stems from the privatization ethos, which is becoming widespread. There can even be opportunity in economic crisis, such as the one which spurred New Zealand's move to drop agricultural subsidies: the public economy was finally over-burdened to breaking point. India's subsidies total over 14 percent of GDP, yet the government wishes to bring down its fiscal deficit to under 4 percent of GDP, thus supplying marked motivation to cut subsidies drastically. There could be parallel scope in the wake of an environmental crisis such as another Chernobyl-type disaster.

Formidable obstacles match these formidable opportunities. There are the special-interest groups, which often feel so addicted to their "entitlements" that they suffer severe withdrawal pangs at talk of cutting back any subsidies, let alone perverse subsidies. They find allies in bureaucratic roadblocks and institutional inertia. Then there can be upsets to equity concerns, especially with regard to who no longer gets what. Finally there is uncertainty about how reduction of perverse subsidies, however rational in principle, will work out in nitty-gritty practice; for instance, will it mean losing a competitive edge to competitors abroad?

There are various ways to overcome these obstacles. One is to formulate alternative policies that target the same subsidy objectives better, while also compensating losers. A related measure is to develop an economic-policy context that encourages subsidy removal through e.g., reducing government controls generally and freeing up markets. A subsidiary measure is to introduce "sunset" provisions that require surviving subsidies to be re-justified periodically, thus avoiding the entrenchment problem. All these measures can be strongly reinforced by promoting transparency about perverse subsidies, especially as concerns their impacts both economic and environmental, and their costs to both taxpayers and consumers.

Perhaps the most important way of all to overcome obstacles to reform is to build support constituencies, especially among the public. The more citizens know that their tax dollars and consumer payments are going down a rathole of perverse subsidies, the more there will be political support for reform. These constituencies—with an interest in the public good rather than sectoral benefit—can engage in information campaigns about the perversity of certain subsidies. Governments cannot deal with perverse subsidies without first learning about the nature and extent of these subsidies. Yet information, especially statistical data, is often incomplete and fragmented across agencies, if it exists at all. An information campaign stands a better chance of success when it stems from grassroots activism, i.e., from the taxpayers and consumers who are penalized by perverse subsidies.

There has been a success story on this front in the United States, where environmentalists such as Friends of the Earth, the Sierra Club and the Wilderness Society have made common cause with economic reformers such as Citizens for Tax Justice, Taxpayers for Common $ense and the Public Interest Research Group. This coalition of 22 NGOs has highlighted perverse subsidies through their periodic "Green Scissors" reports. The most recent report fingers 47 government projects worth $39 billion over five years, with items ranging from over-logging of the Tongass National Forest and price supports for cotton to a royalty holiday for deepwater oil drilling and aid to the Three Gorges Dam in China. The whistle blowing has done much to mobilize the social consensus and political will to tackle the offending subsidies.

In somewhat similar style, the Organization for Economic Co-operation and Development (OECD)—the Paris-based secretariat for developed countries—has run a research program for several years to appraise and evaluate the role of subsidies in advanced economies. The program has published a series of revealing reports, albeit in much more technical form than the public-oriented publications of NGOs. A parallel though more limited effort is being undertaken by the International Energy Agency, also based in Paris.

As a follow-up to information campaigns, there are action initiatives such as (a) regulation via environmental standards, tradable quotas, limits to resource exploitation, the polluter pays principle, and the precautionary principle; (b) user charges for goods and services—whether as concerns energy, transportation, water, timber, etc.—that will encourage more careful use; (c) tradable permits, the largest inside the United States being the 1990 Clean Air Act that allows permits to emit sulphur dioxide; (d) green taxes as a prime mode to change people's behavior toward the environment; and (e) environmental subsidies in support of e.g., agri-environmental measures to support soil conservation and wetland protection.

When once we start to remove perverse subsidies, it will be essential to measure progress. To meet this purpose, the International Institute has formulated a number of principles for Sustainable Development. Performance assessment should (a) be guided by a clear vision of sustainable development as the justifying framework for subsidy reform; (b) include a review of the entire economic sector in question; (c) evaluate the economic, environmental and human subsystems at issue, covering all costs and benefits in both monetary and non-monetary terms; and (d) consider equity factors within communities, also between present and future generations, with focus on such concerns as poverty and over-consumption, also human rights. Taken together, these principles can constitute a "template" for measuring progress toward sustainable development. The task should be undertaken by governments that are ready to devise a consistent framework for statistical analysis of perverse subsidies in all salient sectors, through e.g., a radical revision of their national accounts. Thereafter they will need to standardize and disseminate their information as a routine practice.

The Crux: Covert Costs of Perverse Subsidies

Finally, let us reiterate the many covert costs of perverse subsidies.

- Economically they push up the costs of government, inducing higher taxes (and often higher prices as well). In turn, this means they aggravate governments' budget deficits.

- They divert government funds from better options for fiscal support.

- They distort economies in numerous other ways. For instance, they undermine market decisions about investment, and they reduce the pressure for businesses to become more efficient.

- They tend to benefit few at the expense of many, and, worse, the rich at the expense of the poor.

- They often serve to pay the polluter.

- They foster many other forms of environmental degradation, which apart from their intrinsic harm, act as a further drag on economies.

For all these reasons, perverse subsidies militate against sustainable development. They are a no-no whether economically or environmentally or socially. If they were to be reduced (while still leaving lots of subsidies to placate special interests), there would actually be a double dividend:

1. There would be an end to the formidable obstacles imposed by perverse subsidies on sustainable development.

2. There would be a huge stock of funds available to give a new push to sustainable development—funds on a scale that would be unlikely to become available through any other source. In the case of the United States, for instance, they would amount to more than $300 billion per year. This is larger than the Pentagon budget, $240 billion, and more than twice as large as the federal deficit, $126 billion.

Compare the prospect to a car. Eliminating perverse subsides would be like, firstly, taking the brakes off and moving into high gear. Secondly it would be like giving the engine and all the other major mechanisms such a streamlining that the car would operate with undreamed of efficiency.

PART I

THE CONCEPTUAL
BACKGROUND

CHAPTER 1

INTRODUCTION: WHAT ARE SUBSIDIES?

Subsidies are often difficult to document. Such information as is available tends to be incomplete, imprecise and inconsistent. Trying to pin down the essential information is like putting one's foot on a dozen jellyfishes.

Subsidies are a prime feature of our economic landscape. That much is well understood. Not so widely recognized are "perverse" subsidies, definable here as exerting adverse effects of both environmental and economic sorts over the long run. This report aims to document the problem of perverse subsides in six main subsidy sectors: agriculture, fossil fuels/nuclear energy, road transportation, water, forestry and fisheries. Total subsidies in these sectors, plus a few others, have long been thought to approach $1 trillion worldwide per year *(Panayotou, 1993; United Nations Commission on Sustainable Development, 1994; see also Panayotou, 1993)*. This means that subsidies play a prime role in the functioning of the global economy; and if perverse subsidies amount to a sizeable proportion of subsidies overall, they exert a significantly distortive impact on the global economy.

The Brundtland Report *(World Commission on Environment and Development, 1987)* argued a decade ago that many subsidies are detrimental to the environment. Subsidies for agriculture can foster over-loading of croplands, leading to erosion and compaction of topsoil, pollution from synthetic fertilizers and pesticides, denitrification of soils, and release of greenhouse gases among other adverse effects. Subsidies for fossil fuels aggravate pollution effects such as acid rain, urban smog and global warming, while subsidies for nuclear energy serve to generate exceptionally toxic waste with exceptionally long half-life. Subsidies for road transportation lead to overloading of road networks, a problem that is aggravated as much as relieved by the building of new roads when further subsidies promote over-use of cars; the sector also generates pollution of several sorts. Subsidies for water encourage mis-use and over-use of water supplies that are increasingly scarce in many lands. Subsidies for forestry encourage over-exploitation at a time when many forests have been reduced through excessive

---

In Costa Rica the depletion of soils, forests and fisheries results in a 25-30 percent reduction in potential economic growth.

---

logging, acid rain and agricultural encroachment. Subsidies for fisheries foster over-harvesting of already depleted fish stocks. Hence the environmental consequences of perverse subsidies can be widespread and profound.

This is not to say that subsidies cannot serve many positive purposes. They can overcome deficiencies of the marketplace, they can support disadvantaged segments of society, and they can promote environmentally friendly technologies. The key question is: which subsidies, of what sorts, of what scope and with what impacts, can be viewed as "perverse", i.e., adverse to society's overall and long-term interests? What is their total scale worldwide? Clearly this is a question of major importance, yet it has scarcely been identified as a salient issue of our times, let alone documented and analyzed (except for recent papers by *de Moor, 1997, and Roodman, 1996*).

This report presents findings from a short-term project[1] undertaken with the principal aim of establishing whether there is a significant problem of perverse subsidies worldwide, and if so, determining the nature and scale of the problem. A further aim has been to provide a framework of analysis and evaluation for the generic issue of perverse subsidies. The project has been an exploratory exercise, with no claim to be definitive. To the extent that it demonstrates there is indeed a problem with significance for public policy, the author hopes it will prompt other researchers to investigate the issue in more detail.

This Introduction addresses the preliminary question "What are subsidies?" We cannot determine what perverse subsidies are without an intellectual lock on what constitutes a subsidy at all. It is a complex issue, hence it warrants an extended examination here. There are many sorts and conditions of subsidies, and they come in all shapes and sizes. Indeed they are a pervasive phenomenon of modern economies and hence a deep-seated factor of life both public and private. Not surpassingly, they have become a prime instrument of public policy. How do they arise? In what sectors? What do they cost? Whom do they benefit? Does anybody "dis-benefit"? What is their impact on the economy at both macro and micro levels? Are there better ways to achieve the purposes intended by subsidies?

Definition

A subsidy is a form of government support to an economic sector (or institution, business, individual), generally with the aim of promoting an activity that

---

1   *The research project has investigated the issue in a "first cut" manner. It has been largely a desk project, undertaken from Oxford, England, where the principal output is this book, together with a series of professional papers and popular articles. A parallel project, focusing on economic incentives and disincentives, has been undertaken by Andre de Moor under the auspices of the Earth Council, with findings published as de Moor, 1997, and de Moor and Calamai, 1997. It does not look at forestry or fisheries, and while it documents perverse subsidies extensively, it does not come up with a firm estimate of their magnitude.*

the government considers beneficial to the economy overall and to society at large. Indeed, this is one of the main roles that governments are created to perform: to encourage activities which, if left solely to markets, would occur in unfavorable quantities—or, to use the economist's phrase, less than socially optimal amounts. The subsidy can be supplied in the form of a monetary payment or other transfer, or through relief of an opportunity cost *(Keppler, 1995; Koplow, 1993; Michaelis, 1995; Organization for Economic Co-operation and Development, 1997; Pearce and Warford, 1993; Steenblik, 1995 and 1997).*

Alternatively defined, a subsidy amounts to any government expenditure that makes a resource such as energy or water cheaper to produce than its full economic cost, or makes a product, notably food or education, cheaper to consumers. Energy can be made to look cheaper than it really is if subsidies pay some of its cost. Many developing countries offer "lifeline rates" for electricity, i.e., subsidized discounts on the first increment of electricity bought each month, thus constituting an implicit expenditure. These subsidies are directed at the poor, and the electricity is made cheaper on the grounds that all citizens, no matter how impoverished, should be able to enjoy a modicum of convenient energy. Those people who cannot be reached by electricity are often given a kerosene subsidy instead. Most energy subsidies in developing countries assist consumers, whereas in developed countries they usually support producers.

The subsidies above are all direct subsidies. There can be indirect subsidies too. Consider road transportation in the United States, where direct subsidies for roads, related infrastructure, etc., totaled around $90 billion in 1990 *(MacKenzie et al., 1992).* If the value of free employee parking—largely stimulated in the first place by the car culture, dependent in turn on direct subsidies for road transportation—is included, the figure rises to roughly $140 billion, while some economists would add in the costs of traffic congestion, estimated to be at least $100 billion.

All five sectoral chapters in this report deal with natural resources. In this generic field, subsidies are so diverse that they can include the following: financing or below-market pricing of natural resources such as agricultural lands, fossil fuels, water, forests and fisheries, plus associated infrastructures; commodity price programs; below-market supply of exploration rights for oil, coal and natural gas, together with tax preferences for extraction of these resources; and a lengthy list of minor supports such as tax preferences for private-vehicle travel relative to other modes of transportation. Subsidies can also be taken to include unpaid costs, notably environmental costs that have not been internalized through government policies; by their very nature, they rank as implicit subsidies. For further examination of this latter topic, see relevant sections in this chapter, below, and in Chapter 2.

In addition, government costs of environmental protection can be regarded as a subsidy since these are costs that in a perfect market would be internal to market transactions. There are further subsidy-style incentives to support the environment. In the United States, these include: deductability or direct tax credits for enhanced energy measures (non-polluting and renewable energy sources, energy efficiency and conservation); agricultural set-aside programs; funding of forest replanting costs; tax incentives for preserving open spaces; and government sharing of costs for biodiversity protection *(Toman, 1995; see also Organization for Economic Co-operation and Development, 1995).*

For a look at three main types of subsidies, see Box 1.1; and for a further division into subsidies broad and narrow, see Box 1.2. See also Table 1.1.

Box 1.1

THREE MAIN TYPES OF SUBSIDIES

First are subsidies that provide preferential treatment for a particularly prominent sector. Education, for example, is widely subsidized to ensure that children receive enough schooling for them to make the most of their lives and to contribute to society through their work. This means that education ranks as both a private and a public good: it benefits not only the individual but society too *(Keppler, 1995).*

Second are subsidies that encourage a certain activity or process which otherwise would not be undertaken at a sufficient level. Lead-free gasoline is subsidized in certain countries to encourage motorists to use it rather than leaded gasoline. Similarly, wind power, photovoltaics and other new forms of energy deserve to be subsidized because they are renewable and do not pollute. Recycling schemes and equipment are often subsidized to encourage the re-use of waste. For a host of illustrations, see *Gale and Barg, 1995.*

Third are subsidies that ensure the survival and stability of certain industries of strategic importance, e.g., defence and agriculture. In addition, both sunrise and sunset industries are frequently subsidized on the grounds that such industries would not otherwise survive.

Table 1.1

A: TYPES OF SUBSIDY: ESTABLISHED CLASSIFICATION

Type of Subsidy	Examples
Making direct transfers	Direct grants or payments to consumers or producers; Provision of inputs at below market prices
Changing market prices	Reducing market prices to consumers; Increasing prices received by producers; Import tariffs or barriers
Preferential tax policies	Tax credits, exemptions, deferrals, exclusions and deductions
Reducing input costs	Preferential loans and loan or liability guarantees; Indirect expenditures such as R & D
Reducing the cost of complementary goods	Provision of infrastructure goods

Source: Putnam and Bartlett, 1993

B. TYPES OF SUBSIDY: RECENT CLASSIFICATION

Type of Subsidy	Examples
I. Transfer to Producers	1. Market price support
	2. Payments to producers, e.g., deficiency payments
	3. Payments to factors of production based on:
	a. Use of a variable input, e.g., water at below-market prices; fuel rebates etc.)
	b. Use of a service, e.g., extension services, state-provided pest control
	c. On-site investment, e.g., capital grants, interest concessions
	d. Constraints on factor use, e.g., the U.S. Conservation Reserve Program.
	4. Direct payments to producers, based on
	a. Past support, e.g., the U.S. PFC payment
	b. Past income, e.g., income tax concessions, disaster payments
	c. Established minimum income, i.e., welfare payments
II. Transfers to Consumers	
Other Transfers	General Services; R&D; training and education; Marketing and promotion; Public stockholding

Source: Organisation for Economic Co-operation and Development, 1997a; see also Steenblik, 1995.

Box 1.2

SUBSIDIES BROAD AND NARROW

Subsidies can be both broad and narrow. The conventional or textbook definition of subsidies covers the narrow sense. The broad sense applies when the cost of an activity is not entirely borne by the source of the activity but by some other agent who may not directly and unequivocally benefit from the activity. Scandinavia can be said to be subsidizing Britain's electricity generation by bearing the cost of acid rain which falls on Scandinavia as a result of British sulphur dioxide emissions. This is a way of bringing externalities into the debate—and just as subsidies are a case of government intervention, externalities are a case of what happens when governments do not intervene *(Templet, 1995)*.

Whereas narrow subsidies include only monetary transfers, broad subsidies include transfers both monetary and non-monetary. Precisely because of their "broadness", broad subsidies are often difficult if not impossible to quantify. Nor is it always clear who or what is the cause of a broad subsidy. For instance, the cost of auto pollution is not easily attributable to any particular agent since many parties are involved. In any case, motorists do not intend that the pollution-absorbing environment should subsidize their driving. By contrast, a narrow subsidy, e.g., a payment to farmers, is easily attributable to governments, and its intent is clear.

Precisely because of their varied manifestations, it is not easy to compare subsidies, even though that is required for this report. Too often we run into the problem of apples and oranges. An agricultural subsidy of one dollar in the United States is very different from a similar sum in India. For present purposes, however, it is considered acceptable to view subsidies as essentially of one type, while bearing in mind their highly differentiated nature. The issue here is not to determine that some perverse subsidies should be reduced or eliminated while others should be left alone. The aim is to rid ourselves of perverse subsidies—not on the grounds that they are subsidies but that they are perverse. So we should not be overly concerned with multiple manifestations of subsidies. Nor should we bother too much about pinning down their precise size and values, despite the apples and oranges dilemma. There is little need to calculate our precise speed if we are heading over the cliff.

Equity Concerns

Subsidy support for one activity will cause countervailing effects for other activities. This is a built-in factor. A subsidy is like a cake of limited size, and if one person enjoys a larger slice, other persons have to make do with smaller slices. If everybody receives a subsidy, nobody does. By their very nature, then, subsidies have a marked distributional effect. This means in turn that subsidies carry all manners of equity implications, as would apply to any situation where a group receives financial assistance from the government. Similarly, subsidies can be supplied for social rather than economic reasons, e.g., to relieve unemployment, to offset disease (notably black lung disease in miners), or to correct regional disparities in the notable cases of Canada and the European Union.

It is these equity concerns that make subsidies a politically contentious issue. Whom should governments aim to assist through subsidies: the poor, the unemployed, the socially disadvantaged, rural residents, entrepreneurs in general and innovators in particular, and both sunrise and sunset industries? The list can be long. Should the government target many or few? Future equity questions are equally important. Do we owe anything to our descendants in terms of securing their livelihoods, especially if that is at the expense of our own?

Regrettably, experience shows that in virtually all societies, it is often the powerful who obtain subsidies by causing weaker groups to shoulder some of the costs of their activities: "To him that hath shall be given." In the case of United States agriculture, huge subsidies go to a few "farmers" who are actually millionaire industrialists and rarely set foot on a farm. In Colombia, the largest 1 percent of farmers receive 50 percent of public credits, while the smallest 50 percent of farmers receive little more than 4 percent *(Dasgupta, 1994)*. In Indonesia, kerosene subsidies are supposed to help the poorest people, yet nine-tenths go to richer people *(Hope and Singh, 1995)*. In an international context, annual subsidies for a dairy cow in the United States exceed the per-capita income of half the world's population *(Bovard, 1996)*. Each American farmer receives annual subsidies worth roughly 100 times the income of a corn farmer in Philippines *(United Nations Development Programme, 1997)*.

Despite their distortionary effects, there is nothing necessarily bad about subsidies. Sometimes we need a bit of positive distortion, otherwise we might never get as much as we want of e.g., non-polluting and renewable sources of energy with their many manifold benefits—economic, environmental, political, security, social and ethical benefits. True, these energy sources should be able to make their way in the open marketplace when once they become established—but without help in their opening phase, they might never become established at all because of competition from entrenched energy sources. The same applies to recycling, dematerialization, agricultural set-asides, and a host of other subsidies beneficial to the environment *(Barg, 1996)*. In addition, Certain subsidies

7

should be established simply because they are a good thing. In Chapter 5 on Road Transportation, we shall see that the sector generates huge spillover costs such as traffic pollution, accidents and injuries, and even military supports. These adverse impacts could be countered by subsidies for alternatives to private cars, notably buses and trains. It seems altogether justifiable from economic and social standpoints that there should be sizeable subsidies for e.g., rapid transit systems in San Francisco and Washington DC, even though these two are among the higher-income cities in the United States.

Why Subsidies Are Often Unpopular

Despite their many positive features, subsidies often receive bad press. For one thing, they have grown to be enormously costly for governments. The Indian government spends about $40 billion per year on subsidies, a whopping 14 percent of GDP *(Indian National Institute of Public Finance and Policy, 1997)*. In the United States, direct subsidies for agriculture, fossil fuels/nuclear energy and road transportation amounted in 1996 to $189 billion or 12 percent of the federal budget. The European Union's Common Agricultural Policy puts over $300 onto the average citizen's food bill. If governments were to reduce their spending on subsidies, they would take a solid step toward better balancing of their budgets.

A second and still more significant problem with subsidies is that through their potential feather-bedding effect they encourage inefficiency and waste of all sorts. As concerns environmental resources in particular (farmlands, forests, water, fisheries, etc.), they foster mis-use and over-use of the resources. They perpetuate the status quo in production processes by making it cheaper to continue with existing methods than to adopt costly new technologies. Irrigation subsidies encourage farmers in developed and developing countries alike to persist with inefficient but cheap flooding methods rather than moving on to more expensive but more efficient trickle-drip techniques.

In sum, certain subsidies can promote greater economic efficiency and productivity, as in the case of the New Deal's agricultural subsidies. Or they can foster social equity, as in the case of subsidized transportation for poorer sectors of society. But they can become over-abundant, unnecessary and distortive. For extreme instance, water subsidies in Saudi Arabia (of all countries) are so high that farmers can even afford to shower their cows to keep them cool.

For more on the pro's and con's of subsidies, see Box 1.3. Readers looking for a more extended and technical treatment of subsidies can consult Appendix 1.1.

Box 1.3

PRO'S AND CON'S OF SUBSIDIES

There has been a great expansion in subsidies this century, stemming in part from the two world wars and the 1930s depression. These events have served to generate subsidies of many new sorts, sometimes with multi-billion dollar budgets and often with beneficial purposes. For instance, food subsidies in developing countries improve nutrition among the poor, they ensure markets for farmers, and they help foster socioeconomic equality across income groups. Trouble arises when subsidies are retained long after they have exceeded their shelf life—by which time too they may have expanded way beyond what was originally envisaged. Regrettably, institutional inertia often prevents them from being reduced, let alone eliminated. In any case, ditching them is often perceived to be a vote loser for governments. In fact, subsidies are often used to appease large and politically powerful groups whose support is of special value to the government. Farmers in many countries lobby for agricultural subsidies, and governments are reluctant to disenchant a group that wields exceptional political muscle.

In the United States in particular, special-interest groups are adept at penetrating the political process and using their electoral influence in order to secure subsidies *(Keppler, 1995)*. In Washington DC there are 90,000 lobbyists, plus 60,000 lawyers for back-up, swarming around Capitol Hill, or 280 for every member of Congress. This lobbying costs at least $100 million each month, and is steadily increasing *(Shuldiner and Raymond, 1998)*. Between 1993 and mid-1996, American oil and gas companies gave $10.3 million to political campaigns, and received tax breaks worth $4 billion *(Roodman, 1996)*.

Many subsidies benefit more people than those directly involved. If these side benefits or externalities are not paid for, the subsidized activities may not take place at all, or on a scale smaller than is socially desirable. People who travel by bus or train benefit those who travel by car, because they leave the roads less congested and create less pollution than would be the case if everyone used cars. Unless the car users subsidize bus and train riders in order to pay for the clearer roads, fewer people will use buses and trains than is optimal. To this extent, subsidies make the free market work better. They should be anathema to neither politicians nor voters.

But many subsidies make the market work less well, especially in the long run. Because the amount of a subsidized activity will likely increase, the result tends to be inefficiencies, waste, pollution and other ills whether economic or environmental, often both.

The Scale of Subsidies

Now for a quick look at the scale of the subsidies covered in this report. How do they stack up against other outlays by governments?

- Subsidies for agriculture in OECD countries are in the order of $300 billion per year. Compare it to the estimated cost of upgrading developing-world agriculture, $40 billion per year; and the current inadequate funding of the international network of research centers for agriculture, a mere $235 million per year.

- Subsidies for fossil fuels in just the United States are around $20 billion per year. This is equivalent to 16 percent of the United States federal deficit, or 71% of the annual spending of the World Bank.

- Subsidies for water in developing countries total $48 billion per year. This to be compared with the budget for the proposed Water and Sanitation Decade (only partially implemented due to shortage of funds), $15 billion per year. This latter sum that would have gone far to overcome the many water-related diseases that cause 80 percent of developing-country sickness and that largely lead to several million child deaths per year.

Note too that many subsidies generate knock-on or ripple effects. The energy subsector of oil forms the economic mainstay of several Middle East countries, plus large segments of the economies of Russia, Great Britain, Norway, Mexico, Venezuela, Indonesia and Nigeria. Oil subsidies reverberate through associated sectors such as transportation and agriculture, plus banking interests and many others.

Environmental Externalities

We have looked briefly at indirect subsidies. These make up a good share of conventional subsidies, as one would expect. Not so well recognized are certain other indirect subsidies that deserve a category of their own: the implicit and otherwise "hidden" subsidies of environmental externalities (or spillover costs). When I drive my car and pollute everyone's atmosphere without compensating everyone, I effectively gain a freebie opportunity at everyone's expense. Much the same applies when farmers spray pesticides which then extend their toxic effects into everyone's ecosystems; when industrialists fail to clean up and recycle water taken from everyone's water supplies, which are becoming increasingly scarce in many lands; and when loggers over-exploit forests and deplete the habitats of everyone's wildlife. However little it is acknowledged, these activities amount to implicit subsidies in both spirit and substance, even though they are not dispensed by a government department through actual financial transfer. They are just as economically distorting and socially unfair, as well as environmentally damaging, as are many financial subsidies.

They are also sizeable, and they occur in all walks of life. Consider, for illustration, some externality costs imposed on society by certain corporations in the United States. The health consequences of cigarettes cost the public an estimated $54 billion a year. Similarly, society bears costs through workers who suffer injuries and accidents in unsafe workplaces, $142 billion, or die from workplace cancer, $275 billion. Estimates from a number of studies reveal a conservative total figure of $2.6 trillion per year, roughly five times as much as corporate profits *(Estes, 1996)*. On top of this are the severe and sometimes permanent depletion or destruction of the productive capital of society in the form of environmental resources, as will be demonstrated in this report.

As this report will show, environmental subsidies—or externalities, to give them their technical label—are widespread and significant, and growing fast. The current level of environmental injury is ample evidence that they should be included in a comprehensive assessment of subsidies. In Costa Rica, for instance, the depletion of soils, forests and fisheries results in a 25-30 percent reduction in potential economic growth *(Cruz et al., 1992)*. As we shall see in Chapter 3 on Agriculture, soil erosion worldwide levies unintended costs on society of around $150 billion per year, while pesticides harm society's interests to the extent of $100 billion per year. This means that these implicit subsidies are almost as large as the conventional subsidies in agriculture. In Chapter 6 on Water, we shall see that conventional subsidies of $58 billion per year are widely exceeded by environmental externalities of $175 billion. We shall come across similar instances in the other three sectoral chapters (and in Appendix I on Forestry). These implicit subsidies are environmentally adverse by definition, and their societal costs make them economically adverse too.

Perhaps the most perverse aspect of this is that the GNP method of accounting generally presents such activities as economic pluses—whereas, and as noted, they should be counted as distinct minuses. When soil erosion causes farmers to apply extra fertilizer to compensate for loss of plant nutrients, this is viewed as an economic activity to be recorded as an additional item for GNP—while the costs to society are disregarded. The Exxon oil spill caused clean-up efforts costing $3 billion; the GNP arithmetic counted them as an advance for GNP. When Kobe city was hit by an earthquake, one Japanese economist added up the rebuilding activities and declared the country's economy had actually come out ahead.

We shall take a longer look in Chapter 2 at environmental values and how they are being depleted—and how far that gives rise to many implicit subsidies. Note that these should rank as subsidies in and of themselves. They are not dependent on the "up front" subsidies in the form of financial and other transfers from governments, so we need not ask what proportion of the annual $150 billion "subsidy" from soil erosion is due to conventional subsidy payments to farmers. All environmental externalities are regarded in this report as 100 percent perverse.

At the same time, we should note a salient difference from subsidies as generally understood. Formal subsidies raise problems because of what governments do, while environmental subsidies raise problems because of what governments do not do. Obviously, this has major implications for policy.

Research Methodology [2]

Understandably perhaps, governments are reluctant to admit that they hand out subsidies of myriad sorts in munificent amounts. Still less do they want to concede that some of these subsidies could be ill conceived, out of date, politically dubious, or otherwise off target. In many instances, moreover, governments simply do not compile consistent and comprehensive records on an issue as contentious as subsidies *(Caccia, 1996)*. The consequence for this report is that the author has come up with rather patchy sets of statistics, which nonetheless tell a distinctive tale.

As the 700 references show, there are huge amounts of literature on subsidies— on their nature and extent, their positive and negative features, their costs and benefits, and so on, all as applied to the six major sectors dealt with in this report and as manifested in countries right around the world. Given this abundance of background material, then, it has been surprising that there is no clear, concise agreement on just what subsidies amount to. Every standard definition seems to have several qualifiers, and each of those has its own string of qualifiers. Still less are there specific accounts of how many subsidies apply in each sector, at least on the part of the principal countries involved.

Even in the case of the United States, there are only partial and conflicting data for agriculture and road transportation, notwithstanding that these two sectors account for direct subsidies totaling $157 billion per year. As for specific and precise data by sub-sector, statistical information is still more difficult to track down. When I have asked American economists and other analysts why this should be so, they have told me there are so many covert and indirect subsidies, plus overlapping and otherwise cross-related subsidies (apart from the fact that there is limited consensus on what is a subsidy anyway), that most professionals feel the task of assembling all relevant data would simply be too time consuming.

---

2 *The research has been almost entirely a desk effort conducted through library research, together with papers and reports solicited from colleagues, eventually totaling some 1600 items. The project budget and time frame have made limited allowance for travel to consult experts, though the author has been able through other means to discuss with colleagues in Britain, France, Italy, Switzerland, the United States, Canada, Australia, Indonesia, India, Brazil and Mexico among other countries, and with organizations such as United Nations agencies, the World Bank, the European Commission, and the Organization for Economic Cooperation and Development, also with numerous research centers.*

True, the situation is better for the United States with respect to fisheries. But as concerns water, the information is even more fragmentary than in agriculture and energy, even though water subsidies appear to total "only" $5 billion per year, meaning that this smaller figure could perhaps be expected to be more accurate and precise. There seems little prospect of arriving at a credibly comprehensive figure for just the main subsidies in the water sector without a great deal more background research. This report presents water findings that are far from complete, so the statistical conclusions reflect only part of the subsidies picture in that sector. Not that more research would alter the prime conclusion with respect to water: that subsidies of multiple kinds exert widespread and significant impacts of adverse sort. Even with a research project of several times as much scope as this one, it would be difficult to track down the full array of subsidies in each of the five sectors. This is all the more regrettable in that a main reason why perverse subsidies persist is that few people have a clear idea of how many subsidies are at work, let alone whether they work for good or ill.

The situation is epitomized by the forestry sector. Research has generated volumes of documentation and analysis, but little comprehensive and conclusive. The best research effort over a whole year has produced a total for subsidies worldwide of only $3 billion per year, though this is a very partial estimate due to sheer lack of data from several major forestry countries and only limited data from the rest. Environmental externalities were likewise assessed at no more than $3 billion per year, even though there is much circumstantial evidence to suggest they could be many times more. The grand total for this sector could well be as much as $50 billion per year. Because this sector could be documented and evaluated only at a much lower level than the other five sectors, the author has reluctantly decided to relegate it to Appendix I.2 (to be found at the end of the text), and to omit it from the calculations of subsidies and perverse subsidies overall.

To this considerable extent, the findings presented here are to be viewed as conservative and cautious. The holes in the database mean that many subsidies are only partially assessed or overlooked altogether, which means in turn that many estimates are surely under-estimates. For illustrations of the uncertainties, ambiguities and inconsistencies that seem endemic to data on subsidies, see Box 1.4.

Moreover, the subsidies picture is constantly shifting. In recent years, New Zealand and Australia have gone far to eliminate their agricultural subsidies, while Russia and China have undertaken a parallel effort with their fossil fuel subsidies. At the same time, subsidies for agriculture, electricity and water in many developing countries seem to be expanding. So the author has often found himself aiming at a moving target. Worse: while a sudden reduction of subsidies (in New Zealand, Russia, etc.) is usually well documented if only because it is a remarkable occurrence, a steady rise in subsidies is more likely to go unnoticed among the "background noise" of on-going economics and politics. In addition, certain sets of subsidy figures, notably those for tropical forestry, have been well established for the mid-1980s, but have been largely neglected in the professional literature since then. As it happens, a set of increases in forestry subsidies in one tropical country has often been balanced out by a parallel set of decreases in another tropical country. So the mid-1980s figures for forestry subsidies in tropical countries may not have become much different today, except for a moderate increase to reflect factors such as increased exploitation.

Box 1.4

INCONCLUSIVE STATISTICS

Some of the most important subsidy issues are subject to remarkably variable documentation. For instance, there is doubt about the cost to the United States of defending oil shipping lanes, primarily in the Persian Gulf (an implicit and concealed subsidy to oil users, especially car drivers). Estimates range from the Department of Defence's $1 billion to the Cato Institute's $70 billion per year. The range reflects problems of assessing defense spending in particular regions, and widely differing assumptions about the potential fall in military expenditures were oil protection no longer needed *(Koplow, 1995)*. There is even confusion about the cost to the United States of fighting the Gulf War, estimated to be anywhere from $12 to $30 billion.

Equally surprising are the divergent estimates of energy subsidies in the United States, ranging from $5 to $80 billion per year *(Toman, 1996)*. The Department of Energy cannot make up its mind between less than $5 billion and more than $14 billion per year, while the Alliance To Save Energy puts them at somewhere between $21 billion and $36 billion. In the latter case, the wide variation reflects different definitions. Should subsidies include, for instance, government-funded R & D, and government compensation for past occupational diseases such as "black lung" among former miners? A more remarkable review cites estimates ranging from as little as $5 billion in the entire economy to as much as $174 billion in the transportation sector alone, with only part of the divergence stemming from differences in definition *(Shelby et al., 1996)*.

In the upshot, the author has decided to side-step the problem often associated with ultra-complex topics, viz. the problem of analysis paralysis. He has chosen to go with the best and most recent set of data available for each of the six sectors. This means that he has not been able to come up with an assembly of overall findings for a year as recent as 1995 (though most data are of post-1992 vintage). To that extent, he has often found himself comparing likes with unlikes. But then, a similar problem arises with respect to many aspects of this report. A $1000 subsidy for commercial logging in Alaska is far different from a $1000 subsidy for cattle ranching in Amazonia.

Some observers might feel that a single composite figure for perverse subsidies in all six sectors and for all parts of the world is simplistic. Nonetheless, the author has believed it worthwhile to come up with such a figure (set around with numerous qualifications) on the grounds that political leaders, policy makers and the general public should be appraised of the overall scale of these perverse subsidies—and hence of their adverse impact on both our economies and our environments.

In summary, while it has been difficult to pin down the scale of subsidies in general, it has been still more difficult to do as much for perverse subsidies. The report's findings should be viewed as more than indicative while less than comprehensive (let alone conclusive). The purpose of the research has been limited to demonstrating how far there is indeed a problem of perverse subsidies. The reader may judge for himself or herself whether the case has been made. When the author began the project, he had reason to suppose that the total might well be somewhere between $400 and $800 billion a year (if he did not suspect the total would be in that significant order, he would not have taken on the project). Were the total to have worked out in fact to be somewhere near the median of $600 billion, it would ironically have matched the budget figure proposed for Agenda 21 at the Rio Earth Summit, a figure calculated in support of sustainable development—whereas perverse subsidies foster unsustainable development.

Key Caveat

Herein lies the biggest caveat of all. While it is not overwhelmingly difficult to document the scale of subsidies, it is much more difficult to come with substantive estimates for perverse subsidies. Hardly any of the 1600-plus papers on subsidies consulted by the author tackles the question of how many of these subsidies are perverse. In face of this virtual wall-to-wall lack of data and analysis, the author has had to depend on his own best-judgement assessments, based on such information and illumination as are available. His conclusions may seem rough and ready to many readers, and unduly rough and ready by comparison with the precise findings presented in most reports reviewing major sectors of public policy, whether as concerns the economy or the environment. To some readers, the figures may even appear arbitrary; and some may appear simply off target. The author makes no excuse for this. He considers the exercise has been worth doing, however preliminary, approximate and exploratory the outcome.

He takes this stance because of (a) the size of the problem, and (b) the asymmetry of evaluation. If the perverse subsidies total were not $600 billion but $400 billion (let alone $800 billion), it would still be larger than the GNP of most countries in the world. At this order of magnitude, it is a powerfully distortive factor at the heart of most governments' economic activities around the world. Were these perverse subsidies to be reduced or phased out, that would correct a factor that grossly depletes economies and environments alike, and would release enormous funds for more productive forms of fiscal management. The measure would also open up the six sectors to marketplace discipline, hopefully making them more productive and efficient.

On the grounds of their sheer scale, then, perverse subsidies need to be documented and appraised as far as possible. As long as they remain untackled, there tends to be an implicit presumption that their total must effectively be zero: there is the asymmetry of evaluation at distortive work. Of course, this is not what is intended. But as long as a problem is not accorded adequate attention, it is implicitly viewed as if it is not a problem at all.

These are the twin rationales for attempting to come up with a quantified assessment of perverse subsidies and their magnitude. Again: the estimates of the percentage shares of subsidies enjoyed (sic) by perverse subsidies, together with the dollar estimates of their values, are strictly best-judgement affairs—no more and no less. Future research will no doubt come up with more accurate and precise estimates, and the author hopes this will be both speedy and bountiful. To date, we must make do with whatever is available—and resist the temptation to say we simply cannot appraise perverse subsidies in quantified fashion at all. The reader is asked to attach this qualifier to any quantified assessment he or she comes across in this report. For more on the central question of scientific uncertainty and how to deal with it in the policy domain, see the next chapter.

Now that we have determined what subsidies are in general, we shall go on in Chapter 2 to take a conceptual crack at the character and extent of perverse subsidies. Thereafter we shall review the five main categories of sectoral subsidies in the course of Chapters 3-7. In Chapter 8 we shall consider an assessment of perverse subsidies overall, before going on in Chapter 9 to appraise the scope for policy responses and other ameliorative measures.

CHAPTER 2

WHEN DO SUBSIDIES BECOME PERVERSE?

What governments supply with an environmentally supportive right hand is often taken away by half a dozen left hands wielding subsidies.

How shall we define a "perverse" subsidy, i.e., when does a subsidy become detrimental to both the environment and the economy in the long run? Many subsidies that cause environmental harm may nonetheless meet economic needs through e.g., the provision of jobs in rural areas where there are few other work opportunities, or through lower prices for staple foods in developing nations. The opposite applies to subsidies that are environmentally supportive while economically costly, e.g., financial support to save those threatened species that have no perceived economic value. Some subsidies may be positive in one field and merely neutral in the other. For a subsidy to qualify as perverse, it must exert effects that are demonstrably and significantly adverse in both fields.

Many subsidies have been constructive at the time of their introduction, but have later become perverse. They have completed their original purpose but have not been eliminated afterwards. The American West was settled partly in response to a host of subsidies established by the United States government in the late 1800s. The aim of these subsidies was to encourage settlers to exploit the West's resources as rapidly and widely as possible, which was an eminently desirable goal at the time. Today, however, the West's settlement frontier has long since closed, and its resources are more commonly viewed as a public trust to be carefully managed for all Americans both now and in the future. Resource exploitation has often degenerated into over-logging of forests, over-grazing of grasslands, depletion of watersheds, over-pumping of aquifers, decline of biodiversity, and mining pollution of water and air, sometimes with toxic wastes. Yet many of the original pro-exploitation subsidies remain in place, even though they are now harmful to both the environment and the economy at large and over the long term.

The same applies to a host of government subsidies around the world. Indeed, certain subsidies have become so extensive and entrenched and are so environmentally harmful that subsidy policies may unwittingly represent a prime state-

---

Lobbyists in Washington DC, seeking to retain perverse subsidies among other special interests, now spend over $100 million each month.

The American Petroleum Institute spends for public relations and other forms of lobbying almost as much as the total budget of the top five U.S. environmental groups. During the late 1997 run-up to the Kyoto Conference on Climate Change, fossil-fuel interests in the United States spent $13 million on an ad campaign pushing a do-nothing agenda.

---

ment of a government's environmental policy *(MacNeill, 1994)*. True, governments are becoming alerted to the virtues of the environmental cause, and many are taking safeguard measures. But what they supply with an environmentally supportive right hand is often taken away by half a dozen left hands wielding subsidies. For further treatment of these generic issues, *see de Moor, 1997; Gale and Barg, 1995; Organization for Economic Co-operation and Development, 1995 and 1996; Rogers, 1995; Roodman, 1996; and Serageldin, 1995.*

Consider, for instance, the central function of commercial energy in virtually every economy around the world, and hence the pivotal role played by energy subsidies. These subsidies can harm the environment not only directly, but indirectly by increasing the environmental degradation associated with key sectors such as agriculture, industry and transportation *(Koplow, 1995)*. Artificially cheap energy is the basis of the United States agricultural system, ostensibly the most productive in the world. When measured by output per unit labour input, this may be true, but when reckoned by energy input per food energy output, it is one of the world's least efficient, using nine calories of fossil fuel energy to produce one calorie of food energy *(Pimentel and Pimentel, 1996)*. In addition, energy subsidies for fossil fuels (the main target for such subsidies) rig the market against renewable and non-polluting forms of energy *(MacNeill, 1994)*. In all these ways, many energy subsidies run counter to the interests of both the economy and the environment.

When a perverse subsidy is threatened with removal, however, a host of vested interests are likely to protest that the step will cause profound harm to the economy. These protesters should consider the case of New Zealand, where the government set about eliminating virtually all agricultural subsidies in the mid-1980s. This was a momentous step for a country deeply dependent on agriculture. In the upshot, there have been manifold benefits for both the economy and the environment, and hardly any long-term problems for the agricultural sector *(Reynolds et al., 1993; Shepherd, 1996; and for further details, see Box 3.2)*. This indicates that all the subsidies eliminated could be construed as perverse.

For a short taxonomy of subsidies that are perverse for either economic or environmental reasons, see Box 2.1.

Box 2.1

WHEREIN LIES PERVERSITY?

In general, subsidies are perverse economically when they:

— Maintain production processes that would otherwise be non-starters. Examples include growing rice and alfalfa in California desertlands, and continuing with over-exploitation of fish stocks that are already so depleted that they should be relieved of further exploitation forthwith.

— Reduce costs so far that natural resources are over-exploited or wasted. Examples include over-loading of cropland soils, mis-use of water stocks and over-logging of forests.

— Deter efforts at sustainable exploitation, cost-saving technologies and improved management. For instance, the harvesting of natural forests (such as those in the U.S. Pacific Northwest, Canada's British Columbia, southeastern Australia and Borneo) militates against a shift toward plantation forestry.

— While attempting to benefit one economic area, harm others to the extent that their net impact is negative. For instance, many subsidy costs are eventually passed on to consumers (the people who, as taxpayers, provide the subsidy in the first place.) Agricultural subsidies, especially in the form of protection of domestic agricultural markets, can cause food products to be more expensive. In the United States, consumers pay an average of an extra $260 per year for food that is priced higher than it would be without subsidies. In the European Union, the increased cost is $320 per consumer per year. In New Zealand, however, which has virtually abolished agricultural subsidies, the extra cost is just $66 per person.

Subsidies are environmentally perverse when they:

— Foster activities that result in environmental harm, whether at the site in question (over-logging of a forest, water logging of a rice paddy) or further afield (downstream siltation, acid rain), and whether immediately (urban smog) or later (global warming).

Box 2.1 *(continued)*

— In the agricultural sector in particular, stimulate practices that degrade the natural resources underpinning agriculture, notably soils and water; that encourage over-use of agro-chemicals such as synthetic fertilizers and pesticides; and that reduce biodiversity, especially the natural enemies of insect pests and weeds, plus the genetic variability that enhances crop productivity and resists new diseases.

— Encourage inefficient if not profligate use of fossil fuels with their many polluting impacts; stimulate development of nuclear energy with its many problems of environmental safety and toxic wastes.

— Foster grandscale expansion of the car culture, especially at a time when the many externalities (environmental, social and economic) of road transportation indicate we should emphasize public transportation instead.

— Promote inefficient and wasteful use of water, especially now that water is becoming scarce in many regions.

— Lead to over-exploitation of forests and fisheries, eventually causing stocks to fall away to commercial if not biological extinction.

— Generate gross-scale pollution resulting in acid rain, ozone-layer depletion, and global warming among other climatic dislocations.

Environmental and Economic Values

Are economic and environmental values separate and distinct, and can they can be traded off against each other? Or should they be seen as complementary and mutually supportive for the most part *(MacNeill et al., 1991; Myers, 1997)*? That the second is more likely is demonstrated by the extent to which national economies are set back through environmental problems such as pollution, over-use of natural resources, and the lengthy like. In Japan, 2 percent of GDP is being lost to these problems *(Rylander, 1996)*, and the same in Australia *(Department of the Environment, Sport and Territories, Government of Australia, 1996)*. In the United States, the United Kingdom and Germany, the amount is 4 percent; in most countries of Eastern Europe and the former Soviet Union, 6-10 percent; and in many developing countries, 10-18 percent *(Pearce and Atkinson, 1992)*. In China where the economy is reputed to be expanding by 10 percent per year, the loss to environmental problems is put at 12-15 percent of

---

In China where the economy is reputed to be expanding by 10 percent per year, the loss to environmental problems is put at 12-15 percent of GDP.

GDP *(Smil, 1997; Smil and Yushi, 1998)*. None of these estimates takes account of global warming, so they are all under-estimates, possibly severely so. They show clearly that environmental problems can levy sizeable economic costs—and hence that the fortunes of the economy and of the environment are strongly interrelated. To cite a leading analyst *(MacNeill, 1994)*, "All economic decisions have an environmental consequence, just as all environmental decisions have economic consequences."

So the costs involved should properly be considered as both economic and environmental costs combined. True, there is an operational difference. While economic costs are revealed through the marketplace with many sensitive and accurate signals, environmental costs do not generally enjoy such detailed manifestation since the environmental services (e.g., a watershed function) or resource goods (e.g., a species) are simply not marketed for the most part. This does not mean of course that depletion of the service or good is to be regarded as cost-less, rather that the cost is not recorded in conventional and easily quantified fashion. But non-market values are still values. It seems unduly theoretical, then, to say that economic costs are intrinsically different from environmental costs. They are all costs, and this report views them that way.

Environmental and Economic Costs

Fortunately a good number of environmental costs in question can be shadow-priced or otherwise estimated. Since the environmental values at stake are often large, let us look first at a selection:

> Water shortages, due in part to wasteful use of water by irrigation farmers, industry and municipal consumers, all of which tend to use heavily subsidized water. The shortages problem is particularly acute in developing countries, where 80 percent of all disease incidence is related to water shortages. The economic cost of just worktime lost to disease is estimated to be $125 billion per year *(Pearce, 1993)*. In addition, many women have to compensate for water shortages by spending several hours each day in bringing water from distant collecting points, and the opportunity costs of

---

All economic decisions have an environmental consequence, just as all environmental decisions have economic consequences. (MacNeill, 1994)

---

the time that could otherwise have been assigned to e.g., farm work are put at $50 billion per year *(Myers, 1995)*.

Degradation of irrigation systems: as much as 10 percent of the world's irrigated croplands are salinized *(Umali, 1993)*. This leads to a sizeable loss of crops. Again, the problem derives primarily from subsidies that encourage careless and prodigal use of seemingly plentiful water supplies.

Desertification, which affects one third of habitable lands and levies costs merely through agricultural output foregone to the tune of $42 billion per year *(Glantz, 1994)*. In countries as diverse as the United States, Australia, Spain, Turkey, Mexico, Botswana, Namibia, and parts of the Sahel, the problem lies largely with subsidies that encourage over-grazing by domestic stock and cultivation of inappropriate crops.

Soil erosion, which is widespread around the world, and affects parts of Indiana as much as India. Damages can be measured by the cost of replacing lost water and nutrients on eroded agricultural lands: some $250 billion worldwide per year. In addition, there are off-site damages to human health, private property, navigation, recreation and so on, worth at least $150 billion per year. Thus total costs are in the order of $400 billion per year *(Pimentel et al., 1995)*. In the United States, the two sets of costs amount to some $44 billion per year, whereas control measures would amount to only $8.4 billion per year *(Pimentel et al., 1995)*. Despite these large costs, soil erosion is increasing faster than ever in many parts of the world. Much of the problem is due to subsidies fostering over-use of croplands and pastures.

Mass extinction of species, that deprives humankind of resource stocks for industrial raw materials, new sources of energy, improved forms of present crops and potential future crops, and new drugs, medicines and other pharmaceuticals, among many other goods and services. According to a recent across-the-board estimate biodiversity's value to humans each year can be put at a minimum of $2.9 trillion *(Pimentel et al., 1997a)*. Plant-derived anticancer drugs now save 30,000 lives in the United States each year, with annual economic benefits amounting to $400 billion per year. When we consider all developed countries, the benefits double *(Principe, 1996; see also Mendelsohn and Balick, 1995)*. Tropical forest plants in particular offer many potential sources of potent drugs, and their net present worth is estimated variously at $147 billion *(Mendelsohn and Balick, 1995)*, $420 billion *(Pearce and Puroshothaman, 1993)*, and $900 billion *(Gentry, 1993)*. Suppose 30 plant species with pharmaceutical or medicinal potential are eliminated by 2050; the cumulative retail-market loss from each such extinction would amount to $12 billion for the United States alone *(Principe, 1996)*. The total value of goods and services from biodiversity worldwide is conservatively estimated to be in the order of $2.9 trillion or roughly 10 percent of global GNP *(Pimentel et al., 1997)*. Many biodiversity habitats are being depleted through subsidies that foster over-exploitation.

Tropical deforestation leads to a loss of soil cover, which otherwise offers on-site benefits in India worth $5-12 billion per year *(Chopra, 1993)*. Indian forests also help to regulate river flows and contain floods, a service that is roughly assessed at $72 billion per year *(Panayotou and Ashton, 1992)*. Tropical forests are declining faster than ever, with loss of many environmental outputs; and much deforestation is due to subsidies (Chapter 7). These forests also provide fuelwood for at least 500 million people in developing countries who, due to deforestation, must spend several hours each day in roaming far and wide to find supplies *(Crews and Stauffer, 1997)*, with an opportunity cost of time that could be spent on e.g., tilling crop fields, worth $60 billion per year. Tropical forests supply a still larger benefit in the form of "carbon sinks" that mitigate potential damages from global warming. This function can be roughly estimated at $600-4400 per hectare per year *(Brown and Pearce, 1994)*. To replace the carbon storage service of tropical forests could cost as much as $3.7 trillion *(Panayotou and Ashton, 1992)*.

Environmental Externalities Revisited

Thus far we have looked only at environmental costs that can be directly and demonstrably attributed to specific subsidies. But as we have briefly noted in Chapter 1, there are many other forms of environmental degradation that are not immediately and directly linked back to subsidies but arise in a world where a host of exploitative activities entail environmental costs that spill over onto society at large. Not all these environmental externalities can be readily attributed to subsidies, but any externality, being an uncompensated cost, is effectively a subsidy paid by society. Let us remain aware, however, of a distinctive difference: a formal subsidy can cause problems because of what a government does, whereas an implicit subsidy in the form of an environmental externality causes problems because of what a government does not do. This has profound implications for the government's policy responses when it wants to correct subsidy problems.

Since the externalities in question are exceptionally large, let us look at a few illustrative items of environmental values at stake and hence of what could be some implicit costs when the environmental resources are degraded or destroyed:

> Freshwater systems enable us to dilute pollutants. The value of this in-stream service, as measured by the cost of removing all contaminants and nutrients from municipal wastewater by technological means, can be estimated at $150 billion worldwide per year (the estimate does not cover removal of pesticides, nitrates and other pollutants from agricultural drainage waters) *(Postel and Carpenter, 1997)*. Freshwater bodies also supply transportation services that generate revenues in the United States of

$360 billion per year and in Western Europe of $169 billion per year (lower-bound estimates) *(Postel and Carpenter, 1997)*. In addition again, we can count the freshwater opportunity for sport fishing, worth $46 billion per year in the United States alone. The total global value of fish, waterfowl and other goods extracted from freshwater systems amounts to at least $100 billion per year, possibly several times as much *(Postel and Carpenter, 1997)*.

Agricultural pests cause the loss of over 40 percent of all food grown *(Pimentel et al., 1997a)*. Only a very small number of all insect species, perhaps 9000, rank as pests today, but many more potential pests are currently kept under control by natural enemies in the form of predators and parasites *(Pimentel, 1991; Myers, J.H. et al., 1989)*. These control services are variously estimated to be worth at least $54 billion per year *(Naylor and Ehrlich, 1977)*, and possibly as much as $417 billion per year *(Costanza et al., 1997)*. A good number of these natural enemies are likely to be preferentially eliminated as the mass extinction of species gathers momentum.

Insects also supply pollination services. At least 40 crops in the United States are completely dependent on insect pollinators, with a marketplace value of $30 billion *(Pimentel et al., 1992; see also Buchmann and Nabhan, 1996)*. Worldwide one third of food production depends on insect pollination. Such services are reckoned to be worth between $117 billion per year *(Costanza et al., 1997)* and $200 billion per year *(Pimentel et al., 1997a)*. As pollinator insects are eliminated as part of the species extinction spasm, their services will decline accordingly, with significant economic costs. Already certain American farmers have to hire domestic bees for pollination.

These estimates, like those under Environmental and Economic Costs, err on the cautious side, primarily because the lack of data precludes a comprehensive assessment of what we gain overall from environmental resources—and what we lose when they are degraded and depleted. In any case, there can be no doubt that environmental externalities constitute sizeable subsidies, however covert. As we shall see in the five sectoral chapters, these implicit externalities are sometimes greater in economic terms than the overt subsidies. In the meantime, note that a recent research effort *(Costanza et al., 1997)* concludes that all environmental outputs are worth some $33 trillion, or way more than the world's GNP. This further demonstrates the scope for externalities to grow to exceptional scale when environmental outputs are depleted. For details, see Box 2.2.

A corollary of this section is that the elimination of a perverse subsidy should yield a "double dividend" through benefits for both the economy and the environment. If there were a reduction in subsidies for e.g., road transportation, there would be environmental benefits in the form of less pollution, and economic benefits in the form of less road congestion and hence more efficient travel.

All environmental outputs are worth some $33 trillion, way more than the world's GNP.

The Question of Uncertainty

As has been repeatedly emphasized, there is often uncertainty about how big the costs of subsidies can be, whether direct or indirect subsidies or externalitiy subsidies. Similarly, there is not always a clear idea of where the costs originate, or where they have their greatest impacts. Hence there can sometimes be doubt about whether a subsidy should qualify as perverse. Grey areas abound. But this should not be seen as a salient constraint for policy responses. After all, we confront uncertainty every day in the policy sphere. What, for instance, are to be the ultimate and overall economic returns on today's investment in health, education and defense?

The uncertainty question is so central to this report that it is worth reviewing a little further. What is "legitimate scientific caution" in the face of uncertainty, especially when uncertainty can cut both ways? Some observers may consider that in the absence of conclusive evidence and assessment, it is better to stick with low estimates of subsidies on the grounds that they are more "responsible." But there is an asymmetry of evaluation at work. A low estimate, ostensibly "safe" because it takes a conservative view of such limited evidence as is to hand in documented detail, may fail to reflect the real situation just as much as does an "unduly" high estimate that is more of a best-judgement affair based on all available evidence with varying degrees of demonstrable validity. A minimalist calculation with apparently greater precision may in fact amount to spurious accuracy. In a situation of uncertainty where not all factors can be quantified to conventional satisfaction, let us not become preoccupied with what can be precisely counted if that is to the detriment of what ultimately counts.

This applies especially to issues with policy implications of exceptional scope, as in the case of perverse subsidies. Suppose a policy maker hears scientists stating they cannot legitimately offer final guidance about a problem because they have not yet completed their research with conventionally conclusive analysis in all respects. Or suppose the scientists simply refrain from going public about the problem because they feel, in accord with certain traditional canons of science,

The elimination of a perverse subsidy yields a "double dividend". If there were a reduction in subsidies for e.g. road transportation, there would be environmental benefits in the form of less pollution, and economic benefits in the form of less road congestion and hence more efficient travel.

they cannot validly say anything much before they can say all. In these circumstances, the policy maker may well assume there is, therefore, little to worry about for the time being: absence of evidence about a problem implies evidence of absence of a problem. By consequence, the policy maker may decide to do nothing—and to do nothing in a world of unprecedentedly rapid change can be to do a great deal. In these circumstances, undue caution from scientists can become undue recklessness in terms of the policy fallout: their silence can send a resounding message, however unintentional. As in other situations beset with uncertainty, it will be better for us to find we have been roughly right than precisely wrong.

In the case of perverse subsidies, and by sheer force of circumstance both economic and environmental—a force that is becoming ever-more forceful—it is appropriate to appraise the problem with as much (or as little) information as is available. This is the more pertinent when dealing with an issue of exceptional importance and urgency. The reader should bear this in mind while perusing this report. The writer believes that what follows is a realistic reflection of the problem as we understand it today, less than complete though our knowledge may be in many respects. Where uncertainty arises, the writer has sought to describe the situation with as much "precise imprecision" as possible.

The five sectoral chapters all require that an estimate be made of how big the perverse subsidies are, i.e., what proportion they make up of total subsidies. This is an exceedingly vexed question, and in the upshot the author has often been obliged to come up with an informed guesstimate, proposing somewhere between one half and three-quarters (except for environmental externalities, which are counted as 100 percent perverse). These could well be on the low side. When the author has sent out the chapters to established experts, they have almost all proposed that the proportion should be estimated at 100 percent.

Global Warming

The most prominent instance of uncertainty lies with global warming, partly because of the lack of scientific understanding and partly because it is the biggest environmental problem foreseeable *(Repetto and Lash, 1997)*. It could constitute the number one externality cost to be considered as an implicit subsidy (transfer) from society to those sectors that are the main sources of greenhouse gases, viz. fossil fuels and road transportation. For purposes of this report with its emphasis on cautious and conservative estimates, however, global-warming calculations thus far must be viewed as too limited to warrant inclusion of the phenomenon as an environmental externality. We shall look at it here in a little further detail for what it reveals about uncertainty and how it can be handled in policy terms.

--- *Box 2.2* ---

THE PLANETARY ECOSYSTEM AND THE GLOBAL ECONOMY

Environmental values can be unusually significant—and the same for costs when environments are depleted. Recall the environmental goods and services considered under the headings Quantified Costs: Environmental and Economic and Environmental Externalities Revisted. Let us now expand our analytic purview and consider the planetary ecosystem at large. According to some recent analysis *(Costanza et al., 1997)*, the Earth's environmental outputs altogether could be worth some $33 trillion (range $16-54 trillion) per year, or one fifth more than the world's economic output. Just over half, $17.1 trillion, is made up of nutrient cycling. Waste treatment, including pollution control and detoxification, is reckoned to be worth $2.3 trillion; disturbance regulation, e.g., flood control, storm protection and drought recovery, $1.8 trillion; water supply $1.7 trillion; food production, e.g., hunting, gathering, subsistence farming, $1.4 trillion; control of soil erosion $576 billion; pollination $117 billion; and biological control $417 billion.

We can also assess environmental values by reflecting on the Biosphere II experiment, with $200 million of technological underpinnings for eight people enclosed in an artificial ecosystem that nonetheless failed on several counts of vital environmental services. The cost worked out at $25 million per person. Were we ever to try to replicate such environmental services for the 5.8 billion people now on Earth, the cost would theoretically be $145,000 trillion. Just the annual growth in the world's population would require over $2000 trillion or 71 times more than the world's present GNP.

Or consider the environmental value of a 50-year-old tree. It will have contributed environmental services worth $200,000 at today's values (or an average of $4000 per year), including nutrient recycling, moisture regulation, air pollution control, oxygen generation, biodiversity habitat, and soil protection. The value of the tree in marketplace price is probably no more than what it can be used for as commercial timber; and that price is what the consumer pays. But its cost is what society pays when the tree is eliminated, including the loss of its myriad services *(Hermach, 1996)*.

There have been various economic estimates *(e.g., Fankhauser, 1995; Nordhaus, 1994; Pearce et al., 1996; Repetto and Austin, 1997; Tol, 1995)* of the eventual costs of global warming. These estimates generally propose that the costs may be modest in relation to global GDP, just a few percentage points at most. In the view of many ecologists *(e.g., Daily et al., 1991; Orians, 1996; Woodwell and Mackenzie, 1995)*, virtually all estimates thus far fail to capture the many disruptive discontinuities and synergisms likely to attend global warming, hence they are severe under-estimates. The author strongly agrees with this viewpoint. For further recent analyses along these lines, *see Flavin, 1994; Leggett, 1996; Tucker, 1997.*

As a preliminary and partial proxy of possible costs, note some recent comments by the insurance industry in response to freak weather phenomena such as flooding, droughts and windstorms. These phenomena, widely viewed as portents of global warming, have cost insurers as much as $48 billion during 1990-95, compared with $14 billion during the entire 1980s (though some of the increase is probably due to greater economic activity at risk). Leaders of the insurance industry—which is worth $1.5 trillion per year, just ahead of the fossil fuels industry with $1.4 trillion—are perturbed. To cite the head of the Insurance Association of America, Frank Nutter: were recent weather trends to persist, the industry could face "global collapse" by the year 2000.

These statistics give an opening idea of the scale of possible costs involved in a single dimension of global warming as understood at a time when we may be experiencing only the first signs of global warming. Almost entirely disregarded until just a few years ago, they should give pause to those who assert we know enough about global warming to reckon the ultimate all-round costs will be no more than marginal.

According to a forthcoming study *(Downing et al., 1998; see also Downing et al., 1997a and b)*, which deals extensively with multiple uncertainties, market damages of global warming range from zero to 10 percent of world GDP. When we include non-market damages, however, the additional costs could rise as high as 30 percent of GDP. When we include non-market damages, modest risk factors, potential surprises, and equity issues, the total could soar to 40 or even 50 percent of world GDP, and "it is not unimaginable for impacts to exceed 60 percent of GDP."

Note too that the valuation of global warming effects, and especially the monetary valuations, have an uncertainty range corresponding to at least a factor 20. Thus the "true" value may lie between 5 and 2000 percent of a given estimate *(Maddison et al., 1996)*.

In terms of policy responses, there need be little uncertainty thanks to the "no regrets" option. As has been pithily pointed out by Lovins *(1997)*, protecting the climate need not be costly but profitable, because saving fuel is generally cheaper than buying it (neglecting any further benefits from not burning it). "With market failures corrected, such as the $300 billion of potential annual energy savings in the United States unrealized, huge energy savings can be speedily purchased at current prices. In this context, uncertainties about climate become irrelevant: we should buy energy efficiency merely to save money. The debate then shifts from prices and pain to markets, enterprise, innovation, competitive advantage, and economic opportunity. ... "Those theoretical economists who wouldn't pick up a banknote from the street (if it were real, someone would have done so already) will not capture these profits—alert executives will" *(Lovins, 1997).*

Summation and Conclusion

This report carries the perverse subsidies issue one step beyond two recent publications by Roodman, 1996, and de Moor, 1997. Both review the subsidies phenomenon overall, though from standpoints more restricted than here (and de Moor does not deal with forestry or fisheries). Both present admirable accounts of the subsidies problem writ large, and both assert that a good share of these subsidies can be characterized as perverse. But neither attempts a substantive or firm estimate of how large a share this might be (de Moor suggests it could be anywhere from 35 to almost 80 percent). By contrast, the present report seeks to come up with a substantive estimate of the share, albeit in rough and ready terms.

How rough and ready? As we shall see, there is a solid figure for perverse subsidies in fisheries, backed by authoritative documentation. There are sometimes good figures, sometimes no figures, for agriculture and fossil fuels/nuclear energy. There are patchy and widely disparate estimates for subsidies for road transportation in the United States, a land where the car is king and where one would expect there would be lots of high-quality documentation. In many other countries with large numbers of cars, data are all but non-existent. The situation in forestry is confused and uncertain, though this does not matter much in overall terms since subsidies in forestry are comparatively small. In the water sector, however, there are all too few data for subsidies in many countries, let alone those subsidies that should rank as perverse. In this instance, the author has had to limit himself to a best-judgement estimate, drawing on such limited evidence as can be found. By comparison with the fisheries estimate, it is no more than a guesstimate, and the author readily recognizes the shortcoming in this sector. To refrain from offering a water estimate of any kind, however, would leave the position open to being construed by certain observers as implying that perverse subsidies are negligible—quite the opposite of what seems to be the real-world situation. To reiterate a key point: uncertainty can cut both ways. The author believes that it accords with the intent and spirit of this report to offer a preliminary and exploratory estimate, even a semi-estimate, rather than to let the water sector remain silent on an issue of major moment. In any case, when there is an acute lack of documentation, the assessment tends perforce toward an under-estimate.

To this significant extent, the author considers the estimates for perverse subsidies in the five sectors are valid for present purposes, however uneven their databases. They represent an informed appraisal (vide the 700 references) of our current understanding of perverse subsidies. The rationale is that an exploratory exercise is justified in light of the pivotal part played by perverse subsidies in the way our world works.

PART II

PRINCIPAL SECTORS

CHAPTER 3

AGRICULTURE

The U.S. government subsidizes energy costs so that farmers can deplete aquifers to grow alfalfa to feed cows that make milk that is stored in warehouses as surplus cheese that does not feed the hungry (Hawken, 1997).

Agriculture affects one third of the Earth's land surface, more than any other human enterprise. It also affects the entire planetary ecosystem through the recent intensification of farming practices. More irrigation, pesticides and chemical fertilizers among other forms of modernized farming have achieved higher harvests; and these measures have been widely fostered by subsidies. Many if not most and possibly all such subsidies appear to be costly to the economy, and are often harmful to the environment, especially the natural-resource base that underpins agriculture. For instance, pesticides and chemical fertilizers severely contaminate water supplies; short-rotation cropping and reduced fallows exacerbate soil erosion; high-yielding monocultures cause genetic wipe-out among old varieties of food plants; land clearing for agriculture is the largest single cause of deforestation; and many agricultural activities release greenhouse gases. (This chapter is based primarily on *Batie, 1995 and 1996; Bromley, 1996; Brown, 1996; de Moor, 1997; Faeth, 1995; Gardner, 1996; Lynch, 1994; Organization for Economic Co-operation and Development, 1995 and 1997a; Roodman, 1996; Runge, 1994; and Thurman, 1995.*)

What is the rationale for agricultural subsidies? Why should farmers need a helping hand at all from the government? There are several arguments. First is that governments consider it a prime responsibility to keep their citizens fed, so they feel duty bound to support farmers. Secondly, farmers worldwide have often been among the poorer segments of society, so they have been thought to deserve "a little extra". This applies especially in developing countries, where farmers generally form the majority of the population and governments are keen to keep them in favor. Thirdly, and again in developing countries, many subsidies have been justified in times past as vital foundations of the Green Revolution; they enabled the one third expansion of irrigated lands and the tripling of fertilizer use, thus helping to double crop yields. Overall, subsidies aim to guarantee food supplies, to keep farm prices stable, to maintain farming as a vibrant economic sector, and to support rural communities.

For all these reasons, financial support to agriculture has become an ancient and entrenched tradition in countries right around the world. Farmers have become extremely powerful politically, leaving governments feeling that to reduce agricultural subsidies would be to forfeit a pivotal part of the electorate. Remarkably enough, New Zealand, which is more dependent on agriculture than any other developed country, has grasped the nettle, bringing success for the government, farmers, the economy and the environment (see below).

Agricultural subsidies come in many shapes and sizes. As well as the obvious practice of encouraging farmers to use more inputs (fertilizers, pesticides, irrigation, machinery, etc.), subsidies can simply boost farm income by means of price supports. Less directly, they can facilitate marketing of crops by enhancing transportation networks. They can relieve weather problems and other risks by providing insurance. They can foster credit flows. They can stimulate conversion of wetlands to agriculture. Governments North and South do much to subsidize artificial pesticides and fertilizers. In developed countries, governments typically guarantee minimum prices for crops at levels above the market, while in developing countries governments primarily suppress farm prices in order to keep city communities happy with cheap food.

This last point indicates the technical differentiation between producer and consumer subsidies. The Organization for Economic Co-operation and Development *(1997a)* defines the first in terms of Producer Subsidy Equivalent, being "an indicator of the value of the monetary transfers to agriculture resulting from agricultural policies in a given year. Both transfers from consumers of agricultural products (through domestic market prices) and transfers from taxpayers (through budgetary or tax expenditures) are included." For further details, see *Legg, 1996; Tansley and Worsley, 1995.*

Certain of these subsidies are well and good within particular perspectives. Not so justifiable are subsidies fostering crops grown in regions that would not have grown them at all had a free market existed. Notable examples are ultra-thirsty crops such as alfalfa and rice in California's desertlands. Also irrational are those many subsidies that may have made sense when they were first established but have since become obsolete or bloated, or both. In the European Union, for instance, excess production has lead to milk and wine lakes and butter and beef mountains (not to mention a manure mountain in the Netherlands). In early 1993 cereal surpluses of 30 million tonnes would have been enough to provide an ample diet to 75 million people for one year *(Ritson and Harvey, 1995).* Taxpayers footed the bill to supply the subsidies that boosted these crops in the first place, then they paid again to store the excess stockpiles. Much the same has applied to extravagant food surpluses in the United States, where in a typical year of the early 1990s, the Department of Agriculture obliged farmers to squander 1 billion oranges, half a billion lemons, 100,000 tonnes of raisins and 30,000 tonnes of almonds.

Subsidies generate absurd outcomes in other ways too. Many countries pay their farmers to leave land fallow, whereupon they subsidize them to engage in directly

The European Union has subsidized excess food production until there have been milk and wine lakes and butter and beef mountains (not to mention a manure mountain in the Netherlands). In early 1993 cereal surpluses of 30 million tonnes would have been enough to provide an Italian-style diet to 75 million people for one year. Taxpayers footed the bill to supply the subsidies that boosted these crops in the first place, then they paid again to store the excess stockpiles.

conflicting activities, e.g., to plant crops and practice fallowing simultaneously. Or consider the travels if not the travails of materials needed to make the 150g of daily yogurt beloved by many German consumers. To reach one of the main distribution outlets in southern Germany, ingredients are transported from all around the country, even from Netherlands and Poland. To do the job, a theoretical truck must travel 850 kilometers. It is enabled to do so in part by bountiful subsidies from the European Union's Common Agricultural Policy *(Hird and Paxton, 1994)*. Much more efficient in both economic and environmental terms would be for yogurt producers to utilize local ingredients, but they have no incentive to do so as long as subsidized supplies can apparently do the job more cheaply.

In still more extreme fashion, four airports in Japan have been dedicated to transporting vegetables and flowers, to be followed by another five in 1998 costing almost $30 million in subsidies. To fly 1 kilogram of green onions from Ono in northeastern Kyushu Island to Tokyo costs nearly six times as much as to transport them by road. The airports, paid for entirely by taxpayers, have been built ostensibly to integrate isolated farming communities into the Japanese agro-economy—and more realistically they have served as a sop to the farming lobby after it made concessions to the Japanese government's negotiations for the 1993 Uruguay Round on world trade.

Numerous countries feature inappropriate subsidies for grains, beef, mutton and lamb, pork, poultry, milk and other dairy products, fruits, vegetables, cotton, oilseed and tobacco among a host of other agricultural products. So large and widespread are these subsidies that (and as we shall see in detail below) agri-

Excessive applications of nitrogenous fertilizers, stimulated by extravagant subsidies, are wasteful in economic terms and highly polluting in environmental terms. Indonesia has reduced its fertilizer subsidies from $732 million to $96 million per year; Pakistan from $178 million to $2 million; and Bangladesh from $56 million to zero.

culture has become one of the most distorted and distortive sectors of the global economy.

In addition to economic dislocations, subsidies cause much environmental injury. Pesticides under conventional application regimes cause well-known hazards to human health even as they undermine their own usefulness. Excessive applications of nitrogenous fertilizers lead to washed-off nitrates contaminating drinking water supplies with threats to human health. Intensified farming with heavy machinery aggravates soil erosion, as does the decline of crop rotations. Irrigation agriculture is far and away the largest user of water worldwide, and subsidies encourage farmers to mis-use and over-use water on a grand scale, despite the growing evidence of sizeable water shortages impending (more details in Chapter 6). Many agricultural activities contribute to global warming through emissions of carbon dioxide from fossil fuels, methane from ruminant livestock and rice paddies, and nitrous oxides from disturbed soils. These environmental externalities are widespread and unusually significant, and they merit detailed examination later in this chapter.

The Subsidies Phenomenon

In 1996, financial transfers to agriculture in OECD countries amounted to well over $300 billion *(Organization for Economic Co-operation and Development, 1997a; see also de Moor, 1997).* While this was higher than the 1986/88 average, it was down from the 1993/95 level by $30-40 billion. This recent fall reflected higher grain prices on world markets rather than government efforts to reduce subsidies. When prices slip again, subsidies may well revert to their former level if not higher. These subsidies exerted profound impact on not just the agriculture sector but on the economy at large. They equated to 1.3 percent of the collective GDPs of 24 OECD "core" countries, to more than 2 percent of GDP in Norway and Switzerland, more than 1 percent in the European Union as a whole, and 1.5 percent in Japan. Roughly half were producer subsidies, and of these roughly half were provided through increased prices from consumers: "roughly" because much depends on which categories are included, how they are measured, etc. *(Organization for Economic Co-operation and Development, 1997a; see also Hepher, 1997).*

OECD subsidies for agriculture are worth $300 billion per year. Compare them to the estimated cost of upgrading developing-world agriculture, $40 billion per year; and the current inadequate funding of the international network of research centres for agriculture, a mere $235 million per year.

In 1996, the OECD average subsidy per farmer was almost $14,500. In the United States it was $27,240. In a Western industrialized country, consumers paid an extra food bill of at least $350, and in the United States, $259.

Table 3.1

AGRICULTURE SUBSIDIES IN OECD COUNTRIES,* 1996

Country/Region	Subsidies** (billion $)	Subsidies ($)		
		Per full-time farmer	Per hectare of agricultural land	Per consumer
European Union	120.3	17,474	825	322
Japan	77.4	30,090	15,107	617
United States	68.7	27,240	161	259
Switzerland	6.7	42,701	4,213	935
Canada	4.8	11,225	66	161
Norway	3.4	40,362	3,287	767
Australia	1.6	4,205	4	89
New Zealand	0.2	1,825	14	66
OECD	297.1	14,493	254	334

Source: Organization for Economic Co-operation and Development, 1997a

* excluding Mexico and other recent members
** including increased food prices for consumers

These government outlays were sizeable for individual farmers. In 1996, the OECD average was almost $14,500, in the United States $27,240, in the European Union $17,474, in Japan $30,090, and $42,700 in Switzerland (though in New Zealand only $1825, for reasons explained below). For details of all leading OECD countries, see Table 3.1. The payments amounted to 30 percent of farmers' revenues in the United States, 45 percent in Canada, 48 percent in the European Union, 65 percent in Japan, and 77 percent in Norway, with an average of 44 percent in OECD countries as a whole (though only 15 percent in Australia and 4 percent in New Zealand) *(Organization for Economic Co-operation and Development, 1997a)*. They were sizeable too for consumers because of increased food prices and taxes. In a Western industrialized country in 1996, consumers paid an extra food bill of at least $350; in the United States, $259; in the European Union, $322; in Norway, $767; in Switzerland, $935; and in Japan, $617 (contrast Australia, only $89 and New Zealand $66, both of these countries having eliminated most of their subsidies) *(Hepher, 1997; Organization for Economic Co-operation and Development, 1997a; see also Carmel and Viattae, 1993; Griffiths and Wall, 1993; Morgan, 1994)*. For further details, see Table 3.1.

Later on in this chapter, we shall look at how many agricultural subsidies can be considered perverse. As an interim example of subsidies that are plainly bad news for both the economy and the environment, check Box 3.1 on sugar subsidies in Florida.

Box 3.1

U.S. SUGAR GROWERS

There could hardly be a more extreme case of perverse agricultural subsidies than the U.S. sugar sector. Especially during the last 35 years, the U.S. government has protected domestic sugar against imports by supplying hefty price supports to sugar growers. This enrichment of a small number of such growers causes American consumers to pay sugar prices at least twice the world level *(Bonanno et al., 1994)*. (It also prompts candy manufacturers to move to Canada where they can purchase sugar on international markets.) Sugar growing is concentrated in southern Florida, where it drains water that would otherwise flow into the Everglades, and returns it with eutrophying fertilizer.

The subsidy program costs American consumers $1.4 billion a year. Transferring each $1 of subsidy to sugar producers costs the consumer $2.60 and the economy $0.70. Each sugar grower receives subsidies worth twice as much as the country's average family income *(Bonanno et al., 1994; Center for Responsive Politics, 1995; Krueger, 1988; Maskus, 1989)*.

The United States

The United States is the foremost food producer in the world. Each year the country exports one third of its agricultural products, worth more than $50 billion (which helps it pay for its $60 billion of oil imports). But there is a price to pay for this vibrant activity: in 1996 the American taxpayer underpinned agriculture to the tune of $54 billion in subsidies, and the American consumer contributed another $15 billion in higher food prices *(Organization for*

Economic Co-operation and Development, 1997a). The $69 billion total means that United States agriculture is among the most strongly supported in the world, surpassed only by such super-supported countries as Japan, Norway and Switzerland. Or rather, United States agriculture receives some of the strongest supports in the world; whether that is supportive of the agricultural sector and the United States economy overall, or of the environmental underpinnings of agriculture, is another story. These payments amounted to about one third of farm revenues, or an average of $27,240 per farmer *(Organization for Economic Co-operation and Development, 1997a; United Nations Development Programme, 1996; see also—and for documentation of other parts of this summary assessment— Batie, 1995 and 1996; Faeth, 1995; Gardner, 1996; Moos, 1996; Rocky Mountain Institute, 1992; Roodman, 1996; Runge, 1995; United States Department of Agriculture, 1994).*

The main purposes of these subsidies are to ensure acceptable and stable prices for crops and other produce, and to safeguard the farming community in the United States, especially in the form of family farms and their workforces. These two sets of values seemed to be at exceptional risk during the Great Depression, whereupon the New Deal legislation of the early 1930s saw to it that "No sector of the economy received more systematic federal attention than agriculture; and none received more subsidy for research and development, more technical assistance, more public investment in education, in electrification and in infrastructure, more price stabilization, more export promotion, more credit, and more mortgage relief" *(cited in Schlesinger, 1986; see also Griffiths and Wall, 1993; Soden, 1988).*

In any case, farming had traditionally been seen as a risky enterprise. Insect pests, diseases or bad weather could destroy crops, while prices were subject to marketplace swings and demand changes. All the more, then, prices were to be supported and stabilized by government subsidies—thereby shifting a lot of the risk from the farmer to the taxpayer. When risk was reduced, however, food production was stimulated, usually leading to bulging food surpluses, which in turn caused prices to drop, leading to the need for further price supports. And so on and so repetitiously forth. The basic principles have not changed much today.

In practice, however, things have worked out differently. Whereas the early 1930s saw rural incomes 60 percent below urban incomes, today's full-time farmer may have a net worth more than 10 times the average American household's. But he is far from the family farmer of tradition. Although there are still 350,000 American farms receiving federal farm handouts, almost 30 percent of subsidies go to the top 2 percent and over four-fifths to the top 30 percent. Ironically, if the United States government were to shift its target from the top 30 percent to the bottom 70 percent of farmers, it could save at least $8 billion a year while supplying a competitive boost to lower-income farms *(Faeth, 1995; Roodman, 1996).* As it is, the smallscale farmer has long been under the squeeze.

At the start of this century the farm population made up 43 percent of the United States' population, and in 1950 its share was still 12 percent, but today it has slumped to well under 2 percent. Because farm payments are based on the production of crops and livestock (rather than on the means of production), most subsidies are paid to a few top-bracket farmers. So the decline in farmer numbers reflects the tendency for subsidies to support crops rather than farmers *(Faeth, 1995; Roodman, 1996; Tweeten and Zulauf, 1997).*

Increasingly United States agriculture has become the province of bigger and more efficient farmers, who no longer run farms but agri-businesses. Farmland ownership has become highly concentrated: just 124,000 owners hold half of all farmlands, while 86 percent of farms are now small or part-time operations, earning less than 5 percent of all net farm income. At the other extreme, 5 percent of all farms enjoy sales of more than $200,000 per year, pulling in 84 percent of net farm income *(Gannon et al., 1995).*

United States farm subsidies have been cut back somewhat in recent years. However, they can still be viewed as public policy headed down a blind alley. While intended to stimulate the production of food in general, they induce farmers to plant too much of what is subsidized and too little of the rest. Overproduction of subsidized items drives down prices, whereupon new subsidies are required to pay farmers to leave land idle so as to push prices back up again. But the raised prices undermine farm exports, whereupon exports too have to be subsidized. There is a further whammy: the consumers hardest hit are the poorest people, the ones who spend proportionally most on food.

Many farmers protest that without subsidies, they would have to quit. This brings us to the next vexed question, farm jobs—and another focus of subsidies insofar as they are supposed to safeguard jobs. Today, it is efficiency rather than subsidies that determine whether farm jobs go. Like those other OECD countries where subsidies are overly generous, viz. Japan, Norway and the European Union, it is the least efficient American farms that are losing the most jobs. By contrast, reduced subsidies and farming efficiency in New Zealand and Australia have done much to keep farmers down on the farm.

Subsidies are not only bad news for the United States economy but for the United States environment as well (even the planetary ecosystem via global warming) *(Paarlberg and Orden; Potter, 1997).* Again, this is due to the overwhelming emphasis on ever-more production. (By contrast, subsidies ignore or even discourage low-input and organic farming, which is more environmentally benign.) They encourage farmers to apply excessive amounts of synthetic pesti-

---

One U.S. government agency heavily subsidizes irrigation for crops that another agency has paid farmers not to grow.

---

cides and fertilizers, with widespread pollution of water stocks; indeed this is one of the main forms of non-point water pollution (taxpayers then pay to clean up the rivers and lakes). Water stocks, and especially groundwater supplies such as the Ogallala Aquifer, are also being grossly depleted by intensified agriculture: farms and ranches account for 70 percent of all water consumed in the United States (see Chapter 6 on Water). Subsidies help reduce wildland habitat for bio-diversity—nitrogenous fertilizers and flatulent cattle release greenhouse gases *(Bradshaw, 1995; Faeth et al., 1996; Legg, 1997; Steenblik, 1997; Tolman, 1996).*

Perhaps most important of all, subsidy regulations serve to reduce if not elimi-nate crop rotations. Crop-support programs lock farmers into planting the same crops on the same land year after year. If soil fertility declines, that can be over-come by adding more subsidized fertilizer. This stimulates soil erosion to the extent that it offsets all soil conservation programs put together. Soil erosion is aggravated too by the trend toward bigger farms with fewer shelterbelts, and with increased use of heavy machinery. One third of original topsoil in the United States has already been eroded away, and another 4.5 billion tonnes are lost every year (albeit only 6 percent and perhaps as little as 2 percent of the global erosion total from 11 percent of the world's agricultural lands). On-site costs comprise loss of plant nutrients, moisture and soil depth, while off-site costs consist mostly of siltation of downstream water bodies, plus associated flooding. Both sets of costs together amount to $44 billion per year, increasing production costs by about 25 percent *(Pimentel et al., 1995).*

Most of the above applies to arable crops, but some of it relates to livestock as well, especially on federal lands in the 11 western states making up one third of "the West". Over 20 million beef cattle roam 2 million square kilometers, with 100,000 ranches producing less than one fifth of the country's beef. Yet ranchers using federal lands have long paid less than one third of the average private-land rate. American taxpayers subsidize ranchers to overgraze these rangelands at a charge of just $1.61 per cow per month, less than it costs to feed a cat. Comparable private lands bring in an average grazing fee of $10 per cow per month. These low grazing fees cost the United States treasury over $50 million a year—and the entire federal grazing program, including taxpayer-funded predator control, emergency feed and cheap water, costs Americans at least $500 million a year (without counting the cost of degraded grasslands, eroded soil, muddied streams, trampled vegetation, and scarce water running off). Over-grazing has caused as much as 85 percent of public rangelands to lose their pro-ductivity, thanks to "socialized ranching" on the part of welfare cowboys. Overall the cost of federal grazing permits is some $4 billion *(Gardner, 1997; Meadows, 1995; see also Oppenheimer, 1996; Wald, 1996).*

On top of economic inefficiency, there is social inequity. Many of the biggest ranches are financially marginal sideline investments by wealthy enterprises.

Half of the rangelands are utilized by just 2 percent of all permit holders, these being grandscale operators who make a fortune from the taxpayer. They include 4 billionaires, several oil companies, an insurance company, a California utility and a major brewery. For a sound discussion of the equity factor, see Potter, 1997.

In summary of United States subsidies, note a recent critique *(Hawken, 1997)*: "The government subsidizes agricultural production and agricultural non-production alike, also agricultural destruction and agricultural restoration. [It] subsidizes cattle grazing on western rangelands while it also pays for soil conservation. The government subsidizes energy costs so that farmers can deplete aquifers to grow alfalfa to feed cows that make milk that is stored in warehouses as surplus cheese that does not feed the hungry."

All OECD Countries

In addition to the United States' subsidies of $69 billion in 1996, there are $120 billion on the part of the European Union, $77 billion by Japan, and $31 billion by other OECD countries (not counting Mexico and a few other recent entrants) *(Organization for Economic Co-operation and Development, 1997a; see also de Moor, 1997)*. This makes a total of $297 billion, say $300 billion. For details, see Table 3.1. As discussed earlier, this is down by 10 percent on 1995, but the decline may be temporary if grain prices revert to their erstwhile level.

Non-OECD Countries

Subsidies are pervasive in non-OECD countries too, though not nearly on the same scale. As in OECD countries, they include both producer and consumer subsidies, generally with emphasis on the latter. In fact, agriculture is often taxed to keep consumers, and especially urban consumers, content by e.g., fixing retail food prices or imposing ceilings on producer prices. Price interventions include direct regulation, state trading, tariffs both fixed and variable, and restrictions such as discretionary import and export licenses.

As for producer subsidies, governments often support farm credit programs and salient agricultural inputs such as fertilizer. Fertilizer use worldwide and particularly in developing countries increased by 40 percent per unit of farmland between the mid-1970s and the late 1980s. In Indonesia, for instance, fertilizer subsidies constituted 2 percent of government spending in 1989 (though greatly reduced today), and in India 3.6 percent *(Gupta et al., 1995; Pagiola et al., 1996)*. Producer subsidies also protect farmers through restrictions or tariffs on imported food. The net effect has generally been a huge income transfer out of agriculture *(Schiff and Valdes, 1992; Schiff and Montenegro, 1995; Praven, 1994; Valdes, 1996)*.

Consider the experience of India. Increasingly subsidies have been allocated to inputs such as water, irrigation, fertilizers, pesticides, farm credit, and electricity (mainly for irrigation pumps). By contrast, relatively few subsidies go to non-input factors such as agronomic research, extension services, rural roads and soil conservation. The share of input subsidies in public expenditure increased from 44 percent in the early 1980s to 83 percent by 1990. As a measure of the expected deceleration in productivity due to declining support for research and rural infrastructure, plus lack of attention to problems such as soil erosion, salinization/water logging, and loss of organic nutrients, the demand for cereals is projected to exceed production by 23 million tonnes by 2020, double the largest gap to date *(Kumar et al., 1995)*. Of course the gap will be primarily due to the increase in both human numbers and demands, the latter arising as newly affluent people eat higher on the food chain. Yet despite heavy input subsidies, Indian agriculture is effectively taxed through artificially low prices and high foreign exchange rates. If these basic policies were corrected, there would be next to no need for subsidies at all—as is the case in many other developing countries *(Swaminathan, 1996)*.

Consumer and producer subsidies together in developing countries have accounted for almost 5 percent of annual government spending during the past 25 years—a large slice indeed. In Zambia, for instance, they even soared to 17 percent of the government budget in the late 1980s *(Statz et al., 1994)*. Overall, however, subsidies are small as compared with the OECD countries. A recent estimate proposes $10 billion per year *(de Moor, 1997; see also Schiff and Valdes, 1992; Schiff and Montenegro, 1995; Valdez, 1996)*. This is not so much a cautious and conservative estimate as a gross underestimate *(Dinhem, 1996; Naylor and Ehrlich, 1997; see also Conway and Pretty, 1991; Vorley and Keeney, 1997)*. India subsidizes fertilizer alone to the tune of $2.5 billion per year *(Dixon, 1996)*. For want of anything better, the author posits a minimalist total for non-OECD countries of $25 billion, while believing a more realistic "guesstimate" would be at least $50 billion.

The Environmental Resource Base

The environmental resource base underpinning agriculture is being widely degraded by a variety of farming practices *(Ehrlich et al., 1993; Pimentel et al.,*

Soil erosion worldwide levies unintended costs on society of around $150 billion per year, while pesticides harm society's interests to the extent of $100 billion per year. These two items alone mean that such hidden subsidies are almost as large as the formal subsidies in agriculture.

1996; Pinstrup-Andersen, 1994; Scherr and Yadav, 1996; Swaminathan, 1996). Much of this degradation can be ascribed in part at least to agricultural subsidies that foster over-exploitative agriculture *(Bonnis, 1995; MacNeill, 1994; Maier and Steenblik, 1995).*

Consider soil erosion. During the past 20 years some 500 billion tonnes of topsoil have been eroded away, roughly equivalent to all the topsoil in India's croplands. Currently somewhere between 25 billion tonnes *(Brown et al., 1993)* and 75 billion tonnes *(Pimentel et al., 1995)* of topsoil are lost each year, two-thirds of it from agricultural lands. During the past 40 years, at least 4.3 million square kilometers of croplands have been abandoned because of soil loss, an expanse equivalent to 30 percent of today's croplands *(Kendall and Pimentel, 1994; Oldeman et al., 1990).* Without better soil-conservation practices, between 1.4 and 2.0 million square kilometers (the smaller expanse is equal to Alaska) will lose most of their good-quality soil over the next two decades—and this will apply in parts of Indiana and India alike *(Brown et al., 1993; Daily, 1995; Food and Agriculture Organization, 1993; Pimentel et al., 1995).* If soil erosion is allowed to continue virtually unchecked, it could well cause a decline of 19-29 percent in food production from rainfed croplands during the next 25 years 1985-2010 *(Jarnagin and Smith, 1993; Lal and Stewart, 1990; see also Greenland et al., 1994).*

The on-site costs of soil erosion are borne by farmers themselves, so they are not considered to be a cost pushed off onto society and hence a hidden subsidy. Of course the loss of cropland productivity results in higher food costs for consumers, so to that extent society eventually pays part of the on-farm cost. In the longer run, moreover, soil erosion will impose much higher costs on society if the world without enough topsoil finds itself unable to grow enough food: that would be an externality indeed. Let us limit the calculation, however, to costs borne by off-farm society, these being costs that sooner or later must be picked up by the public at large. Upshot: soil erosion costs are an implicit subsidy from society to farmers. According to recent research *(Pimentel et al., 1995),* the off-farm costs worldwide can be put at $150 billion per year, being just under two-fifths of total costs.

There are other societal costs of intensified agriculture, and these too can be considered as implicit subsidies from society to farmers. They include the health hazards from washed-off nitrogenous fertilizer, polluting public water supplies *(Smil, 1997; van der Voet et al., 1996).* In China, for instance, nitrogenous fertilizer is applied to croplands at rates as high as 1.9 tonnes per hectare per year, and the amount of fertilizer actually taken up by plants is only about 40 per-

---

In China and as a result of fertilizer wash-off (thanks to subsidies), more than half of local groundwater stocks are contaminated above the tolerance level.

---

cent. As a result of fertilizer wash-off, more than half of local groundwater stocks are contaminated above the tolerance level. The same fertilizers cause much eutrophication of water bodies such as lakes and rivers *(Zhang et al., 1996)*. The costs remain unquantified economically.

Another chemical additive, pesticides, can be considered as a final environmental externality. The annual average for global sales of pesticides in the mid-1990s was $30 billion *(Pimentel and Grinier, 1997; see also Naylor and Ehrlich, 1997; World Resources Institute, 1994)*. Many governments, especially in the developing world which accounts for one third of all pesticide use, give outsize subsidies for pesticides. The average is 50 percent, within a range of 15-90 percent *(Farah, 1994; Pimentel, 1997; Vincent and Fairman, 1995)*.

Apart from direct subsidies for pesticides, there is a host of indirect subsidies including below-market interest for loans from state controlled banks, reduced prices for imported chemicals due to over-valued exchange rates, and tax advantages to agro-chemical companies for the import and sale of pesticides *(Organization for Economic Co-operation and Development, 1994)*. These too remain economically unquantified for the most part.

The United States, which has used pesticides longer than developing countries, now applies 10 times more insecticides than in 1945 while crop losses to insects have almost doubled due to a host of factors, including the pesticide-induced demise of pests' natural enemies and the capacity of insect pests to adapt evolutionarily to pesticides ("Every pesticide selects for its own failure"). Since 1945 over 1600 insect and mite species in various parts of the world have developed significant resistance to pesticides *(Naylor and Ehrlich, 1997; World Health Organization, 1992)*. Pests now destroy 25-50 percent of crops worldwide, a proportion that is probably higher than before pesticides were widely introduced in the late 1940s *(Pimentel, 1991; see also Naylor and Ehrlich, 1997; Thrupp, 1996)*.

Farmers find themselves on a chemical treadmill. Insect pests become resistant to pesticides, so next year's pesticides must be still more lethal, despite the ever-greater cost to farmers' finances—also to human health. By definition, these synthetic chemicals are highly toxic, and every year some 3 million people in developing countries are affected to some degree by pesticide poisonings, of which 700,000 people suffer long-term effects and 220,000 die *(World Health*

Every pesticide selects for its own failure. Since 1945 over 1600 insect and mite species in various parts of the world have developed significant resistance to pesticides. Pests now destroy 25-50 percent of crops worldwide, a proportion that is probably higher than before pesticides were widely introduced in the late 1940s.

Organization, 1992; see also Murray, 1994; United States National Research Council, 1995). Unfortunately there is no estimate available of this sizeable cost to society and hence of the implicit subsidy from society to pesticide-using farmers.

Nor are there good comprehensive data for other externality costs from pesticides. In the United States, however, it has been minimally estimated *(Pimentel and Grinier, 1997; see also Farah, 1994)* that the environmental and social costs from pesticides, including groundwater contamination, wildlife and fishery losses, and public health impacts, total at least $8.3 billion per year. American farmers pay $3.2 billion of this cost through on-farm problems arising from the destruction of natural pest enemies and pesticide resistance, meaning that United States society pays the rest, $5.1 billion per year, or say $5 billion. On top of the externality costs listed are many unrecorded losses from destruction of soil invertebrates, microfauna and microflora. Nor do we know the full costs of soil and water pollution or of human pesticide poisonings with effects such as cancers and sterility *(Pimentel and Grinier, 1997).* So the $5 billion estimate is cautious in the extreme.

American farmers use pesticides worth $6 billion per year, or one fifth of the global total of some $30 billion. The same share arises with respect to volume: 0.5 billion kilograms versus 2.5 billion kilograms. But exernality costs in the rest of the world are surely far higher by proportion, if only because of the ratio of pesticide deaths among humans: 20-25 in the United States per year versus 220,000 worldwide. Indeed externality costs overall can be estimated at $100 billion per year, constituting a concealed subsidy from society to agriculture—and even this last figure can be confidently regarded as a severe under-estimate *(Pimentel and Grinier, 1997).*

Agriculture also contributes significantly to what is likely to prove the biggest environmental problem of all, global warming. Both crops and livestock produce carbon dioxide, methane and nitrous oxide. Regrettably there is still no authoritative economic evaluation of the potential impacts of global warming (except for a few minimalist efforts), so the case here must go by default.

In summary of environmental externalities as covert subsidies from agriculture to society, there are $150 billion per year for soil erosion and $100 billion for pesticides. Total, $250 billion per year. If there were data for broadscale pollution by nitrogenous fertilizers, plus biodiversity decline leading to loss of pollination services and natural pest controls, that would raise the total for these implicit subsidies all the more.

Subsidies Worldwide

According to the calculations above, conventional or formal subsidies to agriculture in OECD countries now amount to $300 billion per year, and $25 billion in non-OECD countries, for a total of $325 billion per year. In addition, there are the environmental externalities, $250 billion per year. This makes for a grand total of $575 billion per year.

Box 3.2

THE CASE OF NEW ZEALAND

In the early 1980s, New Zealand took the momentous step of deciding to phase out its agricultural subsidies. This was all the more remarkable in a country with an economy more dependent on agriculture and food exports than virtually any other in the developed world. By 1995 primary agriculture accounted for 5.2 percent of GDP, and related industries bumped up the total to 15.4 percent, while agricultural products accounted for 51 percent of the country's merchandized exports (excluding forestry) *(Chamberlin, 1996; Ministry of Agriculture, Government of New Zealand, 1996)*.

During the brief period 1979-84, supports for agriculture increased from 15 to 40 percent of farmers' gross income, and farm subsidies rose until they were equivalent to 14 percent of the government's budget and 6 percent of GNP—far too high *(Bollard, 1992)*. The government started to eliminate subsidies as part of overall measures to deregulate key sectors of its economy. It cancelled a wide range of support measures, including minimum prices for wool, beef, sheepmeat, and dairy products; and it phased out land development loans, fertilizer and irrigation subsidies, and subsidized credit.

As a result, farmland prices dropped at first by 60 percent and fertilizer use declined by 50 percent. By 1995, however, farmland prices had recovered to 86 percent of the 1982 value in real terms, and fertilizer prices returned close to pre-reform levels. There was a halt to land clearing and overstocking, which in the past had been the principal causes of widespread soil erosion. Whereas stock raising had been encouraged by subsidies to encroach onto erodible hills, it has now intensified on better lands, and the hills have been planted with trees, leading to a 50-percent increase in plantations expanse. The number of full-time farm workers has actually increased. The meat industry has moved from being the least efficient in the world to the second most efficient *(Bollard, 1992; Reynolds et al., 1993; Shepherd, 1996; and Sinner et al., 1995)*.

Box 3.2 *(continued)*

Although there were seven difficult years as farmers adjusted, few of them want to return to subsidies. They prefer the marketplace with its risks, believing it is the only sustainable long-term option. Their country's experience could eventually lead to other governments following suit to some extent at least, however much of the reforms may have been long viewed by certain communities as practically unworkable and politically unacceptable *(Gardner, 1994; Spinelli, 1994; Walker and Bell, 1994)*. Australia has already followed far down the same route, which should provide an easier example for other countries to follow since both the economic and environmental gains are likely to be substantially greater than in New Zealand.

How many of these subsidies shall we consider are perverse? Certain subsidies have sometimes been beneficial in certain local and short-term respects, but many subsidies reveal scope to exert long-run injury on both economies and environments writ large. The documentation in this chapter makes plain that there are many unfortunate repercussions of agricultural subsidies. As can be seen in Box 3.2, New Zealand has eliminated virtually all its subsidies, and the country's economy and environment alike are better off, as is agreed on all sides. To this limited extent, we could reasonably assume that virtually all subsidies in agriculture anywhere are perverse. This would perhaps be pushing the point too far. For purposes of this report and its need to come up with some concluding figure, however far from conclusive, a total for perverse subsidies is proposed that is 65 percent (approximately two-thirds) of the formal subsidies total, viz. $211 billion, or say $210 billion, per year. This is a somewhat arbitrary reckoning, and it is applied to a sector of unusually large financial size. But it is considered a realistic reckoning, and it reflects consultations on this point with established agricultural experts in various parts of the world. The true proportion could be 15 percent higher or lower, which postulates a range of $163-260 billion, per year. The author believes it is unlikely to lie outside this range—unless better-judgement assessments can demonstrate otherwise.

On top of this are the environmental externalities described above, and considered to be hidden subsidies from society to agriculture. Just the two instances documented amount to $250 billion per year. Since they are adverse for the environment by definition and adverse for the economy through their quantified costs, they are all viewed as perverse subsidies.

So the grand total of perverse subsidies is here estimated to be $460 billion per year, within a range of $390 to $520 billion.

Within a broader economic context, these figures must clearly rank as a low estimate. Consider some further indirect costs. Agricultural subsidies do much to distort trade patterns and even to heighten political tensions among the international community, especially as concerns North/South relationships *(Legg, 1993)*. Subsidies in developed countries make it unduly hard for developing countries to compete in international markets, thus reinforcing the inefficiency of their agriculture *(Pearce, 1995)*. Modest liberalization of agricultural trade would be worth $150 billion to the global economy by 2002, most of it due to cutbacks in farm protection; full liberalization would be worth almost $400 billion a year (1991 values). European GDP would be 2.5 percent higher, and some Asia economies could benefit by 8 percent; the United States' balance of trade would be $42 billion better off *(Goldin and van der Mensbrugghe, 1996; see also Johnson, 1991; Maier and Steenblik, 1995; Swinnen and Van der Zee, 1993)*.

These knock-on effects of international trade deserve a further look. Subsidized exports have undermined developing-country livelihoods by flooding local markets with cheap imported food, as witness the impact of European Union beef dumped in West Africa. Pastoral farmers in Mali, Niger and Burkina Faso sell animals in local markets, which during the late 1980s were disrupted by European beef subsidized enough to be sold at one third of the normal price. Also in West Africa, cheap wheat imports have displaced traditional food staples in indigenous diets. Wheat imports into the coastal region have been increasing by over 8 percent per year for the past decade, while per-capita production of sorghum and millet has been falling. By driving down local prices, subsidized wheat exports from developed countries have done much to damage rural livelihoods *(Watkins, 1995)*.

Scope for Policy Interventions

However difficult subsidy removal is reputed to be, there are some success stories available. One of the best is the severe curtailment of pesticides in Indonesia and the introduction of Integrated Pest Management (IPM). This strategy allows for limited use of pesticides as part of an overall plan deploying mixed crops, staged plantings, and natural enemies of pests. As recently as 1985, the government of Indonesia, also those of Senegal, Egypt and several other countries, were covering 80 percent of farmers' pesticide costs. In Indonesia, however, massive use of pesticides from the mid-1970s through the mid-1980s inadvertently eliminated the natural insect predators of a pest, the brown planthopper. This pest had originally been no more than secondary and minor, but pesticides caused it to become a prime pest that cost Indonesia over $1 billion in rice losses by the mid-1980s *(World Resources Institute, 1994)*.

During the brief period 1986-87, the Indonesian government slashed subsidies from 80 percent to zero, using part of the savings of $120 million per year to fund its new IPM program. The government also banned 57 of 66 kinds of pesticides *(World Resources Institute, 1994)*. While rice farmers' use of pesticides plunged by 60 percent, their rice yields rose by 15 percent—a phenomenon that reflected the recovery of the natural predators of the rice pests. During the years 1986-90 there were savings of $1 billion for rice growers and the national economy. The IPM strategy has subsequently been adopted in the Philippines, Vietnam, India, Pakistan, Egypt, Ghana and most Latin American countries *(Denno and Perfect, 1994; Heinrichs, 1994; Moore, 1995; Naylor and Ehrlich, 1997; Rosegrant and Pingali, 1991; Thrupp, 1996)*.

Let us note too that certain agricultural subsidies can generate positive spillovers into other sectors. In India, input supports during the 1980s totaled 17 percent of agricultural value added (25 percent for wheat and 35 percent for rice) *(Gulati, 1989)*. They not only achieved much for the country's Green Revolution, they generated many spin-off benefits as well. From the early 1970s through the early 1990s, agriculture subsidies fed into infrastructure of many sorts, with the result that the length of surfaced roads more than doubled and the number of villages with electricity quadrupled *(Vaidyanathan, 1993; see also Repetto, 1994)*.

Moreover, there are promising signs in a few countries of a shift away from extravagant subsidies. New Zealand has phased out just about all its subsidies (Box 3.2), and Australia has gone far to follow suit. The next most promising demarche, though of far smaller scale, is probably in the United States, where the 1996 Farm Bill makes the most sweeping changes in agricultural policy since the New Deal. It aims to signal a new era when farmer decisions will be dictated by the competitive market rather than by government subsidies. A related bill will eliminate policies that require land to be left idle in some years in order to keep surpluses from depressing market prices. It will also increase spending on conservation of soil, water and on-farm wetlands *(Gardner, 1996; for some earlier analysis of reform needs, see Batie, 1996; Bradshaw, 1995; Faeth, 1995; Repetto, 1995; Sumner, 1995; Ward et al., 1989)*.

In addition, subsidies should not only be delinked from production but relinked to a broad range of crops and environmental services. This should prompt farmers to adopt practices that enhance rather than degrade their farm capital *(MacNeill, 1994; see also Doering, 1992; Just and Bockstoel, 1991; Maier and Steenblik, 1995)*. It would contrast markedly with the present position, whereby price supports unwittingly foster soil erosion among other environmental ills. Indeed subsidies send farmers far more powerful signals about how to use (or mis-use) the land than do all the small grants provided for soil conservation *(MacNeill, 1994)*. Subsidies also encourage over-use of agricultural chemicals such as synthetic fertilizers; reducing subsidies on these fertilizers would promote alternatives such as organic manures in integrated crop and livestock systems *(Pearce and Warford, 1993; see also Lichtenberg and Zilberman, 1986)*.

Particularly helpful would be policy measures that foster environmental safeguards, notably in the form of set-aside programs that divert erodible farmland from crop production in order to protect topsoil. These programs are strongly supported by governments, thus supplying an instance of constructive subsidies. (The measure can also serve to control the supply of food or other commodities and thus to prop up or even raise prices.) There have been some sizeable set-aside programs in recent years: in 1995 alone, 202,000 square kilometers in the United States and 81,000 square kilometers in the European Union (both equating to around 11 percent of arable land), and 7000 square kilometers in Japan, or 16 percent of arable land. In return for setting aside land, farmers receive compensation payments, usually in the range $35 to $125 per hectare, though occasionally as high as $1000 for rice paddies in Japan and $6300 for forestry in the European Union. Participation is usually voluntary, so the compensation has to be as much as a farmer would have received through crops *(Maier, 1997)*.

More helpful still would be measures that prevent the most erodible and otherwise vulnerable lands being put under crops in the first place. But that would require a level of anticipatory land-use planning that does not seem feasible on a broad scale as yet.

This leads to the question of incentives for farmers to safeguard the environmental services they derive from their lands These services comprise non-traded public goods such as aquifer recharge, landscape amenity, flood control, riparian buffer zones and wetland habitats. They could be developed as "crops," providing farm income as well as enriching the landscape. In fact, some American and Canadian farmers are already doing as much through programs such as the North American Waterfowl Management Plan, by which ducks as well as taxpayers foot the bills (at the ostensible behest of duck hunters). In Canada, the revenues have secured nearly 1600 square kilometers of waterfowl habitat in the agricultural region of western Canada, a further 920 square kilometers of habi-

---

The 1996 U.S. Farm Bill makes the most sweeping changes in agricultural policy since the New Deal. It aims to signal a new era when farmer decisions will be dictated by the competitive market rather than by government subsidies.

Eco-agriculture can use 60-70 percent less chemical fertilizer, pesticides and fossil-fuel energy, while maintaining crop yields. It can also generate more jobs and spend more money on local goods and services.

---

tat have been restored, and 2800 square kilometers are being managed for as many as 168 wildlife species. Much of the land continues to produce conventional farm commodities compatible with wildlife production *(MacNeill, 1994; see also Organization for Economic Co-operation and Development, 1995).*

This approach is paralleled in certain sectors of Europe, notably the Alps where Swiss cattle and montane meadows add to landscape attractions as part of a tourist package of expectations. There are many other such examples: the Norfolk Broads in England, the sheep moors of the Lake District and highland Scotland, and the lakes of Sweden and Norway.

All this points the way toward sustainable agriculture, a large component of which is environmentally sensitive agriculture *(Legg and Portugal, 1997; Parris, 1997; Steenblik, 1997; Thrupp, 1997).* "Eco-agriculture" as it is sometimes known can use 60-70 percent less chemical fertilizer, pesticides and fossil-fuel energy, while maintaining crop yields; soils contain 30-70 percent more organic matter, which, apart from the fertility benefit, sequesters carbon from the atmosphere. Sustainable agriculture can also generate more jobs and spend more money on local goods and services *(Maier and Steenblik, 1995; Pretty, 1995 and 1996; see also Bradshaw, 1995; Legg, 1997; Lynch, 1994; Repetto, 1995).*

Pushing this general approach still further, some analysts even envisage the eventual abolition of Ministries of Agriculture, replacing them with Ministries of Land Resources which will look out for conventional agriculture together with forests for timber and recreation combined, uplands watersheds, hedgerows and coppices for wildlife, sports fisheries, and soils and biotas overall as a carbon sink. After all, rural areas are crucial not just in terms of food production but many other forms of enterprise, including leisure activities and even the "spiritual life" of countries concerned *(Ritson and Harvey, 1995).*

To end on a pragmatic note, consider the policy scope to foster agricultural research. If ever there was a niche for government support, this is it. We need agricultural research more than ever before if we are to feed twice as many people within another three or four decades. Hence the calls from the late 1996 World Food Summit for another science-based Green Revolution. Yet the Consultative Group on International Agricultural Research (CGIAR) budget of $319 million in 1992 dropped to $245 million by 1994, even though the network of 14 International Agricultural Research Centers needed $270 million merely to maintain its activities at erstwhile levels *(Greenland et al., 1994).* In light of the returns on research investment which can be as high as 20 or even

40 percent per year, the CGIAR budget is absurdly small *(Evanson and Rosegrant, 1995; Pinstrup-Andersen and Pandya-Lorch, 1995)*. There is all the greater urgency in bolstering research funding at a time when agricultural planners are aiming for an annual 2-percent increase in food production, and given that there is often a time lag of 10-20 years before breakthrough research leads to major harvest increases in farmers' fields *(McCalla, 1994)*. Note that the current CGIAR budget is less than one tenth of one percent of what the OECD countries spend each year on agricultural subsidies.

CHAPTER 4

FOSSIL FUELS AND NUCLEAR ENERGY

The U.S. Clean Air Act has produced net direct monetary savings during the period 1970-1990 averaging $1.1 trillion per year.

Commercial energy—meaning, for the most part, fossil fuels and nuclear power—is the single largest enterprise of humankind, and it is central to most economies worldwide. It can bestow abundant benefits on humankind. It also has great capacity to harm the environment through the pollution impacts of fossil fuels, manifested through urban smog, acid rain and global warming, also through nuclear fuels with their radioactive wastes. Urban smog leads to asthma, emphysema and a host of other respiratory ills, while acid rain imposes extensive damage on biotas. As for global warming, this is widely regarded as the most important single problem in the environmental arena. Similarly, subsidies for fossil fuels and nuclear power can harm the economy through their markedly distortive effects. So the sector as a whole has large potential for perverse subsidies.

A closely associated sector, road transportation, utilizes a fossil fuel, oil, which provides 97 percent of all fuel used in road transportation. At the same time, road transportation features a host of other subsidies, many of which are unusually perverse and unusually large. This entire topic is dealt with separately in the next chapter. Subsidies for oil are considered here only from the standpoint of producing the stuff, as opposed to subsidies for its use in road transportation.

We derive 85 percent of our commercial energy from fossil fuels and 7 percent from nuclear power *(Flavin, 1997; Gelbspan, 1997; World Resources Institute, 1996)*. Only in electricity have alternatives—notably hydropower, geothermal energy and wind/solar power—made much contribution, and except for hydropower they attract little government support. It is fossil fuels and nuclear power that receive the great bulk of energy subsidies. The energy sector also features many indirect and concealed subsidies in the form of environmental externalities. It generates such marked pollution that some analysts *(Cairncross, 1995; Holdren, 1989; Hubbard, 1991; Koplow, 1995; Lovins, 1996)* consider the environmental costs of fossil fuels are at least equal to and possibly much greater than the more conventional and recognized costs. All this, moreover, is without counting what will surely prove to be the biggest environmental externality of all, global warming (see Chapter 2), half of which is due to emissions of carbon dioxide which stem primarily from fossil fuels.

55

Energy—or rather the production and distribution of energy—is often controlled in major measure by the state. This means that many governments play a central role in setting energy prices. The failure of governments to price energy properly means that consumption is higher, grows faster, and is more polluting than it should be. As we shall see, fossil fuels and nuclear energy cost society many billions of dollars more than their users pay directly. There is a plethora of hidden costs: tax policies supply credits, exemptions, deferrals, preferential rates, loans, loan guarantees, exclusions, deductions, R and D programs, depletion allowances, accelerated depreciation, risk insurance, and regulatory costs. (For a brief technical note on the myriad sorts of subsidies, see Box 4.1.) While these tax policies may have served a productive purpose when they were first introduced, many have now exceeded their usefulness, yet they remain on the books. In the United States, depletion allowances were introduced to promote oil production during World War I. This was an entirely valid reason at the time, though it has long run out of rationale even while the tax subsidy persists.

While the fossil-fuel industry is worth well over $1.4 trillion per year *(Heede, 1997)*, it is the second most heavily subsidized of all economic sectors (the first is road transportation, see Chapter 5) *(Lovins, 1998)*. Yet we have only a hazy idea of how large these subsidies are. (Nuclear power, being a much smaller and less diverse industry, should be accurately and precisely documented—but governments, especially those in the former Soviet Union, France and several Asian countries, are even more loathe to divulge information about nuclear energy than about fossil fuels.) Not only are fossil-fuel subsidies large, they are unusually damaging environmentally, entraining heavy economic costs both present and prospective. But as with agriculture and other sectors with huge subsidies, governments simply do not know (or are not saying) how much taxpayers' money they are directing into fossil-fuel energy. Virtually right across the board, the database is uneven in quantity and poor in quality. Worse, such figures which are available often conflict with each other severely. A curious circumstance, and one which makes it unusually difficult to draw policy conclusions.

Hence the following appraisal is partial at best. At least it presents a solid picture of how far the fossil-fuel industry is being propped up by government handouts, even though its prodigious environmental externalities and other societal spillovers suggest it should be heavily taxed. Or, as a minimum, the industry should be subjected to the full rigors of the marketplace: coal and solar energy should demonstrate their prowess on a level playing field, whereas coal is effectively awarded a start of between 10 and 30 goals. Ironically, it is the communist countries of the former Soviet bloc and China that have been doing most to shed this socialistic mode of running an energy economy. One of the most energy profligate and environmentally polluting countries, the United States, has not gone nearly so far to cut its subsidies, limited though they are already in relation to the size of the United States economy and highly beneficial though cutbacks would be in both economic and environmental terms.

The problem of the poor database is helped somewhat by the fact that the fossil fuels sector is concentrated in relatively few producer and consumer countries. The top 10 producers account for 65 percent of oil, 75 percent of natural gas and 87 percent of coal, and the top ten consumers account for 60 percent of oil, 69 percent of natural gas and 82 percent of coal *(British Petroleum, 1997; see also Larsen, 1994; World Resources Institute, 1996)*. For further details, see Tables 4.1 and 2. China accounts for almost one tenth of all production, while the OECD countries account for half of all consumption and the former Soviet Union and Eastern Europe still account for one sixth. To this extent, it is a little easier to track down the major subsidizers.

Box 4.1

ENERGY SUBSIDIES: ALL SORTS AND CONDITIONS THEREOF

There are many direct and well known types of subsidies that have the specific aim of altering market prices. There are also indirect subsidies—probably more numerous while less recognized than the direct subsidies—that operate via fiscal and other measures to affect investment decisions, e.g., favorable tax rates for oil and gas exploration. These hidden subsidies can sometimes be more influential than the direct subsidies. So the term "energy subsidies" sometimes refers to transfers to energy consumers via underpricing, and at other times to transfers to producers via overpricing. It can even be a combination of the two. Given the limited scope of the research project on which this report is based, the distinction is not pursued here.

Similarly, the term "Producer Subsidy Equivalents" comprises direct financial aid from governments to support current production, plus price supports that result indirectly from limits to the use of other fuels to substitute for domestic coal, or from agreements between coal producers and coal users. In other words, the PSE is a direct budgetary subsidy that makes domestic production, at current costs, competitive with imports *(Organisation for Economic Co-operation and Development, 1997b; see also Michaelis, 1996)*.

In 1991 and before the former Soviet Union and a few other countries started to slash their subsidies, just 11 non-OECD countries accounted for over $200 billion of fossil-fuel subsidies, or 92 percent of all such subsidies *(Larsen, 1994).*

Table. 4.1

FOSSIL FUEL PRODUCERS, 1996: THE TOP TENS
(and % of world total)

Country	Oil (million tonnes)		Gas (million tonnes oil equivalent)		Coal	
Saudi Arabia	429	(12.8)	37	(1.9)		
U.S.A.	383	(11.4)	492	(24.5)	565	(25.0)
Russia	301	(9.0)	505	(25.1)	115	(5.1)
Iran	184	(5.5)				
Mexico	164	(4.9)				
Venezuela	162	(4.8)				
China	159	(4.7)			681	(30.1)
Norway	156	(4.6)	37	(1.8)		
U.K.	130	(3.9)	76	(3.8)		
U.A.E.	117	(3.5)				
Canada			138	(6.9)	42	(1.8)
Netherlands			68	(3.4)		
Uzbekistan			41	(2.0)		
Algeria			59	(3.0)		
Indonesia			60	(3.0)		
Germany					70	(3.1)
Poland					87	(3.8)
Kazakhstan					39	(1.7)
South Africa					110	(4.8)
Australia					129	(5.7)
India					141	(6.2)
TOTALS	2185	(65.1)	1513	(75.4)	1979	(87.3)
OECD	1006	(29.9)	918	(45.7)	921	(40.7)
European Union 15			190	(9.4)		
Former Soviet Union	353	(10.5)	602	(30.0)	191	(8.5)
WORLD	3362		2009		2264	

Source: British Petroleum. 1997.

Table 4.2

FOSSIL FUEL CONSUMERS, 1996: THE TOP TENS
(and % of world total)

Country	Oil (million tonnes)		Gas (million tonnes oil equiv.)		Coal	
U.S.A.	833	(25.0)	569	(28.9)	516	(23.0)
Canada	80	(2.4)	66	(3.4)		
France	91	(2.8)				
Germany	137	(4.2)	75	(3.8)	89	(3.9)
Italy	94	(2.8)	47	(2.4)		
U.K.	84	(2.5)	77	(3.9)	45	(2.0)
Russia	128	(3.9)	317	(16.1)	119	(5.3)
China	173	(5.2)				
Japan	270	(8.1)	60	(3.0)	88	(3.9)
South Korea	101	(3.1)				
Netherlands			38	(1.9)		
Ukraine			70	(3.6)		
Uzbekistan			40	(2.0)		
Poland					72	(3.2)
South Africa					82	(3.6)
Australia					43	(1.9)
China					666	(29.5)
India					140	(6.2)
TOTALS	1991	(60)	1359	(69)	1860	(82)
OECD	1976	(59.6)	1064	(53.9)	947	(42.0)
European Union (15)	618	(18.7)	302	(15.3)	226	(10.0)
Former Soviet Union	197	(6.0)	474	(24.1)	181	(8.0)
WORLD	3313		1972		2257	

Source: British Petroleum. 1997.

Roughly $145 billion or 72 percent were in the former Soviet Union (FSU) alone. Thus the FSU was far and away the single largest player in the fossil fuels arena; and while it has engaged in stringent slashing of subsidies since 1991, it still features prominently. In 1991 subsidies in FSU amounted to an astonishing 10-13 percent of GDP, and in Poland, Egypt and Venezuela over 10 percent, though in India they were "only" 2.3 percent and in China 1.8 percent *(Larsen, 1994).*

The United States

The United States possesses only 4 percent of the world's population but it consumes 25 percent of its commercial energy *(World Resources Institute, 1996)*. It consumes roughly twice as much energy per person and per unit of GNP as do Western Europeans and the Japanese *(World Bank, 1996)*. By increasing the efficiency with which Americans utilize energy to Western European and Japanese levels, the country could save over $100 billion per year. The country also emits 22 percent of carbon dioxide accumulating in the global atmosphere. In per-capita terms, it emits twice as much carbon dioxide as Germany, Russia or Japan, almost three times as much as Italy, and ten times as much as China. Fossil fuels contribute 90 percent of the United States' greenhouse gas emissions (plus 90 percent of local air pollution and acid rain, and the great majority of gases leading to smog) *(MacKenzie, 1997)*. So it is worth examining in a little detail.

United States energy subsidies in 1989 were estimated to total over $36 billion (fossil fuels $22 billion), equivalent to $400 per American household. While they have declined a little to perhaps $32 billion—regrettably and surprisingly, it is hard to obtain latest data—the sector spread remains largely the same *(Koplow, 1996; see also D.W. Jorgenson Associates, 1994; Gelbspan, 1997; Hill et al., 1995; Lovins, 1996; McKenna, 1994; see also Repetto et al., 1997; Shapiro and Soares, 1997; Shelby et al., 1995)*. (Even more remarkably, certain estimates vary by an order of magnitude, depending mostly upon definitions and criteria.) The 1989 figure of $36 billion reflected what individuals and private corporations would have had to pay had they purchased these government-provided benefits in the marketplace. Tax benefits in 1989 accounted for $18 billion, agency programs for $15 billion, and two quantified market interventions for $3 billion. Of the $36 billion, 61 percent went to fossil fuels, which supplied 85 percent of all United States energy; 31 percent went to nuclear energy, with 7 percent of all energy; and only 8 percent went to renewable and non-polluting sources of energy (wind power, solar power, hydroelectric, geothermal, etc.), plus energy conservation and energy efficiency. Thus fossil fuels and nuclear power received subsidies totalling 92 percent, or $33 billion, of the total. Within the fossil-fuel category, the smallest subsidy went to natural gas even though it is environmentally cleaner than oil or coal. Some minor subsidies went to a miscellany of items such as government sponsored R and D and general investment tax credits *(Hill et al., 1995; Koplow, 1996; see also Shelby et al., 1994)*. So the figure used here for United States fossil-fuel and nuclear subsidies today is a putative 92 percent of $32 or $29 billion.

United States subsidies are strongly weighted against non-polluting renewables *(Berger, 1997; Lovins, 1998)*. Among the leading biases are: specialized tax benefits for mining coal, oil and gas (including depletion allowances of them as non-renewable resources); exemption from minimum taxation requirements for fossil fuels; public financing for nuclear reactors among other supports for nuclear power; and disproportionate amounts of public R and D for conventional energy sources, primarily fossil fuels. In addition, there is a miscellany of minor supports such as agricultural policies that discourage crop diversification to energy crops. According to the analysis above, the subsidy ratio for renewables versus non-renewables is 1:10 (though some other analysts consider it could be as high as 1:35; *see Johansson et al., 1993; Koplow, 1995; Lovins, 1996*). There is good cause to wonder why the major category of non-renewables, fossil fuels, deserves any subsidies at all.

All OECD Countries

OECD countries as a whole subsidize energy (not just fossil fuels and nuclear power) to the extent of at least $70-80 billion per year (so the United States accounts for 40-46 percent). This includes: coal $30 billion; oil $15 billion; natural gas $6 billion; nuclear $14 billion (could be a considerable under-estimate, due to governments' reticence with data); and renewables $4 billion (could also be a low estimate due to incomplete documentation) *(de Moor, 1997; International Energy Agency, 1995a; Koplow, 1993; Organization for Economic Co-operation and Development, 1997b; Shelby et al., 1994).*

The most extreme instance of subsidies today is probably German coal. See Box 4.2

Box 4.2

COAL SUBSIDIES IN GERMANY

Coal is the most polluting of the fossil fuels, whether through production or consumption, so it should rationally be taxed rather than subsidized. Yet production is heavily supported in industrialized countries such as Germany and Japan, and the same for consumption in many developing countries such as China and India *(Anderson, 1995)*. In 1991 coal subsidies worldwide totalled somewhere between $37 and $51 billion, with at least $17 billion in the former Soviet Union, $10 billion in Eastern Europe, and $6 billion in China and India *(Larsen, 1994; see also Kane, 1996)*.

Box 4.2 *(continued)*

Production is most strongly subsidized in Europe and Japan in order to help high-cost producers compete with imported coal. In Western Europe in the early 1990s, support was worth almost $60,000 per employee per year, compared with only $16,000 per employee in the highly protected agriculture of the European Union *(Radetzki, 1995)*. Coal subsidies now provide a domestic producer price 40 percent higher than the import price in the United Kingdom and France, twice higher in Spain, three times higher in Belgium and Japan, and almost four times higher in Germany *(Anderson, 1995; Ellerman, 1995)*. In the seven main coal producing countries of the OECD—the United States, Germany, Australia, the United Kingdom, Spain, Turkey and Canada—coal subsidies total around $30 billion per year, with Germany accounting for $21 billion (though these figures include many payments and other supports apart from producer subsidies) *(International Energy Agency, 1995)*.

There could hardly be a more remarkable instance of perverse subsidies than coal mining in Germany. (This brief review is based largely on *Anderson, 1995; Data Resources Inc., 1994; DRI/McGraw-Hill, 1994; International Energy Agency, 1995, Steenblik and Coroyannakis, 1995)*. Germany has practically no oil and very little gas, so there is a strong security case in favour of coal. In 1982 the German government supplied subsidies of $30 for each tonne of coal, a figure that by 1995 had soared to $119 (68 percent of production costs), while the subsidies total had climbed from $2.9 billion to $6.9 billion (in terms of producer price supports, but omitting tax credits for anti-pollution equipment and other hidden subsidies). This meant that the subsidy cost of protecting each of 90,000 mining jobs for one year had risen from $15,400 to $72,800 (1995 dollars). The price subsidy for coal as a percentage of the border price is around 230 percent, by contrast with the European Union, 150 percent *(Organisation for Economic Co-operation and Development, 1997; Roodman, 1996)*.

It would now be cheaper for the German government to retire all its miners and pay them their regular salaries to stay at home, leaving taxpayers and electricity users much better off. Making electricity from coal in Germany costs a utility 6 cents per kw hour, but it costs consumers an additional 2 cents for disease and death caused by air pollution *(Roodman, 1997; see also Anderson, 1995; Newbery, 1995; Steenblik and Coroyannakis, 1995)*. (If German utilities had to pay those costs

---

Box 4.2 *(continued)*

too, windpower would suddenly become much more competitive and profitable *(Krupnick and Bertraw, 1997; Roodman, 1997)*. Furthermore the limited contribution of the outsize subsidies is demonstrated by the fact that during the period 1985-95 the German mining workforce still fell by half *(International Energy Agency, 1996)*. Moreover, France and Belgium have virtually eliminated their coal subsidies, while Spain, the United Kingdom and Japan have radically reduced theirs. As a result, coal miners in the United Kingdom now constitute less than 0.2 percent of the national workforce, down from an average of 1.4 percent in the early 1980s; and in France they account for less than 0.1 percent, but they amount to nearly 2 percent in Germany *(Anderson, 1995)*. Since most of these countries are still burning as much coal as ever, however, phasing away subsidies has mostly exported the environmental problems of coal mining to producers abroad.

The Former Soviet Union and Eastern Europe

As noted, the former Soviet Union (FSU) is still a "biggie" in the fossil fuels picture. Of all non-OECD subsidies to fossil fuels in 1991, totalling some $190-245 billion, the largest proportion was in the FSU *(Ingram and Fay, 1994; Larsen and Shah, 1994)*. Just the coal subsidies amounted to 125 percent of the border price—and of course these high subsidies led producers to extract poor quality coal with low calorie content and high polluting impact, while also discouraging consumers from saving energy. The result was that the FSU was hopelessly inefficient in its use of fossil fuels. In 1993, it emitted 502 tonnes of carbon for each $1 million of GDP, way above China's 238 tonnes, the United States' 238 tonnes, India's 183 tonnes, and Japan's 144 tonnes *(World Bank, 1997)*.

Subsequently Russia and several other FSU countries have steadily removed many of their subsidies together with their energy controls and regulations *(Gurvich and Hughes, 1996)*. During the brief period 1990-91 to 1995-96, fossil-fuel subsidies in Russia were reduced by 69 percent, though in early 1996 direct subsidies to the coal industry still amounted to 144 percent of the pithead price and 1.3 percent of GDP *(Gurvich et al., 1996 and 1997; Rajkumar, 1996; World Bank, 1997a; and see Table 4.3)*. Today Russia's energy prices for industry (though not for households, which received two-thirds of energy subsidies in 1994) are moving closer to world market levels *(Gurvich et al., 1997;*

McPherson, 1996). Complete elimination of Russia's fossil-fuel subsidies would reduce energy consumption more than 10 percent from the 1990 level, while carbon dioxide emissions in 2010 would be 14 percent lower and particulate emissions 40 percent lower *(World Bank, 1997a)*. But Russia will find it difficult to reduce its subsidies much further in certain sectors. Complete removal would mean that household costs for heating and gas would have to be raised tens of times over the 1994 level *(Gurvich et al., 1997; see also de Moor, 1997)*.

Table 4.3

REDUCTIONS IN SUBSIDIES FOR FOSSIL FUELS 1990-91 To 1995-96

Country/Region	Subsidies (million1995 US$) (and rates%)				% GDP
	1990-91		1995-96		1995-96
Russia	28,797	(45)	9,427	(31)	1.50
Eastern Europe	13,120	(42)	5,838	(23)	3.19
Asia	29,362	(33)	13,430	(16)	1.19
China	24,545	(42)	10,297	(20)	2.42
India	4,250	(25)	2,663	(19)	1.06
Oil producers	31,067	(56)	19,272	(42)	2.26
Iran	13,076	(86)	9,622	(77)	8.68
Saudi Arabia	3,837	(66)	1,720	(34)	1.42
	3,833	(17)	528	(2)	0.06
OECD	n/a		51		0.25
TOTAL*	n/a		131		0.47

* *all countries*

Source: *World Bank, 1997a; also see text.*

Next, Eastern Europe, where there has been a better than 50-percent cut in fossil-fuel subsidies between 1990/91 and 1995/96. In Poland, industrial coal prices quintupled in January 1990; until then, sulphur dioxide output per head was 2.5 times as high as the European Community average, and pollution of air, water and soils was among the worst in the world. Something similar applied in several other countries of Eastern Europe. Largely as a result of the sudden upheaval in the region's economies from 1990 onwards, however, energy use has declined by about 20 percent across the board and annual fossil-fuel subsidies have declined from $13 billion to less than $6 billion, though several countries have still left their coal prices far below world prices and they use four or five times as much energy per head as countries with the same income levels in Asia and Latin America *(McPherson, 1996; Rajkumar, 1996; World Bank, 1997a).*

Other Non-OECD Countries

China is a fossil-fuel giant to match Russia, mainly because of its coal which provides 73 percent of its commercial energy *(Wang, 1996).* With 30 percent of the world's coal output, China is the number one coal burner, having pulled ahead of the United States (Table 4.2). Every month it installs a new coal-fired power plant with a capacity of 1000 megawatts *(Kane, 1996; see also Flavin and Dunn, 1997).* During the period 1970-90, energy use in China grew by a whopping 208 percent *(World Resources Institute, 1994).* Unfortunately, end users were not encouraged to conserve energy because prices were artificially low, which in turn was due to the government's wish to produce and distribute energy at prices way below production costs. Since the mid-1980s, however, and due to deep subsidy cuts, many fossil-fuel prices have been rising more rapidly than for food, clothing and other daily use articles. More recently, subsidies have been slashed from $25 billion in 1990-91 to $10 billion in 1995-96 (Table 4.3), and since 1984 energy intensity, measured by the ratio of energy used to GDP, has fallen by 30 percent *(World Bank, 1997a; see also International Energy Agency, 1995; McPherson, 1996; Rajkumar, 1996).* In some sectors and regions, China's energy prices are now comparable to those in several OECD countries *(Auer and Ye, 1997).* All this should help to reduce the widespread pollution that is costing the country $54 billion a year through damage to productive resources, plus sickness and premature deaths (178,000 such deaths in major cities each year) *(World Bank, 1997b and c).*

But so extensive are China's fossil-fuel deposits and so ambitious are the country's plans to exploit them, that China projects a three-fold expansion in its energy use between 1990 and 2025 *(International Energy Agency, 1995; World Resources Institute, 1994).* Even if the government were to eliminate fossil-fuel subsidies entirely and even if energy efficiency efforts were to be greatly expanded, China's carbon dioxide emissions would be projected to increase from about 10 percent of global emissions in 1989 to 20 percent in 2010 *(Auer and Ye, 1997; International Energy Agency, 1994).*

Next, consider another leading player in Asia, India, where coal contributes over 70 percent of primary commercial energy *(World Resources Institute, 1996).* India too has reduced its fossil-fuel subsidies, from $4.2 billion in 1990-91 to $2.7 billion in 1995-96 (Table 4.3). The governments were no longer willing or able to sustain large budget deficits, and it likewise wanted to attract capital to meet growing energy demands *(Repetto et al., 1997; see also Flavin and Dunn, 1997; World Bank, 1997a).* All India's petroleum products have risen to world prices or above, with the notable exception of kerosene, a fuel widely consumed by households and especially poorer households *(Bhattacharyya, 1995; Rajkumar, 1996).*

In summary, fossil-fuel subsidies in non-OECD countries, including the FSU and Eastern Europe, totaled $190-245 billion in 1990-91 according to early-1990s estimates. The total has subsequently turned out to be on the high side, and may well have been, according to this paper's analysis based on 1997 findings, more like $150 billion. At all events, the 1990-91 total was reduced to $49 billion by 1995-96 *(World Bank, 1997a)* (another leading analyst, Rajkumar *(1996)*, believes the latter amount could be around $70 billion). For details, see Table 4.3. Russia accounted for $19 billion of the decline, Eastern Europe $7 billion, and China $14 billion, with other sizeable amounts on the part of oil producers such as Saudi Arabia and Iran (Table 4.3) *(World Bank, 1997a; see also Flavin and Dunn, 1997; Rajkumar, 1996)*. On top of this are covert subsidies in developing countries in the form of potential budgetary savings from inefficient energy production, with avoidable power losses amounting to roughly $30 billion *(Ingram and Fay, 1994)*. These various subsidies not only prove a burden on, and hence a hidden subsidy from, the public purse. They have also helped create a host of inefficient and fragile industries, and they have tended to freeze technology, albeit these sizeable costs remain unquantified *(Desai, 1992)*. Conversely, reduction of subsidies has contributed to more rational pricing and reductions in energy-intensity. Brazil, which retains virtually no energy subsidies at all, has one of the lowest energy intensities in the developing world *(World Bank, 1997a)*.

In summary: today's non-OECD total can be put at $79 billion, say $80 billion, per year. This total relates only to fossil fuels. It does not include anything for nuclear subsidies since non-OECD countries do not have (as yet) many of the world's nuclear facilities.

Nuclear Energy

While nuclear energy is an energy source that is eminently renewable, it is subject to major environmental problems in the form of highly toxic and long-life waste products. There is also the risk of accidents like Chernobyl, which is estimated to levy a cost in Ukraine alone by the year 2000 of $100-360 billion, or many times more than the value of all nuclear-generated electricity in the FSU *(Lenssen and Flavin, 1996)*. On top of all this, there is the threat of nuclear materials getting into the hands of terrorists and rogue states. These are formidable externality costs. There is also the question of whether nuclear power can compete in a marketplace with a level playing field. In the United States, no new nuclear power stations have been ordered since 1978: they are not up to commercial snuff. Japan too no longer orders new reactors. Worldwide, 86 nuclear plants have already been retired and decommissioned *(Lovins and Lovins, 1997)*.

66

These problems notwithstanding, nuclear power has attracted much government support in countries such as France and Belgium, both of which are poor in fossil fuels. Altogether there are 400 nuclear plants in 32 countries, including 16 OECD countries with 85 percent of the world's reactor capacity. Nuclear power now provides 17 percent of the world's electricity (and 6.4 percent of all primary energy), compared with hydroelectric power 25 percent, and renewables such as solar and wind power, 3 percent *(World Resources Institute, 1996; for slightly different figures, see Energy Information Administration, United States Department of Energy, 1996).*

Box 4.3

ELECTRICITY

Fully one third of commercial energy is used to generate electricity, and two-thirds of that energy comes from fossil fuels, primarily coal *(Rajkumar, 1996)*. In the United States, almost 90 percent of coal goes to generate electricity *(Kane, 1996)*. Generating and distributing electricity is one of the world's largest businesses, with annual revenues of roughly $800 billion or twice as much as the world's auto industry *(Flavin and Lenssen, 1994)*. So it is worthwhile to consider electricity here as a subsector with subsidies totalling $80-85 billion in non-OECD countries alone in 1991. Of this amount, $34-39 billion was in the former Soviet Union and Eastern Europe, $15 billion in China and $7 billion in India *(Ingram and Fay, 1994; Larsen and Shah, 1994)*. The combined total can still be put today at $80 billion per year *(Ingram and Fay, 1994; International Energy Agency, 1994; Koplow, 1995; Larsen and Shah, 1994; Shelby et al., 1994)*.

Subsidies are still prevalent in those many developing countries that price electricity well below its long-run marginal cost of production and at a level only half that in industrialized countries. In 1988 price controls were driving down electricity prices in developing countries to only three-fifths the true cost of additional supplies. In Brazil and India, for instance, prices did not even cover production costs. In many developing countries, electricity is now sold at an average of only 40 percent of production costs.

In two leading energy consuming countries, China and India, energy policy has been mainly aimed at subsidizing electricity, with tariffs during the 1980s averaging only 40-60 percent of incremental costs

---

Box 4.3 (continued)

(Larsen and Shah, 1994). In India today, prices are still only 40 percent of the global average, and in China only half as much again. Whereas average tariffs in OECD countries rose by 1.4 percent a year in real terms between 1979 and 1988, they fell by 3.5 percent a year in developing countries. A great many energy utilities in the developing world are kept afloat by state handouts, whereupon underpricing encourages careless consumption.

When electricity prices are low, saving energy becomes less attractive. Developing countries use 10-20 percent more electricity than they would if consumers paid the true marginal cost of supply. Some 15-20 percent of the power produced disappears because of transmission losses. To produce one kilowatt hour of energy, developing countries use 20-40 percent more fuel than do OECD countries. In addition, too much capital is spent on energy-demanding projects, while also discouraging investment in new, cleaner technologies and more energy-efficient processes *(Heede, 1997; see also Burtraw and Krupnick, 1996; Krupnick and Burtraw, 1997).*

Electricity is also subsidized in a few developed countries, notably the United Kingdom, Italy and Australia. Direct subsidies amount to at least $10 billion per year, plus cross-subsidies amounting to another $6 billion, or $16 billion in all *(Organisation for Economic Co-operation and Development, 1997; see also Koplow, 1996; Shelby et al., 1994).* This makes for a global total of around $100 billion per year. At least 2 billion people, almost 40 percent of the world's population, still lack access to electricity. We can expect that demand will keep on growing, all the more as developing country populations keep on increasing. There is much scope for governments to pursue a course that allows them to expand electricity supplies with less overall cost to their economies and environments.

Because nuclear energy was viewed in the late 1950s and early 1960s as likely to become "too cheap to meter", many governments subsidized it through R and D outlays, public indemnification of nuclear facilities from accidents, and public management of both the production of nuclear materials and the disposal of nuclear waste. As recently as 1991, the United States government was still expending at least $3 billion in subsidies *(United States Energy Information*

Administration, 1992; see also Koplow, 1993). In industrialized countries as a whole, governments still spend over half their energy research budgets on nuclear power, viz. $4 billion per year (by contrast with less than 10 percent to renewables). All nuclear subsidies in OECD countries amount to $10-14 billion per year *(de Moor, 1997).* If we take a mid-point of $12 billion, that amounts to 15-17 percent of the $70-80 billion in subsidies that go to energy, this being a little less than for oil and only half as much as for coal *(de Moor, 1997).* Regrettably there are no data for subsidies in non-OECD countries, but that does not matter much here since there is little nuclear power there as yet except for the FSU.

Despite its early promise, nuclear energy has not lived up to its expectations. By 2000, it will comprise only one tenth of the lowest official forecasts made a quarter century ago. Today it has become the slowest growing energy source, with less than one percent expansion in 1996 and no prospect of improvement. In the United States, nuclear technology has absorbed $1 trillion in research funding and sundry other subsidies, yet it delivers less energy than wood: "It died of an incurable attack of market forces" *(Lovins and Lovins, 1997).*

Nuclear energy, also much coal, are used to generate electricity—which is itself highly subsidized. It is worthwhile to consider this subsector in a little detail. Certain of its subsidies are decidedly perverse; for instance, support for centralized transmission systems imposes a formidable obstacle to those many renewable energy sources that are decentralized. For a brief review of electricity, see Box 4.3.

Environmental Externalities

Fossil fuels cause many environmental problems apart from the better known forms of pollution, such as landscape scars, mining tailings and oil spills. While these are generally local in scope and often ephemeral in nature, they can cause considerable loss of amenity to immediate communities. Their collective cost, in the billions of dollars worldwide, is not to be dismissed just because it does not match the more widespread injuries deriving from fossil fuels, e.g., urban smog, acid rain and global warming.

It is the grosser-scale types of pollution, however, that we shall consider here, notably sulfur dioxide, nitrogen oxide, particulates and carbon dioxide, all of which stem primarily from fossil fuels. (Certain of these costs in e.g., Mexico City will be covered in the next chapter on Road Transportation, so they are not touched upon here in order to avoid double counting.) In Indonesia, elimination of energy subsidies of $2.5 billion per year would entrain $490 million worth of health benefits, or $0.20 per $1 of subsidy removal. In India, removal of $2.6 billion of energy subsidies would translate into $1.7 billion in additional health benefits, or about $0.65 per dollar of subsidy removed (the pollution intensity of coal is much higher in India than that of subsidized fuels in Indonesia) *(Larsen and Shah, 1994; see also Panayotou, 1997)*. In many other countries too, there would be abundant health benefits from reduction of fossil-fuel subsidies that help generate pollutants such as nitrogen oxides, sulphur dioxide and particulates.

Acid rain has long been attributed to fossil-fuel pollutants among other factors *(Dudek et al., 1997)*. The environmental harm imposed by acid rain is well known, though there are only a few estimates of economic costs, e.g., the health benefits of controlling acid rain in the United States are in the order of $12-40 billion per year *(United States Environmental Protection Agency, 1997)*—to be compared with United States subsidies for fossil fuels, estimated earlier in this chapter at $20 billion per year. (In Britain, a program to reduce sulphur dioxide emissions, the main source of acid rain, confers benefits worth $29 billion per year, mostly in terms of human health *(ECOTEC, 1994)*.) Then there is acid rain damage to forests. In Europe there is an annual loss of commercial timber worth $30-35 billion *(Nielssen, 1994; United Nations Development Programme, 1997)*. There is also some emergent injury to tropical forests, as manifested already in southern China. It should shortly affect several other sectors of tropical forests, notably those with acidic soils and hence very vulnerable to acid rain. with a total expanse of more than 1 million square kilometers or over one eighth of remaining tropical forests *(Rodhe et al., 1992)*. Extensive as this tropical forest damage could be, there is no indication of how costly it could eventually become.

More important is the pollution from fine air-borne particles, i.e., those with an aerodynamic diameter of 10 microns or less, and able to move thousands of kilometers (carbon particulates from smokestacks in Beijing have been tracked to Hawaii), whereupon they cause severe and even lethal respiratory infections. These pollutants (together with other contaminants from fossil fuels) are taking one year off the lives of American people living in cities *(Pope et al., 1995)*, and as many as 60,000 due prematurely each year from particle air pollution *(Shprentz et al., 1996)* with a putative "life value" of $240 billion *(Wilson and Spengler, 1996)*. Relatively small reductions in fossil-fuel emissions worldwide, together with their fine particulates, could save some 700,000 lives annually by 2020. While four out of five of these saved lives would be in developing coun-

---

Fossil-fuel particulates take one year off the lives of Americans living in cities, and cause 60,000 deaths each year, with a putative "life value" of $240 billion. Small reductions in fossil-fuel emissions worldwide could save 700,000 lives annually by 2020 through reduced particulates alone.

Because of fossil-fuel particulates, urban residents in China—one of the most polluted countries—will, under a business-as-usual scenario, undergo health costs rising from $32 billion (or $129 per resident exposed) in 1995 to almost $98 billion (or $197) in 2020. When adjusted to the projected increases in income, the costs in 2020 will total more than $390 billion, or 13 percent of China's GDP.

tries, those in developed countries would equal the number projected to die from traffic injuries. The analysis has not taken account of health benefits through avoidable illness and workdays lost; nor has it considered deaths associated with pollutants other than particulates *(Working Group on Public Health and Fossil-Fuel Combustion, 1997; see also Ostro, 1996; Wilson and Spengler, 1996).*

Because of these fine particulates, urban residents in China will, under a business-as-usual scenario, undergo health costs rising from $32 billion (or $129 per resident exposed) in 1995 to almost $98 billion (or $197) in 2020; these costs include 600,000 premature deaths, 5.5 million cases of chronic bronchitis, more than 5 billion restricted-activity days, and 20 million cases of respiratory illness each year. When adjusted to the projected increases in income, the costs in 2020 will total more than $390 billion, or 13 percent of China's GDP *(World Bank, 1997b and c; see also Working Group on Public Health and Fossil-Fuel Combustion, 1997).*

By far the biggest environmental externality is, or rather will be, global warming. There seems little doubt that it is indeed on its way if not already arriving, and that it is due in major measure to fossil fuel emissions, not just carbon dioxide but methane and nitrous oxide as well. Uncertainties lie with the speed of its onset and its regional manifestations *(Houghton et al., 1996).* Nor is there much doubt about the scale (though not the size) of its economic costs, at least as minimally reckoned in trillions of dollars in the long run (see Chapter 2). Regrettably no estimate can be advanced here, not even in the form of a range, as to the size of ultimate costs of global warming. Suffice it to say that this is far and away the greatest environmental problem we can expect within the foreseeable future. From this standpoint, let alone other pollution impacts, all use of fossil fuels is here regarded as environmentally adverse to significant extent.

During the first half of the 1990s, Russia reduced its fossil-fuel subsidies by two thirds, and China by almost as much.

71

Oil subsidies in the United States prolong the country's risky dependence on foreign supplies, especially from the Persian Gulf, while discouraging private investments in new, cleaner technologies such as hyper-cars and other revolutionary forms of energy efficiency.

Were we to leave aside global warming, we would still find that in the case of the United States, less than 20 percent of subsidies can be classified as improving environmental quality even when "grey" areas are included (and surely far less than 20 percent in non-OECD countries). Those few subsidies that benefit the environment include: financing the remediation and closure of contaminated sites; researching energy-related externalities; addressing energy-related health and safety issues; and accelerating market transition to cleaner energy sources and improved efficiency *(Koplow, 1993 and 1997; see also Steenblik and Coroyannakis, 1995)*. At most, they would have only marginal countervailing impact on the adverse consequences of global warming.

It seems absurd to fail to come up with any quantified estimate of environmental externalities in the fossil fuel sphere in light of its serving as a source of multiple pollutants and in light of its major contribution to the potentially grandscale costs of global warming. Alas, it seems we are stuck with a singular lacuna. The externalities are here reckoned to be effectively nil—purely for lack of quantified evidence. Grotesque as this assertion may seem, it is far and away the most cautious and conservative "estimate" in the whole report. The reader might bear this in mind when evaluating the estimate following with respect to fossil fuel subsidies overall. After all, there is a non-trivial risk that global warming may turn out to be the biggest covert subsidy of all in the future world economy (see Chapter 2).

Subsidies Worldwide

While the OECD countries use most of the world's commercial energy, they appear to employ fewest energy subsidies—though there could be many subsidies that remain undocumented or unidentified. At all events, their fossil-fuel and nuclear subsidies are estimated to amount to at least $65 billion per year *(de Moor, 1997; Organization for Economic Co-operation and Development, 1997b)*. It is the non-OECD countries that feature the most abundant subsidies, which can be put at $80 billion per year *(Gurvich et al., 1997; see also de Moor, 1997, based on Larsen and Shah, 1994; World Resources Institute, 1995)*.

So the present annual total for fossil-fuel and nuclear subsidies worldwide can be put at $145 billion. True, this estimate is not nearly so precise as it seems. It reflects many different modes of analytic assessment by governments with their abundant covert subsidies, leaving the estimate distinctly conservative.

How many of these worldwide subsidies shall we say are perverse by exerting adverse impact on both the economy and the environment? As we have seen in the case of fossil fuels, there is a uniquely negative environmental factor through global warming alone with its potentially largescale and profound impacts. This in itself is enough to designate all fossil fuel subsidies as decidedly perverse from an environmental standpoint.

Fossil fuel subsidies also feature sizeable economic drawbacks insofar as they slow economic development by distorting production and consumption decisions in the energy arena generally—as in the economy overall since they draw capital and labor away from more profitable opportunities *(Bruce et al., 1996; Heede, 1997)*. In non-OECD countries in particular, removal of subsidies would foster economic growth by improving the efficiency with which these countries use their energy resources *(Organization for Economic Co-operation and Development, 1992 and 1997b)*, raising incomes by at least $35 billion or nearly 13 percent of all subsidies *(Larsen and Shah, 1994; see also Burniaux et al., 1992; Shah and Larsen, 1994)*. In just the former Soviet Union, elimination of subsidies would generate a welfare increase of $22 billion per year. In the United States, Western Europe and Japan, the increase would be in the order of $15 billion per year insofar as reduced fossil-fuel prices would imply lower import prices (though some of the welfare increase has already been captured) *(Larsen and Shah, 1994)*. Overall, subsidies seem to cause a sizeable net drag on economies, whether directly or indirectly (and not counting the economic costs of environmental externalities). To this extent, all subsidies can surely be viewed as somewhat perverse from an economic standpoint.

This is not to contend that energy subsidies cannot have any positive impact on the economy. Energy plays a vital part in economic development, and it may sometimes deserve a measure of government support. All depends on the types of energy and support. Subsidies for fossil fuels tilt the energy playing field in favor of energy sources that are heavily polluting, artificially cheap and non-renewable. Fossil fuels are plainly worse than geothermal energy, hydropower, solar energy and wind power; and among fossil fuels, the most polluting is coal, yet it is the most heavily subsidized. Subsidies inflict further economic injury by inhibiting energy efficiency and conservation, and by deferring a shift to renewable forms of energy. While coal and natural gas may remain available in acceptable quantities for a long time to come, oil stocks are likely to become scarce within a matter of decades. The time to start the shift to alternatives is today—and the longer that subsidies work to blind us to the crunch point, the more disruptive will be the inevitable shift when it arrives *(Koplow, 1995; see also Ruijgrok and Oosterhuis, 1997; Steenblik and Coroyannakis, 1995)*.

Subsidies for energy production have further drawbacks. They stimulate energy consumption at a time when there are many benefits to energy conservation and energy efficiency. They encourage the construction of unnecessary power projects. They waste scarce capital on capital-intensive supplies of energy when it is far cheaper to simply save energy through efficiency and conservation. They deepen intergenerational inequities by hastening the depletion of non-renewable resources. On top of all this, they set back the recycling cause, which often saves remarkable amounts of energy, as much as 95 percent in the case of secondary versus primary aluminum *(Gitlitz, 1993)*. They also diminish the value of the energy embedded in the recycled commodity, hindering the substitution of recyclables for primary materials as well *(Koplow, 1993 and 1995)*. In sum, and to cite a stringent critic *(Heede et al., 1985)*, they inflate the government deficit, they cheat the taxpayer, they steer investment dollars into bad options, and they undermine business competition. They also promote oil imports which erode national security, as demonstrated in the next chapter.

There is an employment aspect too. For every $1 million spent on oil and gas exploration, only 1.5 jobs are created, and for coal mining, 4.4 jobs. But for every $1 million spent on making and installing solar water heaters, 14 jobs are created, for manufacturing solar electricity panels, 17 jobs, and for generating electricity from biomass and waste, 23 jobs *(Gelbspan, 1997)*.

It might appear too sweeping in some eyes, however, to count all subsidies as perverse in the sense of this report. The evidence is extensive and substantive, but less than so comprehensive and conclusive as one might wish. Certainly the subsidies reviewed here feature abundant documentation that they are harmful to the economy. In the case of United States subsidies, only 20 percent were shown to be unharmful to the environment even though the United States has built up an impressive record for environmental protection in many areas—a stronger record than most other industrial countries, let alone developing countries. For the sake of being conservative and "safe", let us suppose that 75 percent of all subsidies are perverse. The author considers a strong case could be made for at least 90 percent worldwide. Others might assert that in order to be correctly cautious, one should offer a lower estimate of, say, 60 percent. Clearly the point cannot be established in definitive terms one way or the other. The author believes that on the basis of the substantial but limited evidence above, 75 percent is a defensible estimate, within a range of 60-90 percent. This works out to a worldwide annual total of $109 billion, call it $110 billion, per year.

Policy Options

The predominant purpose must be to reduce and eventually eliminate those subsidies that are harmful to both economies and environments, viz. the perverse subsidies. There are various modes to that end, focusing on (a) removing producer grants and price supports in question, (b) removing consumer subsidies and sales tax exemptions, and (c) removing tax and trade barriers among other restrictions that discourage energy forms with fewer or no environmental injuries *(Michaelis, 1996; Organization for Economic Co-operation and Development, 1997b)*.

Certain of these measures will have the effect of internalizing some of the egregious environmental externalities, notably emissions of carbon dioxide (unevaluated though they remain in agreed economic terms). This can be further helped by direct intervention through reformed pricing policies so that consumer prices reflect all costs, both private and social. There would be plenty of economic advantages, as documented above through analyses of perverse subsidies, without loss of business competitiveness *(Repetto et al., 1997; see also Berger, 1997)*. The principal environmental payoff would lie with the front-rank measure of cutting carbon dioxide emissions, together with a decline in urban smog, acid rain, particulate emissions, and other pollution impacts.

Yet governments seem singularly reluctant to seize the manifold benefits available. In just Western Europe, well over $10 billion has been spent on subsidies for fossil fuels every year since 1990, meaning that since 1992 when the governments signed an international treaty at the Rio Earth Summit to protect global climate, they have spent over $50 billion on fossil-fuel subsidies. By contrast, environment-favoring solutions such as solar electricity, wind power and the like have received only $1.5 billion per year and energy conservation only $3.2 billion per year. Thus subsidies for fossil fuel have been slowing if not suppressing the competitiveness of renewable and non-polluting energy sources, and rejecting the climate safeguards implicit in tackling carbon dioxide emissions *(Ruijgrok and Oosterhuis, 1997; see also Steenblik and Coroyannakis, 1995)*.

Within the overall context of slashing fossil-fuel subsidies, there are two main sets of policy measures available:

1. Cutting carbon dioxide emissions

Were governments to slash fossil-fuel subsidies after the manner of the former Soviet Union, certain countries of Europe both West and East, China and India, would generate major benefits, notably as concerns reduction of carbon dioxide emissions. That much is clear. What is far less clear is the scale of benefits. The problem of statistical divergencies is illustrated by the United States, a country for which one might expect there would be little disagreement. On the contrary, however the economic models display wide divergences of analysis and findings *(Repetto and Austin, 1997; see also Grubb et al., 1995)*. For instance, one assessment proposes that if the United States were to remove its fossil fuel subsidies, this would reduce carbon dioxide emissions by 11-14 percent over 20 years without affecting economic growth *(Organization for Economic Cooperation and Development, 1997b; see also Shelby et al., 1995; Shelby, 1997)*. Another assessment concludes that the same measure would reduce carbon dioxide emissions by only 4 percent while causing GDP to increase by 0.1-0.2 percent (Larsen, 1994). Other estimates are rather less or a good deal less. A carbon tax that induces a 35-percent reduction in carbon dioxide emissions could be expected to raise GDP over its projected baseline level by more than 1.5 percent, or to reduce it by about 3 percent (Repetto and Austin, 1997).

As for all countries, the elimination of subsidies as they were in 1991 (and assuming no change in fossil-fuel prices as a result) would reduce carbon dioxide emissions by 2010 by more than 20 percent in many of the main fossil-fuel consuming countries and by 7.0 percent worldwide—though the emissions would still be more than 40 percent higher than in 1990 *(World Bank, 1995; see also Shah and Larsen, 1992, see Table 4.4)*. In the former Soviet Union, phasing out subsidies would reduce emissions by 25 percent by 2010—though even with this change, carbon emissions per unit of GDP would still be twice as high as in the United States and more than three times as high as in most Western European countries *(Larsen and Shah, 1994)*. In China alone, phasing out subsidies would reduce emissions in 2010 by 5 percent *(Larsen and Shah, 1994)*—though the country's share of global emissions would still increase from about 10 percent in 1989 to 20 percent in 2010 *(Larsen, 1994)*. On the positive side, China's recent slashing of fossil-fuel subsidies has reduced growth in carbon emissions by 40 percent, almost all through greater energy efficiency *(Lovins, 1998)*.

2. *Energy efficiency and conservation*

So much for the carbon dioxide benefits of removing subsidies. A related step is to mobilize policy measures to foster energy efficiency and conservation. With present energy technologies, a saving of 20-25 percent could be achieved, and with more efficient equipment as much as 30-60 percent would become possible *(World Energy Council, 1992), possibly still more (Lovins, 1996; Weizsacker et al., 1997)*.

But again, we have the problem of the playing field tilted by subsidies in favor of fossil fuels. The analysis above shows that in the United States the ratio of subsidies between conventional sources, being largely fossil fuels, and renewable sources of energy is about 14:1 (though an energy expert, Koplow *(1995)*, proposes the ratio is more like 28:1). Most other governments together with development agencies emphasize energy production over energy efficiency. Of energy loans by the World Bank, less than 1 percent has been for increased efficiency *(World Bank, 1994)*, though the Bank is now shifting its emphasis toward energy renewables and efficiency *(Wysham, 1997)*.

Consider what could be accomplished on a level playing field. Were the United States Congress to fund renewable energy with the same amount in tax credits, financial incentives and other subsidies that it provides to coal and oil, renewables would readily become competitive with fossil fuels *(Gelbspan, 1997)*. In fact, a near-complete transition to a renewable-energy economy could be readily achieved for about $25 billion a year over the next ten years—a sum to be compared with the $29 billion of subsidies supplied annually by the government to fossil fuels and nuclear energy *(Gelbspan, 1997)*. An alternative reckoning *(Koplow, 1996)* asserts that the same transition could be achieved for $7 billion less than the government annually assigns in subsidies to coal, oil and nuclear energy.

Meantime, renewables are enabled to supply a mere 2 percent of energy worldwide. If current energy policies persist with their heavy emphasis on subsidies for fossil fuels, we should not expect renewables to supply more than 4 percent of global energy by 2020—though with suitable incentives they could reach 12 percent *(World Energy Council, 1994; see also Berger, 1997)*.

To illustrate the scope for energy efficiency, consider the role of buildings, which altogether use one third of the world's energy with an annual price tag of $400 billion. Cutting this energy use by half through climate-oriented designs could reduce energy pollution by one sixth and save $200 billion per year *(Roodman and Lenssen, 1995)*. American businesses spend almost $100 billion on energy each year to operate their buildings with lighting, heating and cooling systems *(Energy Information Administration, United States Department of Energy, 1996)*. By doing more to use energy-efficient products and operational procedures, they could reduce that energy cost by $35 billion, while improving the comfort and reliability of their buildings.

Over the past 17 years Americans have gained over four times as much new energy from efficiency savings as from all net increases from supply—and of the increases from supply, one third has come from renewables. Americans' energy bills have fallen by $160 billion per year *(Lovins, 1998; von Weizsacker et al., 1998)*. If the United States had adopted energy efficiency in 1974 to match that of Japan, the savings would have been large enough to wipe out the United States national debt *(Hawken, 1997)*.

There are similarly large savings to be made in the electricity field. In Brazil, the Balbina Dam which flooded 2360 square kilometers of Amazonia forest to generate a mere 112 MW of electricity, would not have needed to be built if electricity were sold at a rate that reflected its true cost *(Panayotou, 1997)*. In Thailand, the $10 million investment needed to build a small advanced window factory would, from first year's production alone, save enough electricity to eliminate the need to commission a $1.5 billion power plant *(Gadgil et al., 1991)*. Similarly, if Thailand had pursued energy efficiency rather than build its Moe Moh Lignite power plant, it would have saved $400 million from not having to install anti-pollution equipment *(Panayotou, 1997)*.

Developing countries as a whole could do much to avoid reliance on fossil fuels, also nuclear power, by pursuing energy efficiency and conservation. By investing $10 billion a year over the next 35 years, they could eventually eliminate the need for $1.75 trillion worth of power plants, oil refineries and other energy infrastructure, with gross savings of $53 billion a year for 35 years. At the same time, they would greatly reduce the pollution burden for themselves and for the world at large *(Gadgil et al., 1991)*.

Table 4.4

CARBON DIOXIDE EMISSIONS, 1991 (thousand tonnes)

Country/ Region	Total Emissions from Fossil Fuels	Excess Emissions from Fossil-Fuel Subsidies	Percentage Reduction by Eliminating Subsidies
China and India	3,087,638	169,010	5.5
Other developing countries	274,390	16,787	6.1
Transition economies	674,930	151,964	22.5
Oil exporters	958,158	114,305	11.9
Total	4,995,116	452,067	9.0

Source: *World Bank. 1995.*

CHAPTER 5

ROAD TRANSPORTATION

U.S. gasoline is cheaper than bottled water. In real terms it is cheaper than at any time since Americans started to dig the stuff out of the ground—and only half as costly as in 1982.

The main way by which a fossil fuel, oil, is used by large numbers of people every day is through road transportation. The auto industry is the world's largest manufacturing sector, and of the top 50 manufacturers in all sectors worldwide, no fewer than 13 are auto companies. The industry produces 65 million new vehicles a year to go with the 500 million already on the roads *(American Automobile Manufacturers Association, 1996)*. The latter total is expected to double during the next 20-30 years, mostly in developing countries; in 1996, more cars will be manufactured and sold in Asia than in North America and Europe together. China alone plans to increase its car fleet from 2.7 million in 1993 to 22 million by 2010 *(Jones and Short, 1994; see also Organization for Economic Co-operation and Development, 1992)*.

Road transportation has long conferred sizeable benefits. Without an efficient transport system to "lubricate" modern economies, there would have been far less geographic specialization in production and economies would not have grown nearly as much *(Jones and Short, 1994)*. But the "car culture" is now levying appreciable costs, both environmental and economic. In OECD countries, road transportation causes three-quarters of carbon monoxide emissions, half of nitrogen oxide emissions, and one fifth of carbon dioxide emissions. Economic costs include road building and maintenance, traffic management, congestion and accidents among many other items. To reiterate a point central to this report: it can be artificial if not arbitrary to differentiate between environmental and economic costs, and in the road transportation sector there isn't always a clear-cut division all along the road. Environmental costs often carry monetary price tags, and economic costs often reflect environmental problems (though there is need to differentiate between the two when it comes to policy analysis). *(This review is primarily based on Koplow, 1995; Litman, 1997; Michaelis, 1997; Nadis and MacKenzie, 1993; Organization for Economic Co-*

In OECD countries, road transportation causes three-quarters of carbon monoxide emissions, half of nitrogen oxide emissions, and one fifth of carbon dioxide emissions.

---

operation and Development, 1997; Roodman, 1996; see also de Moor, 1997; Hubbard, 1991; Lowe, 1994; Tunali, 1996.)

At the same time, the sector has become such a lifestyle icon that it has spawned huge subsidies for large cars, cheap gasoline, highway construction plus infrastructure, and a host of other supports (including the implicit subsidies of environmental externalities). Ironically, transportation subsidies can be put to better environmental and economic use than those in most other sectors if used correctly, i.e., in public road transport and railways. Because of their huge popularity with motorists and hence large numbers of voters, these subsidies rank among the most difficult for politicians to control.

The United States

The situation is best illustrated by the United States with its 155 million cars and 35 million trucks, buses and vans for 268 million people, by far the highest vehicle proportion in the world. All Americans could be accommodated in cars at the same time (as often seems the case during rush hour) and nobody would need to be in the back seat. Roads total 6.25 million kilometers, or 1250 times the distance from New York to Los Angeles. They occupy 2 percent of the country's land, more than given over to housing, and with an aggregate expanse greater than Florida. Roads and other vehicle supports such as parking, garages and fuel stations cover between one third and one half of total space in American cities, and in "car saturated" areas like Los Angeles the amount rises to two thirds. Americans drive 3 trillion kilometers per year (an average of 24,000 kilometers per driver), or more than all the world's other drivers put together *(Nadis and MacKenzie, 1993)*. Americans make 80 percent of their trips by car, whereas Europeans make 60 percent of their's by public transit, or by biking or walking *(Gibbs, 1997)*. In China, motor vehicle numbers have been growing at an average of 18 percent per year since 1993 (2 percent in the United States), while in 1994 public transport use decreased by 6.5 percent *(Zhou Fengqi, 1997)*. Similarly the motor vehicle fleet in Santiago, Chile, is doubling every six years, while bus use fell from about 65 percent of trips in 1977 to about 50 percent in 1991. Transport fuel use increased by more than 10 percent per year during the decade 1986-95. Transportation now accounts for 54 percent of all petroleum used in Chile.

Autos and related industries feature one in six jobs nation-wide. Road transportation accounts for 80 percent of energy use in the transportation sector as

---

Americans make 80 percent of their trips by car, whereas Europeans make 60 percent of their's by public transit, or by biking or walking.

---

a whole, which in turn uses 66 percent of all oil consumed in the United States. Road transportation also accounts for 25 percent of the country's carbon dioxide emissions, having become the fastest-growing source of these emissions (as applies in OECD countries as a whole). *(This introductory paragraph, together with the summary review following, derives largely from Delucchi, 1997; Greene, 1995; Haltmeier, 1997; Ketcham and Komanoff, 1993; Koplow, 1995; Litman, 1995 and 1997; Lowe, 1994; Nadis and MacKenzie, 1993; Shelby et al., 1997.)*

This car culture is supported by myriad conventional subsidies, meaning they comprise financial payments and other monetary transfers of the sorts listed in Chapter 1. They are designated "conventional" in order to differentiate them from the hidden and implicit subsidies of environmental externalities. These conventional subsidies, both direct and indirect, conceal the true costs of gasoline and driving. Direct ones include: government funding of programs that primarily benefit the oil industry and the motorist; reduced corporate income taxes for the oil industry; and low sales taxes on gasoline *(Hwang, 1995)*. Indeed, road transportation is directly subsidized right from the initial construction of roads through to the end use *(Shelby et al., 1997)*.

On top of these are indirect subsidies for auto manufacturers, e.g., tax credits for R & D and a new government-led initiative known as the Partnership for a New Generation of Vehicles. In addition, there is government support for iron, steel, aluminum, glass, plastic and other products vital to auto manufacture; and deductible advertising and marketing costs for the auto industry, totalling billions of dollars per year. Then there are subsidies to alternative fuels such as ethanol, which serves as a price depressor for oil. Finally there are the implicit subsidies of environmental externalities that conceal the costs of pollution in many forms. All these covert subsidies make the analysis below more cautious and conservative. Off-setting these many subsidies to road transportation, though only marginally, are subsidies to mass transit, rail, waterway shipping and aircraft.

1. *Road building and infrastructure*

Consider first the conventional and readily recognized subsidies. One quarter of just the costs of road building come from revenue sources unrelated to transportation, hence they serve as a subsidy. Internalizing just this subsidy to drivers through a gasoline tax would cost 20 cents per gallon *(Data Resources Inc., 1993)*. The overall cost of roads, highway patrols, emergency teams and related services, when calculated as costs over and above what drivers pay in fuel taxes and other fees, amounts to more than $91 billion a year, worth 64 cents per gallon of gasoline *(Roodman, 1996)*. That this figure is realistic for 1997 is confirmed by an earlier estimate of $89 billion *(MacKenzie et al., 1992)*. One could also argue that the $91 billion for direct subsidies should be increased to reflect the pressing need for expanded police efforts to reduce vehicle thefts, steadily increasing.

2. *Free parking*

Next, the cost of free parking supplied by businesses for some 80 million American workers *(Shoup, 1997)*. The government allows businesses to assign up to $1860 per year of free parking to each employee tax free, by contrast with a mere $780 for mass transit coupons *(Roodman, 1996)*. Altogether this exemption, being a covert subsidy, is worth somewhere between $20 billion *(Michaelis, 1996; DRI/McGraw-Hill, 1994)* and $50 billion per year *(Pucher, 1990; Shelby et al., 1997)*, or possibly as high as $85 billion *(Ketcham and Komanoff, 1993; MacKenzie et al., 1992; Shoup, 1992)*, while the most recent estimate *(Delucchi, 1997)* posits a range of $49-162 billion. The divergences reflect mainly the estimated value of parking space. This report uses a figure of $50 billion per year.

3. *Road congestion*

The direct subsidies above lead to many indirect subsidies in the form of costs both economic and environmental. For instance, they contribute to road congestion. In 39 metropolitan areas with populations of one million or more, one third of all vehicle travel takes place under congested conditions when speed averages half of the free-flow rate. The delay amounts to 6 billion vehicle-hours each year. Within these congested areas, 75 million drivers average 16,000 kilometers per year, making up 1200 billion kilometers. Through their choices, these drivers demonstrate a willingness to pay an average of at least $1.33 (1994 dollars) to save ten minutes of travel time, or $8 per hour. The annual cost of these driving delays comes to $640 per driver, for a total of $48 billion *(Arnott and Small, 1994; see also Paarlberg, 1996)*. Were congestion delays to be considered in the many other urban localities apart from the 39 metropolitan areas, the total would a good deal larger, possibly twice as large. An alternative reckoning, allowing also for extra consumption of gasoline by idling engines and for wear and tear on vehicles, proposes that Americans lose more than 8 billion hours per year to traffic delays, at a cost exceeding $80 billion *(Krugman,*

In 39 metropolitan areas with populations of one million or more, one third of all vehicle travel takes place under congested conditions when speed averages half of the free-flow rate. The delay amounts to 6 billion vehicle-hours each year, the annual cost of which comes to at least $100 billion.

In 1996, the United States imported more than 46 percent of its oil supply, with twice as much coming from the Persian Gulf as in 1973. The country pays about $17 to the Gulf for a barrel of oil, and effectively several times more per barrel through military protection.

1996). When we include all costs of congestion on roads (though excluding pollution externalities, see below), the total in 1990 came to at least $100 billion *(MacKenzie et al., 1992; see also United States General accounting Office, 1991)*. For present purposes, a figure of $100 billion per year is accepted even though it has surely grown higher today.

Similar findings arise elsewhere. In central London in 1990, each driver in peak traffic cost all other road users about $0.50 in wasted time, or four times as much as the actual expense of driving *(International Energy Agency, 1993)*.

4. *Accidents, injuries and deaths*

A further economic cost and hence an indirect subsidy lies with vehicle accidents and associated injuries and deaths. There are 3.5 million injuries per year with 42,000 fatalities. A detailed estimate *(Miller, 1994; see also Urban Institute, 1991)* proposes a minimum of $139 billion per year in the late 1980s, reflecting the loss of human capital as manifested through market costs, including medical expenses and reduced worker productivity. It also values a statistical death at $500,000, which many analysts consider on the low side, and it invokes similarly low costs for injuries. A second estimate *(Elvik, 1995)* proposes a range of $120-360 billion for the early 1990s. A third calculation *(MacKenzie et al., 1992)* postulates $359 billion per year, this being a comprehensive reckoning that covers reduced quality of life, plus pain and grief, and values a statistical death at $2-5 million together with comparably high estimates for injuries. But the proportion of these costs not directly borne by vehicle drivers involved in accidents, and hence borne by society, is only $55 billion *(MacKenzie et al., 1992)*. This is the figure used for this chapter, albeit relating to conditions in 1988 which are surely lower than today.

5. *Military safeguards*

We should add in the military costs of safeguarding oil tanker shipping lanes from the Persian Gulf. In 1960, United States consumption exceeded domestic production by only 5 percent, since when the amount has grown

---

In 1989 the United States imported 220 million barrels of oil from Iraq and Kuwait—an amount that would have been saved if the U.S. auto fleet had been achieving improved efficiency of just five kilometres per gallon. The oil import bill is expected to increase by some 86 percent during 1996-2005.

---

on average by roughly 0.5 percent per year. "These are the bald facts behind the Gulf War" *(Wallace, 1997)*. In 1996, the country imported more than 46 percent of its oil supply, with twice as much coming from the Persian Gulf as in 1973. In the year 2000 imports are almost certain to exceed domestic production by nearly 25 percent *(Wallace, 1997)*.

In 1995 the United States paid almost $50 billion for its imported oil (half of which came from the Gulf), these imports accounted for 30 percent of the trade deficit *(Energy Information Administration, United States Department of Energy, 1996)*. The country pays about $17 to the Gulf for a barrel of oil, and effectively it pays several times more per barrel through military protection *(Hawken, 1997)*. In 1991, the Department of Defense spent around $50 billion on military safeguards for oil, mostly with respect to the Gulf *(Hwang, 1995)*. (Another estimate *(Carvallo, 1996)* postulates $73-227 billion for all military outlays of whatever sort associated with protection of oil in 1994.) Well over half of the petroleum imported into the United States from the Gulf is used for road transportation, so half of the $50 billion of annual military expenditures, $25 billion, should be allocated to motorists *(Hwang, 1995; see also Koplow and Martin, 1997; MacKenzie et al., 1992)*.

Ironically, in 1989 the United States imported 220 million barrels of oil from Iraq and Kuwait—an amount that would have been saved if the United States auto fleet had been achieving improved efficiency of just five kilometers per gallon (as could well have been stimulated through a rollback in gasoline subsidies) *(Nadis and MacKenzie, 1993)*. Today Americans would have to cut their oil use by only one eighth in order to end their dependence on Gulf imports, and this could be readily achieved by an improvement in fuel efficiency from 32 to 40 kilometers per gallon *(Heede, 1998; see also Hartmaier, 1997; Small and Kazimi, 1995)*. Yet the oil import bill is expected to increase by some 86 percent during 1996-2005 *(Koplow and Martin, 1997; see also Delucchi and Murphy, 1995; see also Koplow, 1995)*.

6. *Environmental harm*

Finally, environmental harm, notably the externality costs of air, water and noise pollution as it affects landscape visibility, agricultural crops and build-

Some 100 million Americans live in cities where vehicle emissions regularly push ozone levels above federal standards.

ings, and climate in the form of global warming. These costs have been calculated for 1991 at $12-50 billion *(Delucchi, 1995; see also Hall et al., 1992; Hwang, 1995; Komanoff, 1994; Small and Kazimi, 1995; Transportation Research Board, 1997)*. A similar estimate *(MacKenzie et al., 1992)* posits $46 billion for 1989, while still another estimate *(Hartmaier, 1997)* proposes $12-35 billion per year for the early 1990s. Due to differences in what is measured and what is omitted, we shall here consider only the first estimate, viz. $12-50 billion per year. This is to be compared with a parallel estimate for the rest of the OECD countries, $181 billion per year (see below).

These figures for the United States are surely under-estimates. According to the American Lung Association, some 100 million Americans live in cities where vehicle emissions regularly push ozone levels above federal standards; and there are several other health hazards from traffic pollution *(Gibbs, 1997)*. For a measure of the scale of values involved in air pollution from autos among other sources, note that the net direct benefits of the Clean Air Act in the United States for the period 1970-90 amounted to somewhere between $5.1 and $48.9 trillion, with a central estimate of $21.7 trillion. Averaged out, this central estimate comes to almost $1.1 trillion per year *(United States Environmental Protection Agency, 1997)*. Of course this assessment covers all forms of air pollution, though those from road transportation (and other uses of fossil fuels) are prominent if not predominant.

Added to this are human morbidity and mortality costs from air pollution, estimated at $42-182 billion for 1991 *(Delucchi, 1995; Hwang, 1995)*. Adding in the other air pollution costs of $12-50 billion makes a total of $54-232 billion per year. This aggregate estimate seems realistic in light of data for air pollution in a single area, the Los Angeles basin. Of course not all pollution there stems from road traffic, but the bulk of it does. A report on the health benefits from meeting the federal public health standards for ozone and particulates shows that over 30 million "restricted activity" days and 1600 deaths would have been averted annually in the late 1980s. The

In the Los Angeles basin, over 30 million "restricted activity" days and 1600 deaths would have been averted annually by road traffic controls. The value of such health gains in a population of 12 million is estimated to be $14.3 billion, or $1200 per Los Angelino.

value of these health gains in a population of 12 million is estimated to be $14.3 billion *(Hall et al., 1989)*.

It is unfortunate that estimates for human health costs should span such a broad range, $42-182 billion, while being large relative to other hidden costs. That is to say, this single component of a single sector is unusually significant for the entire report. The broad range reflects the uncertain methodology employed to calculate human health values, and until it can be better substantiated and refined, we must live with it as best we can.

Note that the overall estimate (like the other two) is very conservative. For instance, it considers that the factor that could eventually turn out to be the biggest environmental externality of all, possibly worth all the rest put together, viz. climate change and global warming *(Houghton et al., 1996; Repetto and Lash, 1997)*, is worth no more than somewhere between $2.5 and $22 billion per year. This does not do justice to recent IPCC calculations and other preliminary estimates of the putative costs of global warming (e.g., Fankhauser, 1995; see also discussion in Chapter 2). In any case, all assessments feature an uncertainty range such that the "true" value may diverge from a given estimate by anywhere from 5 to 2000 percent *(Maddison et al., 1996)*. For further appraisals of environmental externalities, broadly consistent with the figures above, see Hwang, 1995; Ketcham and Komanoff, 1993; Koplow, 1993; Lowe, 1994; Miller and Moffet, 1993; and Roodman, 1996.

For purposes of the present analysis, the author proposes the median figure of $143 billion within the range of $54-232 billion per year. Rough and ready, but reasonable in the absence of anything better. A recent estimate for externalities worldwide, albeit a preliminary and approximate estimate *(von Weizsacker et al., 1997)*, postulates a total of $1 trillion.

Total United States subsidies

The estimates presented above are set out in Table 5.1, with an overall total of $464 billion per year. Many of the supporting calculations date from the early 1990s, and today's total is likely to be higher. The figure is not exceptionally high, even though it constitutes 51 percent of global subsidies in this sector. It is to be compared with another recent assessment *(Litman, 1996)*, calculating that total road costs are $2.4 trillion, with over $800 billion being external costs. Still another recent estimate *(Delucchi, 1997)* puts the total at $1.9-2.8 trillion, with by far the biggest component being made up of private vehicle costs. Yet another up-to-date estimate *(DeCicco, 1996)* postulates total costs at $1.5 trillion, of which environmental costs amount to $115 billion. None of these estimates, including the one used in this report, considers land-use impacts, aesthetic degradation, and social costs such as equity and mobility loss for non-drivers in auto-dependent communities.

Table 5.1

U.S. SUBSIDIES FOR ROAD TRANSPORTATION ($ billion, 1991)

Subsidy Type	Amount
Direct	91
Indirect	
Free parking	50 (range 20-85)
Congestion	100
Accidents, injuries and deaths	55*
Military safeguards	25
sub-total	321
Environmental externalities	143 (range 54-232)
Total	464 (range 345-588)

*   The proportion of $360 billion not directly borne by drivers

Note: the total of $464 billion is 51% of the global total of $917 billion.

Sources: *MacKenzie et al., 1992; also see text.*

The estimate presented here for the unpaid costs of road transportation, $464 billion per year, is equivalent to just over $1700 per American, and more than 6 percent of United States GDP. Indeed, if Americans were to cover the entire costs of their car culture, including environmental externalities and especially global warming, they could find themselves paying much more than they now pay for their largely "free ride," courtesy of the hefty subsidies to road transportation. Passing the concealed costs back to drivers would require a tax of almost $3 per gallon of motor fuel. Such are the ultimate costs of a car culture that, through its abundant and munificent subsidies, amounts to a form of super-socialism.

Whatever the true figure, it says much about the "high" present price that Americans pay for their gasoline. Around $1.20 per gallon today, it is actually cheaper in real dollars than for 60 years; it costs only half as much as milk and

The 1993 price of U.S. gasoline was 74 percent of Canada's and 64 percent of Australia's, both geographically large countries like the United States, a factor which supposedly requires extended auto driving (though 80 percent of Americans' trips are less than 15 kilometres).

cheaper than bottled water. Americans might compare their gasoline expenses with other countries. The 1993 price was 74 percent of Canada's, and the tax component was 27 percent of the price whereas Canada's was 46 percent. Similarly, the 1993 United States price was 64 percent of Australia's, where tax made up 45 percent of the price. Both Canada and Australia are geographically large countries like the United States, a factor which supposedly requires extended auto driving (though 80 percent of Americans' trips are less than 15 kilometers). Moreover, the 1993 United States price was only 34 percent of Italy's, where tax makes up 72 percent. Not surprisingly, gasoline consumption per person in the United States amounted to 1,600 liters, in Canada 1,124 liters, in Australia 936 liters, and Italy under 400 liters *(United Nations, 1995)*.

Box 5.1

ROAD TRANSPORTATION COSTS
IN THE UNITED KINGDOM

In the United Kingdom, a country with 59 million people and 21 million cars, roads and their verges occupy 3.3 percent of land area whereas railways occupy only 0.2 percent *(U.K. Royal Commission on Environmental Pollution, 1994)*. Well over half the population is exposed to substantial noise pollution. Road vehicles account for 90 percent of carbon monoxide emissions and 24 percent of carbon dioxide emissions, the latter proportion increasing fast *(U.K. Royal Commission on Environmental Pollution, 1994)*. At least one in five and possibly one in three persons in England are at risk from poor air quality, though not all the pollution comes from road transportation. Premature deaths due to air pollution from traffic total 6000 a year, double the rate of deaths from traffic accidents. Asthma affects every seventh child, and is widely thought to be due in major measure to the recent rise in vehicle emissions; the costs to the economy were in the region of $6.2 billion in 1990 *(Cookson and Moffat, 1997; Strachan et al., 1994)* (similar costs are reported for other European countries *(Lenney et al., 1994)*).

Box 5.1 *(continued)*

Altogether the health effects of traffic pollution are estimated to be $24 billion per year *(U.K. Department of Health, 1995)*, while road congestion imposes further costs of $26 billion per year *(U.K. Royal Commission on Environmental Pollution, 1994)* (it now takes longer to cross central London by motor vehicle than in the days of the horse and cart). Road accidents impose costs on society of over $16 billion per year. The grand total according to this reckoning is $66 billion per year, a total to be compared with another recent estimate *(Maddison et al., 1996)*, over $80 billion per year. Because the $66 billion is a partial reckoning, we shall go with $80 billion.

In Western European countries generally, subsidies tend to be quite a lot lower thanks to higher fuel prices and taxes, which in Germany are as much as 70 percent, in Netherlands 110 percent and in France 120 percent. Certain European countries such as Italy pay over $3 per gallon in taxes, and the amount is being ratcheted up year by year at a rate considerably faster than inflation. In Britain and Germany (also Japan), motorists now pay between $3.50 and $4.00 per gallon, and in Italy almost $4.50.

Other OECD Countries

How about other OECD countries and their subsidies, both direct and indirect? In the United Kingdom, cars, trucks, vans and the like are estimated to be costing the country more than $80 billion a year *(Maddison et al., 1996; see also Kageson, 1993)*. For details, see Box 5.1. In Japan there is a net direct subsidy to road users of $16 billion *(Morisugi, 1997; Organization for Economic Co-operation and Development, 1997)*. But this does not include free parking, and uses only very low costs for road-related services such as traffic police. The real total could be as high as $50 billion *(de Moor, 1997)*, and that is the figure accepted here. In Germany, a bare minimum estimate for direct subsidies in 1991 was $12 billion *(de Moor, 1997)*, while the true figure remains entirely uncalculated. Let us suppose that the same proportion, 213 percent, as in Japan should increase the known figure, $12 billion,; then it becomes $38 billion per

---

In the United Kingdom, cars, lorries, vans and the like cost the economy more than $80 billion a year, or $1300 per citizen (the European Union $290 billion; France $47 billion and Italy $40 billion).

---

year. By contrast, road users in a few OECD countries pay more than the costs of providing roads and associated services: in Netherlands 110 percent and in France 120 percent. When we include indirect subsidies, however, we find that road transport in all countries is heavily subsidized *(EcoPlan, 1992; Hubbard, 1991; Lowe, 1994; Roodman, 1996)*. The aggregate total for 17 countries of the European Union is estimated to have been $290 billion in 1994 (including France $47 billion and Italy $40 billion) *(Maddison et al., 1996; see also Rothengatter and Mouch, 1994)*. As with the United States's figures, there is little reason to think these estimates have fallen by 1997.

Total Subsidies in OECD Countries

The totals for the United States, the European Union and Japan —cautious or even minimalist reckonings as they mostly are—come to $804 billion per year. These 19 countries comprise 784 million people, meaning that the collective total of $804 billion works out to $1025 per person per year. If we assume that the same average applies for three other OECD countries (Canada, Australia and New Zealand, though omitting Mexico and other new members) with their 52 million people, these three countries account for $53 billion of subsidies. Thus we get an OECD total of $857 billion per year for subsidies to road transportation. This is to be compared with a recent estimate *(de Moor, 1997)* for just three countries, the United States, Germany and Japan (with populations totalling 57 percent of all traditional OECD countries), of $85-$200 billion per year. This latter estimate does not include any component for externalities, which the literature suggests could be anywhere from $350 billion to $1.4 trillion per year *(de Moor, 1997)*.

Subsidies in non-OECD Countries

If it is difficult to come up with accurate estimates for subsidies in OECD countries, it is even more difficult to find much data at all on subsidies in the transition economies of Eastern Europe and the former Soviet Union, and yet more difficult to establish much evidence in developing countries. A fact frustrating in the extreme, but a fact.

All one can say is that in Russia, the cost of rehabilitating the roads network would be at least $5 billion per year *(Bousquet and Queiroz, 1995)*. Plainly this must constitute only a part and probably a small part of direct subsidies. Regrettably there is no information on indirect subsidies, nor on implicit subsidies in the form of environmental externalities. It would be surprising if the true total were not in the region of $50-100 billion, but in the absence of any substantive evidence, we must stick with the gross underestimate of $5 billion per year. As for other countries of the former Soviet Union and Eastern Europe, let us postulate a further $5 billion per year. Again, this must surely err on the low side several times over, as any observer would agree after experiencing the lamentable state of transport infrastructure overall.

As long as we lack any indication of the true situation in the countries in transition, we must settle for a joint total for road transportation subsidies of $10 billion per year. The author would not be surprised if a comprehensive reckoning proved to be ten times greater.

As for developing countries, both the economic spillovers and the environmental externalities tend to be even worse than in developed countries, due to the larger populations in many cities, the inadequate infrastructure, the lower safety standards, and the higher accident rates and pollution levels *(Zegras and Litman, 1997)*. Developing-country cities are legendary for their congestion and pollution, and rural areas are equally legendary for the disrepair of their roads. In Bangkok there are long periods every day when traffic moves at an average speed (if that is the right word) of 3 kilometers per hour, and cars spend an average of 44 days per year stuck in traffic, costing $2.3-9.6 billion in lost worker productivity, plus $1.6 billion of energy wasted in idling car engines. Only 37 percent of trips are made by public transportation. Private auto fuel use is projected to nearly triple during the period 1990-2005, while traffic congestion is projected to reduce fuel use efficiency by at least half. There are one million respiratory infections each year linked to air pollution, and cancer rates are three times higher than in other parts of Thailand *(Du Pont and Egan, 1997; Lovins and Lovins, 1997; Midgley et al., 1994; Poboon et al., 1994; Shaefer and Victor, 1997)*. These costs will eventually have to be met by the public purse, and should count as unwitting subsidies.

Mexico City's air pollution, largely stemming from motor vehicles, is often so severe that health costs are estimated at $1.5 billion per year *(World Resources Institute, 1996)*. In New Delhi, the World Health Organization estimates that an average of 7500 people die prematurely from traffic pollution each year, and 1.2 million people receive medical treatment for pollution-derived ailments. Much the same can be said for Manila, Santiago, Sao Paulo, Cairo and Lagos, yet private vehicle numbers are increasing at unprecedented rates in many developing countries *(Gibbs, 1997; International Institute for Energy Conservation, 1997)*. In China, the growth rate has been an average of 18 percent per year

---

In Bangkok there are long periods every day when traffic moves at an average speed (if that is the right word) of 3 kilometres per hour, and cars spend an average of 44 days per year stuck in traffic, costing $2.3-9.6 billion in lost worker productivity, plus $1.6 billion of energy wasted in idling car engines.

---

since 1993 (the United States, 2 percent), while in 1994 public transport use declined by 6.5 percent *(Zhou Fengqi, 1997)*.

In addition, the World Bank believes that half of developing countries' roads are in such poor state that governments need to spend $15 billion per year simply to rehabilitate their road networks, let alone to expand them for farmers wanting to get their produce to market: more of those effective though hidden subsidies. A coffee farmer on the eastern slopes of Kilimanjaro in Tanzania finds the value of his crop drops by half by the time it makes its way along dismal roads to the export ship in Mombasa. In Africa as a whole, one third of $150 billion invested in roads has been lost due to poor maintenance and management, and the potential annual cost savings (an effective subsidy) amounts to $1.5 billion *(Heggie, 1995)*.

This means of course that governments effectively subsidize their road users by charging them only a small part of the costs of constructing the roads and keeping them in tolerable condition. Indeed Bangladesh and Tanzania require road users to cover only 19 percent of direct costs; Bolivia 20 percent; and Mexico 41 percent (improbably precise though these figures seem). Conversely, China charges its road users 120 percent of the costs and Turkey 217 percent *(de Moor, 1997)*. But in none of these countries is there any estimate of indirect costs, let alone externalities.

Both these latter two items can be costly. Traffic-accident deaths in India are believed to total at least 500,000 per year, and the rate per 1000 people is two to five times as high as in Europe *(Button, 1993)*. If all such deaths in all developing countries total several million each year, and regardless of how the value of life is computed, the cost and hence the covert subsidy must be exceptionally large. Regrettably it remains unquantified for present purposes.

What are total subsidies in developing countries? The parlous lack of information is so severe that it is difficult to come up with much meaningful. But to offer no assessment on the grounds that we have no "realistic" basis for saying anything, is to deny the real world. We could reasonably offer a few judgements with respect to environmental externalities. For instance, we could say that traffic congestion Bangkok-style levies costs of $20 billion per year in all developing countries (the actual total could readily be several times greater). The same for air pollution and health costs along the lines of Mexico City: conceivably $15 billion (again, this is surely a gross underestimate). Then there is the $15 billion for unrepaired roads as cited above. This all amounts to a total of $50 billion, and is the figure accepted here, even though its small size seems to fly in the face of common sense. Could the environmental externalities be only a small fraction of those in OECD countries, instead of a lot larger?

Subsidies Worldwide

Overall reckoning for subsidies in this chapter: $857 billion per year in OECD countries (range $738-$981 billion), at least $10 billion in countries of the former Soviet Union and Eastern Europe, and at least $50 billion in developing countries. Grand total: $917 billion (range $798-$1041 billion), of which $558 billion are conventional subsidies and $359 billion environmental externalities (Table 5.2). A more realistic and less minimalist estimate for the former Soviet Union/Eastern Europe and for developing countries could well increase the total by $100 billion each, perhaps much more.

How much of this $917 billion (and the range) should count as perverse subsidies? Recall that not all conventional subsidies are to be viewed as perverse; there are beneficial and neutral subsidies as well as adverse ones. So for the final summation (see below), we shall count only a proportion of the conventional subsidies. By contrast, the implicit subsidies of environmental externalities are regarded as 100 percent perverse (for rationale, see Chapter 1).

What proportion of conventional subsidies should be considered perverse? The economic case is readily recognized, viz. that road transportation imposes sizeable direct costs. Let us first note, however, the positive aspect. There is the prima facie argument that road transportation serves as a basic "lubricant" for economies at many levels of development (see opening paragraph of this chapter), hence there will often—though certainly not always—be a need to build more roads and otherwise support the car culture. In addition, we shall continue to need regulation of traffic through highway patrols and the multiple like. So not all subsidies are economically adverse. At the same time, the severe overloading of road systems through the rapid increase in vehicles, leading to congestion, traffic accidents, etc., demonstrates that while increasing numbers of vehicles can liberate the individual, they can eventually enslave society (to cite the graphic phrasing of *de Moor and Calamai, 1997*). As the reader will recognize from his or her own experience, driving in many cities and on rural roads is no longer a benefit but a burden. Like the Red Queen, we seem to have to run faster to stay in the same place. Of course this is not always the case, but increasingly, and in increasing parts of the world, it is.

Even small subsidies can "leverage" a large amount of vehicle travel.
Conversely, even a limited reduction in subsidies can leverage a comparatively sizeable reduction in driving.

Table 5.2

WORLDWIDE SUBSIDIES FOR ROAD TRANSPORTATION
($ billion per year)

	Total	Subsidies Conventional	Perverse*	Environmental Externalities**
USA	464	321	161	143
Rest of OECD	393	212	106	181
Total OECD	857	533	267	324
	(range 738-981)			
Total Non-OECD	60	25	13	35
Grand Totals	917	558	280	359
	(range 798-1041)			

* *perverse subsidies 50% of conventional subsidies*
** *perverse subsidies 100% of environmental externalities*

Now for the environmental side of conventional subsidies. Road building has its adverse environmental factors, such as despoiling of landscapes; in the United States, an expanse the size of Florida has been taken over for roads. Traffic congestion can likewise be said to have an adverse environmental dimension. The same applies, though sometimes in more marginal sense, to the other categories of conventional subsidies. (This much is apparent; perhaps not so obvious is that if the problem were entirely environmental, it would rank as an environmental externality and thus become an implicit subsidy.) There are many adverse environmental aspects to conventional subsidies, even if some of their costs, notably their non-monetized costs, can be characterized in only qualitative fashion.

One would be somewhat justified in concluding that virtually all conventional subsidies exert adverse impacts both environmentally and economically, and thus are perverse subsidies. Let us allow, however, for the net benefits that still accrue from subsidies in certain circumstances, even though they may often be in accelerating decline in relation to the "disbenefits". Let us note too that while the replacement of subsidies in the United States for example, through e.g., targeted user fees and gasoline taxes, would reduce carbon dioxide emissions by 11-14 percent over 20 years (a major environmental benefit, boosted by reduction of urban smog, acid rain and other pollution forms), it would often induce the parallel benefit of relieving traffic congestion and other economic ills *(Organization for Economic Co-operation and Development, 1997)*. The picture is decidedly mixed, with all kinds of factors operating in some positive as well as many negative senses. On the whole, however, the evidence is decidedly downside.

As a best-judgement assessment, let us conclude that a sizeable proportion of conventional subsidies are perverse. After reviewing all the evidence, the author decides that the proportion is somewhere between an absolute minimum of one third and a more likely two-thirds (if not more—the transportation experts who critiqued this chapter considered that 100 percent would not be unrealistic). It is difficult indeed to narrow the one third/two-thirds range in strictly objective fashion. As a thoroughly informed but less than finally accurate estimate, the author proposes that roughly half of the $558 billion conventional subsidies are perverse, viz. $279 billion, rounded to $280 billion per year (Table 5.2).

True, this assessment is arbitrary in the extreme. Is it any more arbitrary, though, than the "assessment" now being imposed by the individual calculations and choices of the world's road users? It is idle to say that in the absence of conclusive evidence one cannot or should not offer any estimate at all of what the proportion should be. What one can truly say is that one cannot offer a definitive estimate. For want of a better assessment, one half seems appropriate.

To this must be added the environmental externalities, which are 100 percent perverse. In the United States, as we have seen, they are estimated to be $143 billion per year. In the European Union they are estimated *(based on Maddison et al., 1996)* to be 46 percent of total conventional subsidies, and this proportion is arbitrarily but realistically extrapolated to the rest of the OECD countries, for a total in the latter (all OECD countries apart from the United States) of $181 billion per year. In non-OECD countries, and as we have seen, the total is $35 billion per year. These make up a total of $359 billion per year, and 100 percent of this figure is taken to be an implicit and perverse subsidy.

In summary, conventional perverse subsidies are $280 billion per year, and environmental externalities are $359 billion per year. Grand total, $639 billion, or say $640 billion, per year (Table 5.2). This is 44 percent of the global total of all perverse subsidies, $1.5 trillion. The author has repeatedly asked his expert colleagues if the calculations are inflated, and the response has been a resounding "No." Indeed several of them assert that the share of conventional subsidies represented by perverse subsidies should not be 50 percent but 100 percent. Moreover, where a particular subsector, e.g., road accidents in the United States, features a range of estimates, the author has usually chosen one of the lower estimates. Certain of the statistics derive from the early 1990s or the late 1980s, and the figures for 1997 would surely be higher. For all these reasons and for others that reflect the generally cautious and conservative approach to this chapter's assessment, the estimate of $640 billion for perverse subsidies seems realistic, even though it is far and away the largest for the six sectors considered in this book.

Policy Responses

It is commonplace to limit the listing of policy proposals to fuel taxes and "fee-bates" among other policy instruments and management measures, plus specific actions such as promoting unleaded gasoline. Instead, we start here with what could now have become the most productive and urgent option of all. In fact, it could well be worth all the other proposals put together.

1. We need to get a secure quantified handle on all subsidies both direct and indirect, with emphasis on their numerous externalities. It is absurd that we are ostensibly expending in the region of $917 billion per year through subsidies, let alone some $640 billion through perverse subsidies, yet we have hardly a working idea of how accurate these figures are (the limited evidence suggests on several counts that both figures could be well on the low side). The first is a sum equivalent to 3.3 percent of the global economy. It is like saying that an individual with an annual income of $30,000 is paying out a special tax of over $1000 per year with only the haziest notion about its existence, or of whether the actual amount is more, possibly a good deal more. Or suppose you were buying a car for $15,000, and then you find that it would be subject to all manner of additional payments that increase the purchase price by hundreds of dollars. You would protest that it would be both fairer and more efficient for you to be told the true overall price in the first place.

   We need to firm up the calculus from all angles, and with due dispatch. (For the latest extensive survey of this complex and contentious issue, *see Organization for Economic Co-operation and Development, 1997.*) Until we know just what is the nature and extent of the problem we are grappling with, there is limited mileage (so to speak) in formulating solutions.

2. When once we have gained a firm understanding of the scale of subsidies, we can then take measures of suitable scale to require road users to pay the full costs of what they do. In particular, we can do more to internalize the superscale externalities inherent in road transportation. A good start could be made with rigorous implementation of the Polluter Pays Principle.

3. At the same time, we should bear in mind the potent impacts of subsidies in this sector. Because road transportation is co-produced by users (who supply the vehicle and driving effort) and society (which supplies roads and many support services), even relatively small subsidies can "leverage" a large amount of vehicle travel. Conversely, even a limited reduction in subsidies can leverage a comparatively sizeable reduction in driving. For instance, the cost of building and maintaining roads is only about 5 percent of the total monetary cost of automobile travel, not counting the many non-monetary costs. Yet road investments determine per-capita automobile travel rates *(Litman, 1997).*

4. We need to consider that simple increases in fuel taxes will not do the job alone. Nor is it correct to say that if automobile users could be obliged to pay an amount equal to the total costs they impose, that would square every last circle. It would not address economic efficiency, which requires that prices equal marginal costs. Not only should users pay the correct amount, but the pricing mechanism should correlate as closely as possible with the costs imposed. Fuel taxes do not capture many additional costs such as parking subsidies, accident risk, traffic congestion, etc. Rather, we need to understand the full range of costs and apply pricing to capture each *(Litman, 1997)*.

5. There is much scope for traffic management. When employees can decline free parking in favor of a cash payment of equal value, automobile commuting declines by 20-40 percent *(Shoup, 1994)*. Making auto insurance a variable cost can reduce driving by 5-14 percent in the short term and 16-14 percent in the long term *(El Gasseir, 1990)*. Eliminating underpricing of auto travel can reduce vehicle use by 33 percent or more—and the same for environmental impacts such as air and noise pollution, even allowing for no new technologies *(Maddison et al., 1996)*.

6. The most productive way to reduce carbon dioxide and other pollutant emissions is to charge for road use during peak hours and in the urbanized environs of major cities. Surprisingly, however, this does not generally seem to reduce car use—though within the European Union an increase in excises of $1.5 per liter can decrease car use by 38 percent and carbon dioxide emissions by 61 percent *(de Moor, 1997)*.

    Singapore is one of the most prosperous communities in the world, and one would expect traffic to match bumper-to-bumper Bangkok. On the contrary, the government taxes cars heavily and auctions the right to buy them. It engages in area licensing, plus a $3-6 daily user fee for cars entering the city's central zone. These various measures have decreased traffic during peak periods by 75 percent *(World Resources Institute, 1996)*. Similar policies for demand management in Mexico City could, it is estimated, reduce emissions by some 70 percent *(de Moor, 1997)*.

The Singapore government taxes cars heavily and auctions the right to buy them. It engages in area licensing, plus a $3-6 daily user fee for cars entering the city's central zone. These measures have decreased traffic during peak periods by 75 percent.

97

7. The transportation playing field should be leveled or even tilted in favor of rail and water transport, which are usually competitive commercially and far less harmful environmentally. There is also good reason to promote the use of buses with their many advantages over private cars.

CHAPTER 6

WATER

Humans already use 54 percent of available water runoff, and they use it wastefully by courtesy of subsidies.

The water sector features abundant subsidies, making it crucial for this report. The subsidies are diverse, scattered and often concealed, hence they are difficult to track down. Because they are so large, however, a review is essential, even if its findings are approximate and exploratory in some respects.

In this sector probably more than in other sectors, there is a premium on equity for all water beneficiaries. After all, water is a basic component of life processes, and should be readily available to all users, especially the poor. This generally means that water should be subsidized for the poorest. Conversely, we cannot expect to see sound water management when subsidies are munificently dispensed to rich and poor alike, often in inconsistent fashion. The hard-scrabble rice farmer on one side of the road should not have to pay for water if the car manufacturer, the chemicals the swimming pool owner and the golf player on the other side of the road do not pay the full cost of their water—or pay the full cost of waste water treatment, flood protection, storm drainage, and a host of other ancillary services which support water supplies for the entire community *(Frederiksen, 1997)*.

Water Demand and Supply

Humans withdraw water from rivers, lakes and other freshwater bodies for three main uses: household/municipal, industrial and agricultural (mainly irrigation). Worldwide, household/municipal takes 10 percent, industry 25 percent, and agriculture 65 percent (Table 6.1) *(Pimentel et al., 1997; Postel et al., 1996; Serageldin, 1994; World Bank, 1992)*. In developed countries, agriculture accounts for less than 40 percent of total use, whereas in many developing countries it is over 90 percent. Most of the funds spent on the water sector each year go to financing irrigation schemes, as is appropriate given that irrigated croplands make up only 17 percent of all croplands but supply 38 percent of our food *(Jones, 1995; Pimentel et al., 1997; for further general reviews of the water sector, see Falkenmark, 1994; Gardner-Outlaw and Engelman, 1997; Gleick, 1993, 1996 and 1997; Postel, 1996, 1997a and b; Rosegrant, 1997)*.

Of all agricultural water used, the developing world's share is almost 80 percent. In developed countries, by contrast, industrial use of water tends to be higher than agricultural use *(World Bank, 1993a)*. In the United States, the single biggest user is the thermo-electric power industry (fossil fuel and nuclear plants), which requires huge quantities of water for cooling purposes, albeit much being returned to source in semi-satisfactory state. Other big industrial users are pulp and paper, iron and steel, chemicals, and petroleum. Yet industry is not always obliged to treat its waste water—a factor which serves as a salient example of the many major uncounted subsidies in the water sector. The same applies to waste water from domestic households. Both these sets of covert subsidies arise in developed and developing countries alike *(Roodman, 1996)*.

Table 6.1

MAIN USES OF WATER WORLDWIDE

Households/municipal	10%
Industry	25%
Agriculture	65%
in many developing nations	90%

During the next 30 years we need to produce an extra 60-100% more food, half of it from irrigation

To produce I kg of corn takes 1000 kgs of water; to produce 1 kg of beef takes 100 times as much.

Sources: *Gleick, 1996; Pimentel and Pimentel, 1996: Postel, 1997a and b.*

How much water does a person use each day? Counting all three main purposes, the average worldwide is 1800 liters. An American gets through 400 liters for personal and direct purposes, and 5100 liters when we reckon in all forms of use *(Postel, 1996)*. The latter figure primarily reflects an American's consumption of grain in both direct and indirect fashion, an average tonne of grain requiring 1000 tonnes of water and 1 tonne of beef requiring 100 times as much *(Pimentel and Pimentel, 1996)*. One tonne of water is equivalent to one cubic meter or 1000 liters. Were the worldwide average daily water use to amount to 2740 liters per day, that would work out to 1000 cubic meters per year. So a global average of 1800 liters per day equates to just over 650 cubic meters per year *(Postel, 1996, 1997a and b)*.

We can reckon this another way. A nutritious and low-meat diet requires about 1600 cubic meters of water per person per year or 4400 liters per day. Worldwide water use for household and industrial purposes averages about 240 cubic meters per person per year, or 660 liters per day. By reducing this level through more careful consumption and more efficient technologies, we can assume an average of 200 cubic meters per person per year or 550 liters per day. When we add in water for food production, the total rises to 730 cubic meters per person per year or 2000 liters per day. A portion of water runoff must remain in rivers, however, in order to dilute pollution and meet other "instream" needs. Thus the total amount of runoff must be two to three times higher than the amount required to meet the three main purposes. So let us postulate an average total requirement of 1700 cubic meters per person per year or 4660 liters per day *(Postel, 1996, 1997a and b)*.

When water use falls below 1700 cubic meters per person per year, a country encounters "water stress" through a lack of adequate supplies. When water use falls below 1000 cubic meters, there is "water scarcity", meaning a significant and often a severe restriction on material welfare at individual level and on development prospects at national level *(Falkenmark, 1994; see also Gleick, 1996 and 1997; Postel, 1996)*.

True, some countries manage with a good deal less than the cut-off level of 1000 cubic meters. Israel, for example, gets by with a renewable per-capita water supply of only around 400 cubic meters *(Engelman and LeRoy, 1995b; see also Gleick, 1997)*. In part, the country manages to do this by importing much of its grain, which has been referred to *(Allan, 1995)* as "virtual water" since one tonne of grain requires 1000 tonnes of water (see above). The Middle East as a whole, which is the most concentrated region of water scarcity in the world, is fortunate in that its oil exports allow it to import 30 percent of its grain *(Postel, 1997a and b)*.

Producing food takes a lot of water. An average tonne of grain requires 1000 tonnes of water, and 1 tonne of beef requires 100 times as much *(Pimentel and Pimentel, 1996)*. One kilogram of lettuce takes over 800 kilograms of water, one of rice takes almost 2000, and one of chicken 3500 kilograms (grain fed) *(Pimentel et al., 1997c)*. One cup of orange juice takes 220 liters of water, one kilogram of pasta 2850 of water, and one hamburger 2775 kilograms *(Kreith, 1991)*. One of the thirstiest crops of all, albeit not a food crop, is cotton: one kilogram needs 17,000 kilograms of water *(Kendall and Pimentel, 1994)*.

Whatever the limitations on water supplies today and still greater shortages in the future through population growth alone, they could become even more stringent because of global warming. If mean annual temperatures rise, as is expected through a "business as usual" scenario, by as much as 3-4 degrees C,

---

Producing food takes a lot of water. An average tonne of grain requires 1000 tonnes of water, and 1 tonne of beef requires 100 times as much.

---

rainfall in the United States cornbelt could well decline by 10 percent *(Downing and Parry, 1994)*. This will be accompanied by increased evaporation, meaning still greater loss of moisture. Worldwide, global warming could step up irrigation needs by one quarter simply to maintain the production level of the early 1990s, without allowing for increased human numbers and improved diets *(Postel, 1992)*. In addition, there could be many more droughts: those that have only a five percent frequency today could increase to 50 percent by 2050 *(Rind et al., 1990)*.

Yet we need to produce 50-60 percent more food during the next 30 years simply to keep up with the projected rise in human numbers and the rise in human appetites. Since at least half of this increase is scheduled to come from irrigated croplands, this places a premium on more efficient and careful use of water. It is, after all, a renewable resource, available for repeated recyclings and thus contrasting strongly with other natural resources such as topsoil and fossil fuels. Almost everywhere, however—from California and Britain to Mexico and India—water is mis-used and over-used, in major measure because of subsidies that discourage people from making efficient and careful use of water. Fortunately, and through vigorous policy reform of subsidies among other measures, developing countries—these being where water shortages are likely to become most pronounced—could eliminate almost two thirds of their present water losses due to inefficient and profligate use of water. This would be equivalent to increasing their actual water supplies by a full one quarter *(Serageldin, 1995; see also de Moor, 1997)*.

Water Waste and Subsidies

There can hardly be a country in the world that is more dependent on a natural resource than Egypt is on water. At the time of the 1994 Cairo Conference on Population and Development, the conference grounds were regularly watered at midday when the temperature was over 30 degrees C. So too in California's Central Valley where it is often the practice for highly inefficient water sprinklers to irrigate croplands at midday when the temperature is not much lower than in Cairo. The reason in both cases is that government subsidies encourage wasteful use of water, and eliminate any incentive to use it sparingly, let alone repeatedly. These subsidies typically range from 75 to 99 percent of full costs; in the irrigation sphere, governments collect an average of under 10 percent of irrigation services via user fees (Tables 6.2 and 6.3) *(Gleick, 1996 and 1997; Postel, 1996; Serageldin, 1994; Xie, 1996)*. Almost as bad, wasteful use of water means that money is spent on lobbying and other forms of persuasion to secure further supplies of cheap water, causing subsidies to create a second-order source of waste *(Repetto, 1986)*.

Table 6.2

WATER PRICES AS SHARE OF MARGINAL COST OF SUPPLY

Israel	60%-+
China	25%
Algeria, Egypt	20%
United States	17%
Pakistan, Indonesia, South Korea	13%
Mexico	11%
Philippines	10%
Nepal	4%
Thailand	3%
Bangladesh	1%

Sources: Gleick, 1996; Postel, 1996; Serageldin, 1994.

Table 6.3

IRRIGATION SUBSIDIES IN DEVELOPING REGIONS, 1983-93
(million $)

	Total annual costs	Irrigation subsidies	
Africa	6,281	5,909	(94%)
Latin America	3,598	3,386	(94%)
Asia	13,263	12,480	(94%)
Total	23,142	21,775	(94%)

Water subsidies often amount to 75-99% of full costs.

Governments collect an average of less than 10% of irrigation services via user fees.

Amount of irrigation water available to plants, generally   40%;
    Through efficient irrigation systems   60-90%.

Over the past 30 years Israel has achieved a five-fold increase in the value of crops grown with a given amount of water.

Sources: Gleick, 1996; Postel, 1997a and b; World Bank, 1997a.

One person in ten is short of water. He/she uses less for all daily needs—cooking, washing, sanitation—than an affluent person uses with each flush of the toilet.

A potent political reason for subsidizing irrigation water in developing countries is that agriculture often employs over half the workforce *(Gupta et al., 1995; Sampath, 1992)*. This often helps to justify government measures to build yet another irrigation project or a further hydro works. To oblige its farmers, China plans to divert five percent of the Yangtze River's flow to its dry northern provinces, while Mexico proposes to pump water as much as 1000 meters up into its Central Valley.

In short, subsidies give rise to a host of problems: chronic excess demand for water, especially through grandscale water projects; poor operation and maintenance of water systems; inattention to scope for water conservation; and many other problems. The upshot *(to cite Repetto, 1986)* is "inefficient, inequitable, fiscally disastrous, wasteful use of increasingly scarce water, and environmentally harmful. [Because of subsidies,] neither farmers, local governments, irrigation agencies, nor international banks are financially at risk for the success of irrigation investments, so pressures for new capacity lead to a proliferation of projects, many of them being of dubious worth."

Table 6.4

WATER TRENDS WORLDWIDE

During 1950-90, water use has tripled; 1991-2010, demand is expected to double.

Humans already use 54 % of available water runoff.

People experiencing water shortages today:	550 million
expected in 2025	3 billion

Principal areas at risk: most of Africa and the Middle East, also parts of Pakistan, India and China.

Source: *Engelman and LeRoy, 1995b.*

All this is the more unfortunate in that water is becoming scarce in many parts of the world. Humans already use 54 percent of available water runoff, and new dams will increase this runoff by only about 10 percent over the next 30 years— a period during which population is projected to increase by 40 percent *(Postel et al., 1996).* Global water use has tripled during the four decades 1950-1990, and demand is expected to double again during the two decades 1991-2010 (Table 6.4). In 88 developing countries with 40 percent of the world's population, the problem has become a serious constraint on development, and the number of people experiencing water shortages is projected to reach three billion by 2025 (range, 2.8 billion to 3.3 billion), or more than one person in three worldwide (Table 6.4) *(Engelman and LeRoy, 1993 and 1995b; see also Gardner-Outlaw and Engelman, 1997; Gleick, 1996; Postel, 1997a and b; Serageldin, 1995).* It is unlikely that demand will be met if only because of practical upper limits of usable and renewable freshwater stocks.

The principal areas at risk include (though are not confined to) parts of China, India, Pakistan, the Middle East, Mexico, and much of Africa. (This analysis takes no account of further shortages brought on by global warming.) By 2020 China is projected to more than triple its domestic water withdrawals and to increase industrial withdrawals four-fold over the 1995 level (supposing the water is available). In Southeast Asia, there is expected to be a doubling of domestic water withdrawals and a 290-percent increase in industrial demand by 2020. The largest increase in water demand, 309%, is likely to be in India.

Adverse Consequences

Water shortages cause major problems for irrigation agriculture, industry and public health. A full 80 percent of developing-nation disease, or four billion cases, are due to lack of clean water for household use, and six million deaths per year stem from water-related diseases such as malaria, cholera, schistosomiasis, yellow fever and river blindness, and especially diarrhea *(Pimentel et al., 1997c; World Health Organization, 1992).* There are one billion episodes of diarrhea annually in developing countries. Moreover, when a person experiences diarrhea, malaria or other disease, some 5-20 percent of food intake is needed simply to offset the disease's impact on nutrition *(Pimentel et al., 1997c).* These water-related diseases are estimated to levy a cost, just through workdays lost to sickness, of $125 billion a year (late 1970s value) *(Pearce, 1993),* by contrast with the cost of supplying both water and sanitation facilities, $50 billion a year *(Christmas and Rooy, 1991).* Thus the subsidized abuse of water exacts high costs from national economies in the health sector alone. This effectively amounts to a concealed subsidy of egregious scale, though because of its very indirect nature it is not considered further in this analysis.

Fully 80 percent of developing-nation disease are due to lack of clean water for household use, with costs just through workdays lost to sickness of $125 billion a year (late 1970s value).

Industrially contaminated wastewater used for irrigation in northern China causes a loss of 5 million tonnes of grain a year.

There are many other instances of broad-scope externalities from water pollution. Industrially contaminated wastewater used for irrigation in northern China causes a loss of 5 million tonnes of grain a year *(Gardner, 1996)*. Pollution of groundwater in Yingkou, China, has almost doubled the cost of new water supplies, while in Shenyang, also in China, similar pollution will cause the cost of new supplies to almost triple during the period 1988-2000 *(Jones, 1995)*. Worldwide, pollution externalities of various sorts must collectively amount to tens of billions of dollars of covert subsidies per year, but they remain unquantified by economists and hence unconsidered by policy makers. To this sizeable extent, of course, the subsidy estimates in this chapter are to be viewed as all the more cautious and conservative.

Water subsidies also exert adverse effects on the environmental cause writ large. Foremost (and as noted above) is the wasteful use of a natural resource that is coming into ever-greater demand and ever-tighter supply. Other effects include, in terms of irrigation water alone, widespread agricultural pests (as well as a lengthy list of diseases); disruptions of river hydrology; water-caused soil erosion; siltation of water bodies; draining of wetlands; depletion of fish stocks; and building of unnecessary dams. All these adverse effects arise because governments find it politically easier to provide new water sources than to make users pay a price that reflects the true costs of supply, thus inducing consumers to treat water negligently if not prodigally *(Repetto, 1986)*. In India alone, 95,000 square kilometers out of 420,000 square kilometers of irrigated croplands have been lost to cultivation through waterlogging, and 70,000 square kilometers are affected by salinization. In Pakistan, more than half the Indus Basin canal system, some 120,000 square kilometers of irrigated croplands, is waterlogged and 26 percent is salinized. Worldwide, 454,000 square kilometers out of 2.8 million square kilometers (16 percent) are salinized enough to reduce crop yields, with crop losses worth almost $11 billion per year *(Ghassemi et al., 1995; see also Dregne et al., 1991; Jones, 1995; World Bank, 1992)*. Waterlogging and salinization may now be taking as much old land out of irrigation as is added through new irrigation networks *(Seckler, 1995; Serageldin, 1995)*.

There are other environmental problems from excessive irrigation. In some regions, so much water is withdrawn from rivers that they start to run dry. In Asia, which will see most population growth and greatest rise in food demand within the foreseeable future, many rivers are largely or completely tapped out during the drier part of the year, precisely when irrigation is most needed. They include most rivers in India, including the Ganges; also China's Yellow River,

---

In Asia, which will see the greatest rise in food demand, it is not shortage of land or fertilizer or machinery that will cause the biggest problem, it is shortage of water.

---

whose lower reaches have run dry for an average of 70 days a year in each of the last 10 years, and for 122 days in 1995 *(Postel, 1996)*.

At the same time, heavy irrigation leads to a decline in water tables. As far back as 10 years ago, more than one fifth of the United States' 100,000 square kilometers of irrigated lands was being watered only by lowering water tables, especially that of the Ogallala Aquifer *(Gleick et al., 1995)*. In parts of the north China plain around Beijing and Tienjin, the water table is currently dropping by one to two meters a year. This area, roughly China north of the Yangtze River, contains nearly half a billion people or almost 40 percent of the country's populace. It also encompasses half of China's croplands, yet it features only one-fifth of the country's surface water. This situation explains, even if it does not justify, the Chinese government's action in subsidizing water for agriculture *(Postel, 1992; see also Gardner, 1996)*. In India, excessive water pumping means that water tables have fallen precipitously in many areas (in parts of Tamil Nadu State, by as much as 25-30 meters during just the 1970s), drying up the more shallow tubewells, while in certain coastal areas the over-use of freshwater has sucked in seawater, destroying freshwater aquifers permanently *(Brown and Kane, 1994)*. In India's bread basket of the Punjab, water tables have recently been falling by 20 centimeters per year *(Postel, 1996)*.

Falling water tables affect urban communities too. Water for Mexico City used to be supplied at a price that implied an annual subsidy of $1 billion. This encouraged excessive pumping, with the result that the water table has fallen by 80 meters, aquifers are being compacted, and many parts of the city have been sinking (in some localities, as much as eight meters, damaging the city's underground infrastructure of pipes, cables and sewers, and increasing potential earthquake damage) *(Postel, 1992)*.

Perhaps the best known example of subsidy-driven degradation of a water resource has occurred in the former Soviet Union, in the form of the Aral Sea's decline. Much of the water basin centered on the Sea—once the world's fourth

---

In parts of the north China plain, the water table is currently dropping by one to two metres a year. This area contains nearly half a billion people or almost 40 percent of the country's populace. It also encompasses half of China's croplands, yet it features only one-fifth of the country's surface water.

---

largest lake—was given over in the late 1950s to cotton growing with heavily subsidized irrigation water, requiring the diversion of two of the Sea's main feeder rivers. As a result, the lake's expanse declined by 50 percent and its water volume by three-quarters between 1960 and the early 1990s. The lake's fishery, once worth 44,000 tonnes a year, has all but disappeared, taking with it 60,000 jobs. Within another decade or two, the Aral is likely to dwindle to a few residual brine lakes, worsening water shortages in an extensive sector of Central Asia and contributing to political tensions *(Aral Sea Program Unit, 1994; Elliot, 1991; Postel, 1996)*. To rehabilitate the area's salinized lands could cost at least $1 billion *(Serageldin, 1996; see also Glazovsky, 1995)*.

There are still further environmental problems from water subsidies, albeit of less precise and graphic impact. For instance, subsidies foster agriculture on marginal lands where cultivation requires excessive use of chemicals, hence contributing to degradation of rivers, contamination of aquifers, destruction of wetlands, and toxic pollution of fish and wildlife *(Sinclair, 1987)*. Yet these environmental externalities, like the others listed above (rivers running dry, water tables plunging, etc.), remain almost entirely unquantified in economic terms and hence unnoticed in policy terms—even though they effectively constitute perverse subsidies of exceptional size.

Another way to get a handle on what is at stake is to consider the putative value of major benefits derived from water, and then to reflect on what will be lost as water supplies decline in relation to fast-growing demand. According to a recent assessment *(Costanza et al., 1997)*, water supplies from watersheds, aquifers and reservoirs generate benefits worth $1.7 trillion per year, and water for agricultural irrigation, industrial processes and waterway transportation is worth $1.1 trillion worldwide per year. Even if these benefits totalling $2.8 trillion were reduced through water waste, pollution etc., by only 1 percent per year, the annual loss would be $28 billion.

That the $2.8 trillion estimate is in the right ballpark is demonstrated by a further recent assessment. This shows that the dilution of pollutants, as measured by the cost of removing all contaminants and nutrients from wastewater by technological means, is worth $150 billion worldwide per year (this estimate applies to municipal water only, and does not consider the dilution function that removes pesticides, nitrates and other contaminants from agricultural drainage water). Then there is the value of transportation by freshwater, generating revenues in the United States of $360 billion per year and in Western Europe by $169 billion per year, this being a lower-bound estimate that also does not consider the rest of the world. In addition there is the value of freshwater systems for sport fishing, worth $46 billion per year in the United States alone; the global value of fish, waterfowl and other goods takes from freshwater systems amounts to at least $100 billion per year, possibly several times as much. The marginal value of these benefits is increasing in many countries as more people spend time and money on outdoor pursuits, and as freshwater systems become more scarce. The economic value of the services listed amounts to $779 billion per year, while "The entire benefits and services provided by freshwater systems almost certainly amount to several trillion dollars annually" *(Postel and Carpenter, 1997)*.

Finally, consider what could prove to be the biggest potential externality of all: water wars. This is not so improbable within the foreseeable future *(Gleick, 1993; Serageldin, 1995)*, mainly because of water stocks that straddle international frontiers. Of 214 major river basins around the world, three-quarters are shared by two countries and one quarter by three to 10 countries (Table 6.5). Almost half of Earth's land surface is located within international river basins, supporting 40 percent of the world's population; two-thirds of these basins are in developing countries with generally less water per citizen than do developed countries. Nearly 50 countries have more than three-quarters of their territory within such areas. Within countries too there is scope for conflict. In India's Punjab, there have been constant violent clashes as Sikh nationalists claim that too much of their water has been diverted to the Hindu states of Harayana and Rajasthan.

Tensions and violence have erupted too in the river basin of the Mekong, shared by Thailand, Laos, Cambodia and Vietnam; in that of the Amur, shared by China and the former Soviet Union; in that of the Parana, shared by Brazil and Argentina; in that of the Lauca, shared by Bolivia and Chile; and in that of the Mejerdah, shared by Tunisia and Libya *(Myers, 1987)*. Were confrontation over water shortages to give way to conflict and outright violence, this would likely be the biggest and most costly single externality of all, yet it does not figure in the economic calculations of policy makers in the water sector.

Water as a Free Good

Why this dismal state of affairs from both economic and environmental standpoints? Much of the essential reason is that nations and people alike tend to regard water as a free good, which places an ostensible burden on governments to supply it without charge. (The free-good approach is explicitly enshrined in the Koran, which may account for grossly wasteful use of water in Muslim lands of the Middle East—though in the largest Muslim country, Indonesia, the government gets round the problem by charging for the container that brings the water.) The overall result is that water is generally used inefficiently because it appears to cost next to nothing if not nothing at all. What is priceless is then taken to be value-less. As a further result, governments squander large amounts of taxpayers' money building new water-supply systems *(Cairncross, 1995; see also Briscoe, 1996; Yep, 1995)*.

Table 6.5

DEPENDENCE ON INTERNATIONAL WATER SUPPLY

Country	Share of Total Water Flow Originating in an Upstream Country/Countries (%)
Egypt	97
Botswana	94
Uzbekistan	91
Cambodia	82
Syria	79
Sudan	77
Iraq	66
Bangladesh	42
Thailand	39
Jordan	36

Sources: *Gleick, 1993; Postel, 1997a and b.*

A subsidiary reason is that all governments recognize a basic responsibility to make sure their citizens are fed, preferably with home-grown food. A full one third of our food is produced on irrigated lands, even though they comprise only one sixth of all croplands. But if agriculture were to compete openly with industry and domestic needs for water, it would often be out-priced. So governments support agricultural water with one subsidy after another, certain of them of indirect character, difficult to discern. In particular, governments sponsor water-demanding crops. In California's Central Valley with its desert-like climate, three of the main crops are alfalfa, cotton and rice, crops more suitable to a much moister climate. In an increasing number of semi-arid countries, the main use of water is to grow crops that are worth less than the water itself. In Cyprus, for example, three-quarters of crops grown are uneconomic, produced only because of water subsidies *(World Bank, 1993)*. In Jordan, one of the driest countries anywhere, subsidies encourage over-use of irrigation water, whereupon strict rationing is required to allocate the resulting scarcities *(Rosegrant,*

In many semi-arid countries, subsidies encourage the use of water to grow crops that are worth less than the water itself. In Jordan, one of the driest countries anywhere, over-use of irrigation water results in strict rationing to allocate the resulting scarcities.

Whether in California, Mexico and Indonesia, or along the banks of the Nile, the Ganges or the Yangtze, farmers rarely pay more than one fifth and sometimes only one tenth of the operating costs of irrigation schemes, let alone their capital costs. Much the same applies in the United States, Australia, Canada, Greece, Spain and Italy.

1995). A further subsidy lies with the electricity used to drive irrigation pumps, a virtually universal practice in developing countries.

In most thirsty regions, water management can account for as much as 14-18 percent of all public investment. This should supply a massive incentive to ensure farmers make best use of every last drop of water. But whether in California, Mexico and Indonesia, or along the banks of the Nile, the Ganges and the Yangtze, farmers rarely pay more than one fifth and sometimes only one tenth of the operating costs of irrigation schemes, let alone their capital costs *(Gleick, 1993; Postel, 1996)*. Much the same applies in the United States, Australia, Canada, Greece, Spain and Italy, though most other developed countries cover their government outlays with consumer charges (whereas capital costs are often subsidized to an average of 20-40 percent) *(Herrington, 1987; Repetto, 1987; United States Department of Agriculture, 1994)*. In Australia, the government of Victoria State recovers only two-fifths of the delivery costs of irrigation water, and the government of New South Wales manages even less. Because of massive over-use of water, irrigated lands in New South Wales' portion of the Murray Darling Basin—specially important because they produce 90 percent of the country's irrigated food with just 6 percent of the country's water runoff—feature broadscale salinization, water pollution, rising water tables and soil erosion *(Armstrong, 1996; Mussared, 1995)*.

Inefficiency and Waste

Let us take a closer look at the degree of subsidy-induced inefficiency and waste in many developing nations. In China, water prices are believed to be only 25 percent of the marginal cost of supply, while the cost of infrastructure (dams, piping, etc.) is left out of account altogether. In Algeria and Egypt, supply-cost recovery is 20 percent or less, in Pakistan, Indonesia and South Korea it is 13 percent, in Mexico 11 percent, in Philippines 10 percent, in Nepal 4 percent, in Thailand 3 percent, and in Bangladesh 1 percent of water supply's full economic cost to the government (compare the United States, 17 percent) (Table 6.2). Irrigation charges as a percentage of economic benefits to farmers work out in Mexico to 26-11 percent, in Indonesia 21-8 percent, and in Pakistan 6 percent *(Falkenmark and Suprato, 1992; Gleick, 1993; Pearce and Warford, 1993;*

Postel, 1992; Sampath, 1992). This means that were governments to steadily increase the cost of water supply, it would make only marginal difference to farmers' overall costs.

Because farmers are implicitly encouraged to be prodigal in their use of irrigation water, it is generally the case that only a small fraction of water actually becomes available for plants' use—typically no more than 40 percent, compared to 60-70 percent in more advanced systems. The rest of the water seeps or evaporates from unlined or obstructed canals and distributories *(van der Leeden et al., 1990)*. So wasteful is water use by outmoded irrigation systems that they often use twice as much water per hectare yet achieve crop yields only one third as high as advanced counterparts *(Falkenmark and Widstrand, 1992; Serageldin, 1994)*.

Even in more efficient irrigation systems, however, generally crop plants use only half the water. Farm distribution systems lose 15 percent, irrigation systems lose another 15 percent, and field application methods lose another 25 percent *(Food and Agriculture Organization, 1994)*. Irrigation efficiency can be improved by several techniques, including the simple expedient of irrigating at night in order to reduce evaporation *(van der Leeden et al., 1990; Verplaneke et al, 1992)*. This is not to say that farmers do not value their irrigation water, rather that the situation discourages them to value it much at all in financial terms. In India, farmers in areas with irrigation water supplied by private instead of public bodies have been willing to pay six to nine times the water charges levied for official supplies *(Mundle and Rao, 1991; Shah, 1993)*. This means of course that subsidies are strictly unnecessary insofar as farmers are willing to pay highly for their irrigation water.

The same applies to inefficiency and waste in municipal communities. The water supply in Manila loses 58 percent of its water through leakages from pipes between the treatment plant and the consumer, whereas Singapore with its hefty water charges loses only 8 percent. In most Latin American cities, water losses through pipe leaks and other sources of "unaccounted for" water amount to 40 percent, while the average municipal loss in many countries rises as high as 50 percent. As a result, Latin America as a whole foregoes $1-1.5 billion in water revenues each year *(Serageldin, 1994)*. As noted, developing countries could readily avoid two-thirds of their water losses.

Three Case Studies

1. India

Some 93 percent of India's water use is for agriculture, mostly for irrigation. Revenues from irrigation farmers cover only 7.5 percent of the cost of operating and maintaining irrigation systems, while subsidies cost Indian tax-payers $735 million in 1991 *(Pachauri, 1994; see also Mundle and Rao, 1991; Shah, 1993)*. Yet there is not enough public money even to repair and desilt irrigation canals, so the whole canal network is deteriorating. The system encourages farmers to mis-use and over-use irrigation water, and years of excessive soaking of irrigated farmlands have led to much water-logging and salinization (as detailed above).

There are further subsidies at work in India, this time indirect ones. State electricity boards supply electricity for irrigation pumps at a 1992 cost to the states of around $1.5 billion a year, yet farmers pay only one eighth of the cost (in three southern states, the power is given free) *(Pachauri, 1994; see also Mundle and Rao, 1991; Shah, 1993)*. Ironically farmers could cut back on irrigation water use by 15 percent without reducing crop yields simply by eliminating over-watering *(Faeth, 1993)*. Since water charges are typically 2-5 percent of the harvest's value, they have very little impact on the farmers' financial planning.

The two figures, $735 million and $1.5 billion, add up to $2.2 billion. They date from 1992 and 1991, and at the time of the author's latest visits to India in early 1996 and early 1998, there was no sign of the subsidies being reduced—rather the opposite. Allowing for expansion of the subsidies (and not counting other subsidies, notably the many indirect and otherwise concealed items), we can suppose a realistic minimum estimate for India's irrigation subsidies in 1996 was $2.5 billion. This is the same as was alternatively estimated for 1992 *(Bahatia and Falkenmark, 1993)*.

2. *Israel*

Israel is an instance of a country that tries to do things properly, or at least better. It has come a long way, but has quite a way to go. Over the past 30 years it has achieved a five-fold increase in the value of crops grown per unit of water, yet in a flooded or spray-irrigated field, at least half the water never reaches plants' roots but seeps underground or evaporates. This is to be contrasted with an Israel-innovated technique, drip irrigation, utilizing long lengths of hose with pin-holes that drip water close to plant roots; the technique cuts water losses by half *(Pearce, 1992)*. As far back as the early 1980s, drip irrigation and other efficiency techniques were watering at least 5000 square kilometers of irrigated lands. True, this area was small compared to the total expanse under irrigation, but half of remaining irrigated lands were being subjected to a moderately efficient technique known as micro-irrigation *(Meybeck et al., 1989)*. It is a measure of Israel's pioneering efforts that only one percent of irrigated lands worldwide feature any form of trickle-drip irrigation *(Verplaneke et al., 1992)*.

In addition, Israel recycles 65 percent of its domestic wastewater for use on farms, where wastewater accounts for 30 percent of all water supply (a figure planned to rise to 80 percent by the year 2025). As a measure of the significance of Israel's efforts, note that if all countries were to recycle 65 percent of their domestic and municipal wastewater, they could theoretically boost their agricultural output by 350 million tonnes of wheat or almost 20 percent of all grain grown today *(Postel, 1996)*.

Due to excess pumping from water reserves over many years, however, Israel now faces an acute hydrological deficit *(Cohen and Plaut, 1995)*. The source of the problem lies with water subsidies of numerous sorts, plus special interests' control over water-use decisions, faulty pricing assumptions, and rigid use patterns that penalize users of low-cost stocks of water. Water subsidies amount to $120 million annually, the most expensive subsidy in the country apart from that for public transportation, but they reduce the price of agricultural water by only 17 percent after tax exemptions. On top of this, there is an indirect subsidy with respect to the under-pricing of the pumping and distribution services of the main water agency, Mekerot Ltd. *(Pearce, 1992)*.

In marked contrast, Saudi Arabia spent $40 billion during the 1980s on developing its farming, thanks largely to extravagant subsidies, mostly for water. The country also spent $10 billion on desalinization plants which provide just 15 percent of drinkable water for its citizens, the rest coming from groundwater. Due to poor irrigation techniques, more than two-thirds of water pumped to the surface to irrigate fields of wheat, alfalfa and date palms never reached plants' roots but was lost to evaporation *(Pearce, 1992)*. Yet the country contrived to increase its wheat output from virtually nil in 1980 to more than 4 million tonnes in 1992, even producing an exportable surplus thanks to huge subsidies that reduced the price from a level 10 times that of American wheat *(Pinstrup-Andersen, 1994)*. Following the recent decline in oil prices, however, the Saudi government has slashed its agricultural subsidies and wheat output has dropped by half.

3. *United States*

Irrigated lands in the United States account for one ninth of croplands and one third of the value of agricultural output *(Gleick et al., 1995; Pimentel et al., 1997b)*. They also feature some of the largest irrigation subsidies in the world. Since the cost recovery from Bureau of Reclamation irrigation projects in the early 1980s averaged only about 17 percent of total costs, the implied subsidy to farmers using Bureau water was about $1 billion per year *(Repetto, 1986; see also Congressional Budget Office, 1983)*. There is little rea-

---

Subsidized irrigation in the United States is used primarily to grow crops that are officially in surplus and subject to other expensive federal programs to reduce production.

---

son to suppose the subsidy has declined significantly since then *(Gardner, 1997; Gleick et al., 1995; Roodman, 1996)*.

Remarkably enough, it is impossible to estimate the total value of all United States water subsidies because government agencies (others are involved besides the Bureau of Reclamation) do not maintain the records that would permit such calculations. There is general agreement, however, that irrigation subsidies alone in the western United States alone amount to $4.4 billion per year *(Pimentel et al., 1997b; see also United States Department of Agriculture, 1994)*. Well over half of all federally irrigated lands are in the West (three-fifths of that total in California). In this dry region, irrigation accounts for 86 percent of water use *(Carlson et al., 1993)*. Ironically, irrigation is used primarily to grow crops that are officially in surplus and subject to other expensive federal programs to reduce production *(Anderson, 1995 and 1996; Jones and Dyer, 1995; see also Frederiksen, 1997; Gaffney, 1995; Gardner, 1997; Reisner, 1996; Wahl, 1989)*.

To gain a clearer picture of subsides at work, consider California and its Central Valley Project. So extravagant are subsidies here that one hectare of agricultural land can sometimes use roughly as much water as one hectare of houses and offices (albeit most farmers get their water from groundwater wells rather from subsidized sources). Although agriculture accounts for only 3 percent of the state's economic product, it consumes 85 percent of the water. Were urban users to cut their water consumption by one third (swimming pools and all), that would do no more than farmers cutting their consumption by a mere 10 percent. Grandscale irrigation enables California to grow 8 percent of United States agricultural output (and half of all fruits and vegetables) on less than 1 percent of United States farmland. Each California farmer feeds 130 people, of whom nearly 100 are Americans and the rest are foreigners. But without virtually unlimited supplies of artificially cheap irrigation water, most farmers could not continue with their traditional cropping patterns (though there is plenty of scope for them to shift to less water-demanding crops and to use scarce water more productively) *(Gleick et al., 1995; Reisner, 1996; see also Frederiksen, 1996; Miller, 1994)*.

The water subsidies derive from cheap 50-year contracts signed early this century, which are still in operation even though they have long exceeded their "shelf life". By the mid-1980s, farmers had repaid only 4 percent of the original capital cost of almost $1 billion, with United States taxpayers footing the rest of the bill. The subsidies ensure that many farmers now pay around $25 per hectare-foot for water that costs 10 times as much to pump it to them, by contrast with $575 for the same hectare-foot in San Francisco and more than $750 in Los Angeles. On top of that, California farmers still collect direct subsidies of $400 million to grow such thirsty crops as rice, cotton and alfalfa *(Department of Water Resources, State of California, 1994; Gaffney, 1995; Jones and Dyer, 1995; and for some historical background, see LaVeen and King, 1985; Reisner, 1996)*. This curious circumstance is by no means confined to California; in neighboring Arizona, farmers pay only one twenty-fifth as much for their water as do residents of Phoenix *(World Bank, 1993)*.

Fortunately there is vast scope for water savings in California, and not just in agriculture. They are urgently needed. Demand already exceeds supply, and a "business as usual" scenario projects that the gap will steadily increase until at least the year 2020. But through water-use efficiency and conservation, fostered by water markets (see below), supply could easily exceed demand by 2020. Thanks to existing technologies, industrial water use efficiency could increase by 20 percent over today's level within 25 years; residential water use could decline by 46 percent; and use of reclaimed water could expand fivefold *(Gleick et al., 1995)*. There is potential for similar grandscale savings throughout the United States. Were subsidies to be phased out and Americans required to pay the full social cost of their water, they would then feel more inclined to install efficient technologies. Fitting improved showerheads alone would effectively save water equivalent to the output of 10 large dams, while the resulting electricity savings would equal the output of three Chernobyl-sized power plants (they would also reduce CO_2 emissions by 20 million tonnes a year) *(Hawken et al., 1998)*. The cost of water from a plumbing-retrofit program is only half the average cost through conventional suppliers.

So attractive are water savings that the Seattle Water Department is relying on improvements in water efficiency as the sole source of additional water for its expanding population during the 1990s. It will actually give away efficient showerheads. It will also audit homes, promote the installation of efficient toilets, and implement many other similar water-saving programs. By 2002, this will supply over 30 million liters of water per day at an estimated cost of almost $16 million, whereas water from conventional sup-

---

The United States has recently established standards for faucets, showerheads and toilets, with water savings of 35 percent expected over the next 30 years.

---

plies, notably by diverting a river, would cost almost three times as much per liter *(Jones and Dyer, 1995; see also Gladstone, 1992)*.

Subsidies Worldwide

What is the scale of water subsidies worldwide? To reiterate a key point: governments do not usually keep systematic records, of all their financial supports for any of the three main categories of water use. So the true total remains a black hole. For purposes of this report, however, it is pertinent to attempt a best-judgement estimate in order to indicate the scale of these government outlays.

We have just noted the annual $4.4 billion for irrigation in the western United States. Let us suppose that other irrigation subsidies in the United States bring the United States total up to $5 billion (could be much more). Let us suppose too that several other developed countries such as Japan, Australia, Russia and Ukraine (leaving out other former Soviet Union republics in Asia) practice irrigation subsidies of the same scale. That makes a developed-world total of $10 billion (probably much more) per year. This is rather a "heroic extrapolation", but it is surely justified when we consider that the reckoning reflects no other kinds of water subsidies beyond irrigation. It is almost certainly well below the true figure, but there is no way to establish that with worthwhile accuracy.

In developing countries, the cost recovery of providing water for household use averages around 35 percent. The fiscal burden of this underpricing can be conservatively calculated at $13 billion for 1993 *(de Moor, 1997; see also World Bank, 1994; Yep, 1995)* (rather more today if only because of the booming growth of cities and other urban communities). Then there are savings to be made from eliminating illegal connections, worth perhaps $5 billion in 1993; also savings available through increased efficiency, worth $4 billion. This all makes a total of $22 billion for 1992 *(World Bank, 1994; see also de Moor, 1997; Roodman, 1996)*. By late 1997 the total could well have risen to $25 billion per year, and this figure is used for present purposes.

More important than subsidies for household use in developing countries are those for irrigation, particularly in Asia. In the Indian State of Tamil Nadu, electricity subsidies for irrigation pumps total at least $316 million per year. The cost recovery throughout developing countries ten years ago was no more than 20 percent at best, often only half as much *(World Bank, 1993; see also Bahatia and Falkenmark, 1993; Briscoe and Garn, 1994; Tsuar and Dinar, 1995)*. There is scant reason to suppose it is better today except in a few countries, and abundant evidence to suggest it is worse in most countries. Given total costs in 1985 of $25 billion, and using the conservative recovery figure of 20 percent, irrigation subsidies in 1985 could effectively be put at $20 billion *(Xie, 1996)*.

Thirteen years later they are likely to have risen to perhaps $25 billion if only because there are an extra one billion people in developing countries, over 60 percent of them in the humid zones of Asia where most rice is grown. That this figure of $25 billion is conservative, perhaps extremely so, is demonstrated by five-year old estimates of $2.5 billion per year for each of India and Egypt *(Bahatia and Falkenmark, 1993)*, while China in 1997 is estimated to feature total costs of $16 billion, of which only 25 percent are recovered from users, meaning an effective subsidy of $12 billion *(Hongliang, 1997)*.

Thus subsidies in developing countries are here estimated to be at least $50 billion and in developed countries at least $10 billion, for an overall total of $60 billion per year. (The figure of $50 billion per year for developing countries is to be compared with a World Bank estimate for minimum water investments in these countries over the next decade, an average of $60 billion per year *(Serageldin, 1995)*.) The true subsidies total could readily be twice as big, conceivably several times bigger were we to consider all forms of water use. Given the harm that these subsidies impose on economies and environments alike, at least three-quarters of them or $45 billion are considered to be perverse. True, this is a very preliminary and approximate estimate, even an exploratory guesstimate, though it reflects a strong consensus of opinion among water experts consulted in Europe, North America, Israel, India, China and Australia. It is advanced solely with the aim of getting a handle, however crude, on the scale of a matter of paramount importance to developed and developing countries alike.

In addition to these formal or conventional subsidies are the implicit subsidies of environmental externalities. Notable instances are water pollution and water deficits, both of which relate strongly to disease in developing countries. The 1991 cholera outbreak in Peru cost the country at least $1 billion, while the 1994 Indian plague deprived airlines and hotels of some $2-5 billion. We have already noted the cost of workdays lost to water-related diseases, $125 billion per year *(Pearce, 1993)*. A further way to shadow price the cost of water shortages is to estimate the numbers of people—at least 500 million *(Engelman and LeRoy, 1995b; see also Falkenmark, 1994; Postel, 1997; Reddy et al., 1997)*—who must spend several hours a day in fetching clean water to their homes, then to reckon their time opportunity costs at a minimum of, say, 25 cents an hour. Result, an externality cost of at least $50 billion a year. These two implicit subsidies alone total $175 billion per year, or three times more than the formal and conventional subsidies. As argued in Chapter 1, these implicit subsidies are to be counted as 100 percent perverse. So the total subsidies figure for the water sector amounts to $60 billion plus $175 billion, i.e., $235 billion per year.

Scope for Policy Reform

The main priority is to reduce and eventually phase out water subsidies. This chapter has demonstrated there is plenty of scope to do this, especially in agriculture. California landowners can buy water for only one tenth as much as it costs the federal government to deliver it—and it can be worth six times as much on the open market *(Roodman, 1996; see also Gaffney, 1992)*. Nor need farmers fear the gradual elimination of subsidies. For most agricultural commodities, water is such a small component of overall costs that steady climbing water prices would have negligible effects on crop prices. Far from undermining farming, the disappearance of subsidies would foster more sustainable agricultural practices in the long term. In fact, by growing less thirsty crops and making more careful use of water, farmers could increase their revenues by 12 percent while using 12 percent less water *(Gleick et al., 1995)*.

There is lots of scope too in the urban and industry sectors. An increase in the water tariff in Bogor, Indonesia, from $0.15 to $0.42 per cubic meter has resulted in a 30-percent decline in household demand for water. In the industrial sector, increased water prices led to investment in water recycling and conservation technology. In Goa, India, increased water tariffs have induced a 50-percent reduction in water use by a fertilizer factory over a five-year period. In Sao Paulo, Brazil, three industrial concerns have reduced water consumption by 40-60 percent in response to effluent charges *(Rosegrant, 1995)*. (See also Box 6.1 on South Africa).

Water conservation in households can also be achieved through efficiency standards. The United States has recently established standards for faucets, showerheads and toilets, with water savings of 35 percent expected over the next 30 years. Similar standards have been adopted by a number of other governments, including Mexico and the Canadian province of Ontario *(Postel, 1997a and b)*. This is not only better for the resource, it is generally cheaper than looking for new supplies of water. Reducing demand through efficiency and conservation costs 2-45 United States cents per cubic meter, while treatment and re-use of waste water for irrigation runs at 36-60 cents. By contrast, desalination of brackish water costs 43-68 cents, and desalination of seawater 98-148 cents. Development of marginal water sources comes in at 52-83 cents—a high cost partly because there are few good dam sites left *(Postel, 1996)*.

It is sometimes objected that to reduce water subsidies for household use would penalize the poor. There is much evidence, however, that these people are willing to pay highly for dependable water supplies. In many developing-country cities, street vendors sell water at prices four to 10 times higher than those of public utilities *(Bahatia and Falkenmark, 1993; see also Rosegrant, 1997; Serageldin, 1994)*.

119

Box 6.1

SOUTH AFRICA—A SUCCESS STORY IN THE MAKING?

South Africa has long been a thirsty country. Two-thirds of the country receives less than 500 millimeters. of rainfall per year, regarded as the minimum for sustainable dryland farming, and evaporation is often greater than precipitation. Only 13 percent of the country is suitable for cultivation. Due to water shortages, the industrial sector sometimes endures months of water restrictions. One third of all citizens lack access to drinkable water, and one half do not enjoy water-borne sanitation. At the same time, the population is growing at 2.3 percent per year, and its current total of 46 million is projected to surge to 58 million as early as the year 2010. Regrettably there is little incentive for consumers to use water sparingly, given the multitudes of subsidies pushing him or her in the opposite direction. Farmers pay some of the cheapest water prices in the world.

Much depends, however, on how many people want how much water. An affluent citizen consumes at least 1,750 liters of water per day for household purposes alone, whereas a shantytown dweller makes do with only 15 liters, equivalent to a single flush of the rich citizen's toilet. In Metropolitan Cape Town and the rest of the Western Cape region, there are 400,000 households, plus schools and the like. If they were all to switch to low-flow showerheads and dual-flush toilets, they would save more water than is to be delivered by a huge new dam, and do it at one quarter of the capital investment and with none of the operational costs. The dam is being built primarily to satisfy the "needs" of affluent Cape Towners, comprising 5 percent of the populace.

Fortunately the new Minister for Water is embarking on a program to (a) phase out those many subsidies that encourage abuse of water, and (b) charge consumers the "full economic costs" of water, i.e., the cost of replacing each liter consumed. He is also encouraging water marketing, and mandating that water suppliers adopt conservation measures such as recycling.

Waste markets epitomize the saying "Water flows uphill to money."

A further policy initiative lies with water rights and water markets *(Anderson, 1995; de Moor, 1997; Frederiksen and Perry, 1995; Postel, 1996 and 1997a and b; Roodman, 1996).* As we have seen with respect to areas as disparate as California, central United States, India, China, and central Asia, when farmers have motivation to view water as "cheaper than dirt", they treat it as such. They also face the choice of "use it or lose it", meaning that if they behave with public spirit and reduce their consumption through conservation measures, the water merely becomes available to other users. If, by contrast, the farmers could sell their water to higher-value users, the opportunity cost of using the water would immediately rise, and the farmers would have an incentive to conserve it. But they will not be willing to consider this positive prospect unless they are accorded some form of ownership of their water. Hence the vital issue of water rights *(Anderson and Snyder, 1997; Cohen and Plaut, 1995; Keller et al., 1995; Rosegrant and Schleyer, 1995; Seckler, 1993).*

Fortunately these rights are now being made available in many areas, and in turn this opens up the scope for a highly promising phenomenon: water markets. As soon as water rights become tradable, they achieve several things: they empower water users, provide investment motivation, improve water use efficiency, increase flexibility in resource allocation, and reduce incentives to degrade the environment *(Anderson, 1996; Frederiksen and Perry, 1995; Keller and Keller, 1995; Pinkham and Chaplin, 1996; Postel, 1996; Rosegrant et al., 1995; Seckler, 1996).*

Water markets state in effect that water is an economic good and should be treated as such—whereupon there are many opportunities for imaginative husbandry of the resource. The gap between the value of a liter of water to a farmer and to a thirsty city dweller is so large, and agriculture's use of water so extensive as well, that there is abundant opportunity for trading deals *(Anderson and Snyder, 1997; Rosegrant et al., 1997).* Since the late 1970s, a vigorous water market has sprung up in the western United States, allowing urban authorities to buy up farmers' water rights and thus provide extra water for city communities. Los Angeles has done a deal with Imperial Valley farmers: by paying for improvements to reduce wastage from irrigation channels, the city has acquired more water at less than half the cost of the cheapest alternative, while farmers have received cash and suffered no reduction in their irrigation supply *(Cairncross, 1995).* Annual savings of more than $200 million could be achieved in California through regional reallocation of water from agriculture to urban areas *(Howe, 1996).*

This all epitomizes the saying "Water flows uphill to money." Similar water markets are emerging in other parts of the United States, also in Australia, New

Zealand, Algeria, Morocco, Tunisia, Brazil, Peru, Mexico, Chile, China, India and Pakistan *(Roodman, 1997)*. In Chile, for instance, water companies supplying urban communities with their fast-growing numbers can now buy water from farmers with surpluses thanks to their efforts to improve efficiency *(Postel, 1997a and b)*. In 1994 the Mexican government turned over some 25,000 square kilometers of irrigated land, being 78 percent of all such lands under federal management, to water-user organizations; farmer water fees in several districts soared by 50-180 percent, thus reportedly lifting the nationwide rate of irrigation financial self-sufficiency from around half to three-quarters *(Gorriz et al., 1995; Postel, 1997a and b)*.

As a measure of how far water markets can stimulate conservation, note that farmers in northwest Texas, trying to cope with falling water tables through depletion of the Ogallala Aquifer, have reduced their water use by 20-25 percent by adopting more efficient sprinkler technologies, surge valves to even out distribution, and gravity systems among other water-saving practices. Farmers in a variety of countries who have switched from furrow or sprinkler irrigation to drip systems which deliver water directly to the root of crops, have cut their water use by 30-60 percent *(Postel, 1992 and 1996)*.

That irrigation subsidies can be removed with benefit to the economy and environment alike is demonstrated by the experience of several republics of the former Soviet Union, where these subsidies have been largely ended, leading to a marked shrinkage of irrigated areas. During just the period 1990-93, Russia phased out more than 7000 square kilometers of irrigated cropland, or 13 percent of its former expanse. This contraction is expected to continue for perhaps another decade or however long it takes for governments in the region to recover their fiscal health *(Gardner, 1996)*. It is reported *(Frederiksen, 1997)* that the governments of Vietnam and Indonesia, both heavy water users, have recently legislated to recover all costs of water supplies.

Let us conclude this chapter with a remarkable success story through innovative policy measures, albeit with respect to water for city use rather than irrigation agriculture *(Chichilnisky and Heal, 1998)*. New York City has found its water demand rising so much that it has faced the prospect of having to build a new filtration plant. The plant would have been the largest in the world, with a capital cost of $6-8 billion plus running costs of another $3 billion over ten years. Fortunately there was an alternative. The City could rehabilitate a watershed in the Catskill Mountains where water purification has traditionally been carried out by the vegetation's root systems and soil microorganisms offering filtration functions sufficient to cleanse the water to EPA standards. In recent years, soil pollutants in the form of local sewage, fertilizer and pesticides have reduced the efficacy of the process below EPA standards. So the City has been faced with a choice: build an expensive new filtration plant, or restore the watershed ecosystems. In other words, invest in either physical capital or natural capital.

Investment in natural capital meant buying 5200 hectares of land (15 times more than Central Park) in and around the watershed so that the land's use could be restricted, for instance no more pollutant farming. The investment would also entail subsidizing the construction of better sewage treatment plants for the homes of watershed residents. The total cost would be $1-1.5 billion, between one sixth and one eleventh of the alternative. This would give an internal rate of return of 90-170 percent and a payback period of 4-7 years—a return an order of magnitude higher than is normally available, particularly on relatively riskless investments. Moreover, these calculations were conservative since they considered only one service of the watershed, viz. water purification, even though watersheds generally provide other important services such as flood control, biodiversity habitat, and recreational facilities. In 1996 the City floated an environmental bond issue, using the proceeds to restore the functioning of the watershed ecosystems and to undertake better sewage treatment for watershed residents. The cost of the bond issue is to be met by savings produced, viz. the avoidance of a capital investment of $6-8 billion plus annual $300 million running costs.

The Environmental Protection Agency estimates that over the next 20 years, ensuring safe and adequate drinking water throughout the United States will require infrastructure investments of $138 billion (the equivalent figure worldwide will be in the trillions of dollars). Watershed conservation could cut the investments substantially, while securitization or privatization could ensure that much of the balance remaining is provided by the private sector *(Chichilnisky and Heal, 1998)*.

CHAPTER 7

FISHERIES

The ocean fisheries catch—well above sustainable yield—costs more than $100 billion to bring to dockside, whereupon it is sold for some $80 billion, the shortfall being made up with government subsidies. The result is depletion of many major fisheries to commercial extinction, plus bankruptcy of fishing businesses and sizeable job losses.

As fisheries expert Carl Safina has pointed out *(1995 and 1998)*, there is no longer as much truth as there used to be in the proverb "Give someone a fish and you feed them for a day, give them a net and you feed them for a lifetime." Marine fisheries are fading in many regions, primarily because of massive subsidies from governments that foster over-fishing.

Marine Fisheries in Decline

These fisheries have been producing a worldwide catch averaging around 85 million tonnes during the 1990s. After four decades of steadily expanding catches, they appear to have exceeded their sustainable output in many instances despite—or rather, because of—fishing fleets becoming bigger than ever and with fishing technology more sophisticated than ever. Worse, there have been marked declines for fish such as cod, haddock, plaice and other species that make up the bulk of the catch and are the preferred species for human consumption *(Grainger and Garcia, 1996; McGoodwin, 1995; Milazzo, 1997; Safina, 1998; Weber, 1994)*.

The declines are regrettable not only from the conventional economic and environmental standpoints. Some 20 million fishermen and their families, and ultimately as many as 200 million people depend directly on ocean fishing for their livelihoods *(Botsford et al., 1997)*. Of the 1993 catch of 84 million tonnes, 56 percent was taken by just eight nations: China with 10.1 million (12.0 percent), Peru 8.2 million (9.7 percent), Japan 8.1 million (9.6 percent), Chile 6.1 million (7.2 percent), the United States 6.0 million (7.1 percent), Russia 4.5 million (5.3 percent), Spain 1.8 million (2.1 percent), and Canada 1.5 million (1.8

As many as 200 million people depend directly on ocean fishing for their livelihoods, and it supplies almost 20 percent of all animal protein.

---

percent). For documentation of these data, and for other information presented in this chapter generally, see *Botsford et al., 1997; Food and Agriculture Organization, 1993a, 1994, 1995 and 1997; Porter, 1997; Safina, 1994, 1995 and 1998; Thorpe et al., 1995; Weber, 1993 and 1994. For additional broad-scope information, see Bonino, 1996; Earle, 1995; Engelman and LeRoy, 1995; Gimbel, 1994; Holden, 1994; Kaczynski, 1992; Norse, 1993; Sutton, 1996; Thorne-Miller and Catena, 1989; United States National Research Council, 1995.*

Still more to the point, marine fishing supplies almost 20 percent of all animal protein consumed *(Botsford et al., 1997; Food and Agriculture Organization, 1992)*. It is the prime source of animal protein for one billion people in developing countries, where it supplies 86 percent as much animal protein as the four terrestrial animal groups combined viz. cattle, sheep, pigs and poultry *(Safina, 1994; Weber, 1994)*.

Since 1950 the world's marine fish catch has increased from 22 million tonnes to around 85 million tonnes in the mid-1990s. But as noted, the steady 40-years growth appears to have peaked. Worse, if the catch were measured by value instead of by weight, the decline would be even more marked: as the most valuable stocks are fished out, fishermen have to hunt other, less valuable species. Most fisheries are fully exploited if not heavily over-exploited, and many are depleted to varying degrees. Indeed, nine out of 17 major fishing grounds are in precipitous decline, and four are commercially "fished out" *(Food and Agriculture Organization, 1993, 1994 and 1995; Earle, 1995; Holden, 1994; Safina, 1995; Weber, 1994)*.

For illustration, the Northwest Atlantic catch has fallen by almost one third during the past 20 years. Such is the decline of cod and other stocks in the once-bountiful fisheries of the Grand Banks and the Georges Banks off Newfoundland and New England that following 4 years of fleets heavily exceeding their quotas, the fishing grounds were closed in 1992, at a cost of 42,000 jobs and $8.1 billion in unemployment payments *(Safina, 1995; Shrank, 1997; Sissenwine and Rosenberg, 1993)*. In Europe's North Sea, stocks of cod and haddock fell by 83 percent during 1971-1990 and the stock of mackerel crashed 50-fold during 1960-1991, while the herring fishery, closed altogether in 1977-82, and has not recovered to anywhere near its former levels. Catches in the Gulf of Thailand have been maintained only because an expanding trawler fleet has been fishing the stocks ever-more intensively, a situation that cannot persist indefinitely *(Food and Agriculture Organization, 1994)*.

Nine out of 17 major fisheries are in precipitous decline, and four are commercially "fished out".

Such is the decline of cod and other stocks in the once-bountiful fisheries off Newfoundland and New England that the fishing grounds were closed in 1992, at a cost of 42,000 jobs and $8.1 billion in unemployment payments.

Worse, a depleted fishery may not recover regardless of how long it is relieved of exploitation pressure. Other species may fill the ecological niche of the former fish, and keep the recovering stock from resuming its previous place in the ecosystem. There is much evidence to support this, as witness the North Sea haddock population which was wiped out in the 1950s and has never recovered, plus similar ecosystem shifts in the Baltic, the Northeast Arctic, the Gulf of Thailand, and the Grand Banks *(Botsford et al., 1997; Norse, 1993)*. This all results from a steady decline over recent decades in the mean trophic level of species groups in major fisheries, reflecting a steady transition in landings from long-lived, high-trophic-level pisciverous bottom fish toward short-lived, low-trophic-level invertebrates and planktivorous pellagic fish, especially in the northern hemisphere *(Pauly et al., 1998)*.

Because of the unpredictable variations and unknown status of many fishery stocks, many experts now believe that even with optimum management the ultimate maximum sustainable yield could probably not exceed 100 million tonnes per year, and the annual catch should be limited to about 80 million tonnes *(Garcia and Newton, 1995; Grainger and Garcia, 1996; Milazzo, 1997)*. As a result of the failure of stagnating supply to match fast-rising demand, the worldwide per-capita consumption of seafood, which rose from 9 kilograms in 1950 to 19 kilograms in 1989, declined by 8 percent by 1995. As a further result, international prices for seafood have been rising by 4 percent per year in real terms over the past decade. Whereas export prices for pork in late 1991 were 55 percent above the 1975 price, and for beef 75 percent above, those for marine fish were 335 percent higher. Demand for fish in 2010 is projected to be at least 45 percent higher than in 1990, meaning that prices can be expected to climb even higher *(Botsford et al., 1997; Food and Agricultural Organization, 1997)*.

There is a further problem, significant in some areas while not comparable to the decline of fisheries overall. Modern industrial fishing can lead to disruption and degradation of marine habitats through e.g., dredging, trawling, long-hauling and explosives, all of which deplete structural formations on otherwise relatively featureless sea floors. There can also be widespread destruction of tropical coral reefs, temperate oyster and polychaete reefs, and seagrass beds and epibenthic organisms *(Botsford et al., 1997; Norse, 1993; Northridge, 1991)*.

Reasons for Decline

The fundamental issue here is the "tragedy of the commons", plus the related problem of obstacles to collective action. These generic problems probably do not have a more graphic, widespread or intractable manifestation than through marine fisheries *(Broadus and Vartanov, 1994; Cairncross, 1995; Wieland, 1992)*. For much of fishing's history there have been enough fish in the world's oceans and there have been sufficiently few fishing enterprises for each country to take its catch without depleting the stocks. The built-in inducement for a country to take more than its "share" has proven too potent, however, since the benefit has accrued exclusively to the over-fishing country while the cost has been borne by all fishing countries. Once a single country has begun over-fishing, others have followed suit. The upshot is today's deeply depleted stocks. In addition to the problem of a common property resource vulnerable to "open access" or free-for-all exploitation, there is a problem with the market rate of discount, which has generally been high enough to further encourage fishermen to view the fisheries within a foreshortened time horizon and to over-exploit the resource. For a fine exposition of these two inter-related problems, see *Clark, 1994*.

Subsidies Worldwide

One might suppose that the fisheries decline would send a clear message to governments that they should reduce their excessive fishing. On the contrary, however, they have preferred to put off the day of reckoning by stepping up their subsidies to the fishing industry. Once fishermen's livelihoods are in danger, governments provide plentiful incentives for them to catch more rather than fewer fish—thus exacerbating the problem from top to bottom. The solution lies with a severe reduction and an eventual phasing out of subsidies, paralleled by a collective decision to protect remaining fish stocks through collective action, suitably enforced.

Instead governments have been inclined to engage in ever-heavier subsidies—which only serves to prolong the agony. Subsidies have proliferated both in types and quantity. They have included financial contributions from governments in the form of transfers of funds (grants, loans, equity infusions), potential transfers of funds (loan guarantees), foregone government revenues (tax preferences), goods and services (other than general infrastructure), and payments to a funding mechanism or to a private body to perform any of the above. On top of these financial contributions have been price-and income-support programs (other than tariffs) *(Food and Agriculture Organization, 1993a; McGoodwin, 1995; Porter, 1997; Weber and Gradwohl, 1995)*.

These state supports have helped primarily to pay for more and larger boats. The global fishing fleet has expanded from 585,000 registered vessels in 1970

Subsidies have helped supply longer and larger nets, a typical trawl net being one kilometer long and big enough to hold 12 jumbo jets. Some nets scoop up 400 tonnes of fish at a single go, or 80-90 percent of a fish population in a year. Sophisticated technology means that only half of the world's fishing fleet would be needed to catch the maximum sustainable yield of fish.

---

to 3.5 million in 1993, worth $320 billion *(Food and Agriculture Organization, 1993a; Matthiasson, 1996; Safina, 1996)*. Other subsidies have helped supply longer and larger nets, a typical trawl net being one kilometer long and big enough to hold 12 jumbo jets. Some of these nets scoop up 400 tonnes of fish at a single go, or 80-90 percent of a fish population in a year *(Safina, 1995)*. Other advanced equipment includes radar and remote-sensing devices. Given the sophisticated technology of the 1990s fishing industry, only half of the world's fishing fleet would be needed to catch the maximum sustainable yield of fish.

According to calculations by the Food and Agriculture Organization *(1993)*, the 1989 catch was worth around $70 billion at the dockside. Yet the fishing effort to land the catch—boats with their crews, equipment, etc.—cost $124 billion. The difference, viz. $54 billion, was almost entirely made up of government subsidies including price controls, fuel-tax exemptions, low-interest loans, and outright grants for gear and other infrastructure *(Food and Agriculture Organization, 1993; Safina, 1995 and 1998; see also Engelman and LeRoy, 1995c; Thorpe et al., 1995; Weber, 1994)*.

Such, at least, was the understanding of fishery subsidies during much of the early 1990s. But critics have been pointing out that the 1993 assessment did not define or analyze the subsidies themselves, it merely inferred them from revenues and costs in 1989. A recent assessment *(Milazzo, 1997; see also McGinn, 1998; Porter, 1997)* has engaged in a more detailed and comprehensive review, and it concludes that the 1993 calculation was too high. It shows that while subsidies conform for the most part to the categories listed, their total is more likely to be $16-22 billion per year. Note too that this estimate reflects a highly conservative analysis; for instance, it takes only incomplete account of environmental externalities, it accepts that certain countries such as Japan, Russia and China might be severely under-reporting their subsidies, and it acknowledges that not all countries are included in the reckoning *(McGinn, 1998)*. So for purposes of this report, the author accepts the higher figure, $22 billion.

Subsidies arise from the efforts of governments to preserve their fishermen's jobs. Regrettably these incentives have long induced investors to finance more industrial fishing ships than the fish stocks could possibly sustain. During 1970-

1990, the world's fishing fleet grew at twice the rate of the global catch, until it amounted to twice the capitalized capacity needed to catch what the oceans could sustainably produce after allowing for re-building of fish stocks *(Safina, 1995 and 1997; see also McGoodwin, 1995; Weber, 1994).*

Because this excessive capacity has rapidly depleted the amount of fish available, profitability has generally plunged, reducing the ships' value. Unable to sell their chief assets without major financial loss, ship owners have found themselves forced to keep on fishing, or rather over-fishing, in order to repay their loans. They are caught in an economic trap. In response, they have mobilized political pressure on governments to refrain from cutting the inflated fishing quotas *(Safina, 1995 and 1997; see also Food and Agriculture Organization, 1994).*

The costs to fisheries are substantial. If, in the case of the United States, the principal fish species in question were allowed to rebuild to their long-term potential, sustainable harvesting would add $8 billion to GDP and provide some 300,000 jobs *(Sissenwein and Rosenberg, 1993).* Within United States federal waters, today's catch is only 60 percent as valuable as it could be if fish stocks were allowed to recover *(United States National Marine Fisheries Service, 1992; see also Weber, 1995; Wise, 1991).*

In addition, subsidies encourage gross wastage. Fishermen make enough profit on their subsidized operations, albeit at the cost of progressively depleted fisheries, that they throw away many fish that could be marketed but do not command best prices. For details on this "by-catch", see Box 7.1.

As noted, total subsidies today are estimated to be $22 billion per year *(Milazzo, 1997).* If one is cautious, one can view perverse subsidies primarily as those which enhance the capacity and effort of fishing fleets, making up some 80 percent of all subsidies, or almost $18 billion per year. But virtually all subsidies can be considered perverse, for three reasons: 1, because subsidies are far and away the principal cause of over-fishing; 2, because of the parlous and fast-deteriorating state of fisheries, a state that is worsened by subsidies; and 3, because of the adverse repercussions of fisheries decline for both economies and natural resources concerned. Indeed the recent review *(Milazzo, 1997)* concludes that "just as trade experts insist that ... all subsidies are bad from a trade point of view, ... practically all subsidies are bad from a conservation standpoint." Thus the figure for total subsidies, $22 billion per year, is accepted as the figure for perverse subsidies.

If, in the case of the United States, the principal fish species in question were allowed to rebuild to their long-term potential, sustainable harvesting would add $8 billion to GDP and provide some 300,000 jobs. Today's catch is only 60 percent as valuable as it could be if fish stocks were allowed to recover.

Nevertheless, the subsidy figure, being 27 percent of revenues, means that ocean fish are hardly more supported than other protein foods, notably rice 86 percent, wheat 48 percent, coarse grains 36 percent, sugar 48 percent, lamb and mutton 45 percent, beef and veal 35 percent, pork 22 percent and poultry 14 percent *(Milazzo, 1997)*.

Box 7.1

FISHERIES BY-CATCH

Every fourth creature taken from the sea is unwanted. Worldwide these discards total at least 27 million tonnes per year, equivalent to one third of fish landings (the amount could be a lot higher, even as much as one half, since fishermen have little incentive to report all such by-catches) *(Alverson et al., 1994)*. In fact, if we were to include all sea urchins, sponges and other marine life hauled up with commercial fish and then discarded, the amount could readily be several times greater *(McGinn, 1998)*. Discards of king crab in the Bering Sea in 1990 amounted to 16 million individuals, more than five times the number landed, and weighing 340,000 tonnes. Off the northern coast of Norway in the 1986-87 season, as many as 80 million cod, weighing almost 100,000 tonnes, were discarded because they were too small. In Europe's North Sea, about half of the haddock and whiting caught for human consumption each year is discarded, usually because the fish are too small or of inferior quality *(Bonino, 1996)*. In some U.S. shrimp fisheries, 10 or even 15 tonnes of fish are dumped for every one tonne of shrimp landed, making up 175,000 tonnes per year; during the past 20 years, this by-catch has contributed to an 85-percent decline in Gulf of Mexico populations of sea-floor species such as snappers and groupers *(Safina, 1994)*. Most of the by-catch is thrown back either dead or in such a weakened state that it forms easy prey for predators *(Alverson et al., 1994)*.

Subsidies encourage waste. Every fourth creature taken from the sea is unwanted. Worldwide discards total at least 27 million tonnes per year, equivalent to one third of landings. In some U.S. shrimp fisheries, 10 or even 15 tonnes of fish are dumped for every one tonne of shrimp landed; this by-catch has contributed to an 85-percent decline in Gulf of Mexico populations of sea-floor species such as snappers and groupers.

Policy Responses

While the $22 billion figure is small as compared with perverse subsidies for agriculture, fossil fuels/nuclear energy and road transportation ($460 billion, $110 billion and $639 billion respectively), the fisheries sector is nonetheless the most politically volatile of all sectors reviewed. This is evident from the numerous fishing disputes during the past few years, notably the conflicts over tuna in the northeastern Atlantic, over crab and salmon in the North Pacific, over squid in the southwestern Atlantic, and over Pollock in the Sea of Okhotsk.

Fortunately there are signs of improvement in the situation, albeit far less than required *(Garcia and Newton, 1995; Gimbel, 1994; Grainger and Garcia, 1996; Safina, 1998)*. The Canadian government is spending CAN$2 billion for unemployment handouts for its fish workers laid off through a government effort to restore depleted fish stocks. While a much more sustainable gesture would be to offer alternative employment to these workers, retraining them if need be, the measure does at least supply scope for the fisheries to recover and perhaps supply employment for future fishermen. Iceland has cut back its subsidies enough to reduce its domestic fishing by 50 percent. The European Union (E.U.) is planning to phase out sufficient subsidies to effectively decommission 40 percent of its fishing vessel capacity, at a cost of $4 billion for idled fishermen. Were the E.U.'s fisheries allowed to rebuild, they could eventually yield a further $2.5 billion worth of fish a year. At present the E.U. spends nearly $780 million a year on fishing subsidies, almost all of it to support the bloated fishing fleets. Why not use the $780 million to retrain fishermen who are put out of work through reduced catches—whether reduced through declining stocks or through policy shifts (for a detailed discussion, see *Bonino, 1996*). If governments feel politically obliged to make payments to their fishermen, they would do far better to create incentives such as retraining for alternative employment, rather than fostering ever-greater capacity to chase ever-fewer fish *(Cairncross, 1995; Weber, 1994; World Wide Fund for Nature International, 1997)*.

Governments could also go far to reduce fishing capacity while increasing employment at the same time. The key this time is to redirect subsidies, converting them from perverse to constructive, by for instance phasing out the more highly mechanized ships and using the released funds for more productive purposes *(Gates et al., 1997)*. Each $1 million of investment in industrial-style

---

Iceland has cut back its subsidies enough to reduce its domestic fishing by 50 percent. The European Union is planning to phase out sufficient subsidies to decommission 40 percent of its fishing vessel capacity, at a cost of $4 billion for idled fishermen.

---

fishing provides only 1-5 jobs, whereas the same investment in smallscale fishing could employ anywhere from 60 to 3000 people. The United States has been leading the way in promoting management efficiency through catching inefficiency. In the Chesapeake Bay, for instance, oyster-dredging boats are now required by law to be powered by sail alone. Similarly, half of the United States bluefin-tuna fishery is now allocated to the least capable gear such as handlines or rod and reel, whereupon almost 80 percent of jobs are supplied by ships with labor-intensive tackle, by contrast with 2 percent on the part of ships with large nets *(Safina, 1995; see also Sissenwine and Rosenberg, 1996; United States National Fish and Wildlife Foundation, 1995; United States National Marine Fisheries Service, 1995).*

The United States' fisheries situation has been helped too by the 1996 Fisheries Conservation and Management Act. But it is crucially limited in that it does not define and prohibit over-fishing. Nor does it direct fishery managers to take a series of other vital steps: to rebuild depleted populations, to protect habitats for fishery resources, to reduce wasteful and harmful by-catch of non-target organisms, and to consider predator-prey and other important ecological relationships *(Safina, 1998).*

There are still further policy initiatives and management options available to governments. They are not directly related to subsidies, but they would certainly be helped if undertaken in conjunction with phase-out of subsidies. Only 10 percent or so of the world's catch is found in international waters, the rest being within 200 nautical miles of some nation's shoreline. Yet governments do not generally charge fishermen for the right to catch off their shores. The few governments that impose such charges set the price far too low, typically no more than 5 percent of the catch's value. If governments were to charge fishermen an appropriate price for access to their fisheries (and if they were also to manage their fisheries as communal rather than commons resources), the results would be formidable. For instance, mostly foreign fleets exploit the Falkland Islands' fisheries. When the Islands introduced charges of up to 28 percent of the catch's value, the result was vigorous protest from foreign fishermen. But the increased fees yielded revenues enough to quadruple the Islands' GDP—and they supplied a stream of revenues that could be used to pay for still better management and policing of the fisheries.

A final policy response could lie with tradeable fishing rights to individual fishermen, a system known as Individual Transferable Quotas (ITQs). Again, this would be reinforced if accompanied by a reduction of subsidies, and would be much less useful if perverse subsidies continued to pull in the opposite direction. ITQs can help both to curb over-fishing and boost fishermen's incomes. The strategy would allow individual fishermen to buy and sell rights to shares in a fishery's potential catch, and thus give them a financial stake in the fishery's health. It also means that those fishermen obliged to leave the industry would receive implicit compensation by being able to sell their rights to those fisher-men remaining.

An approach along these lines—controversial as it is in some quarters, and largely unproven as yet—could hold promise for matching fishing investment with fishery productivity and sustainable catches. A number of pilot programs have had some success, e.g., a 30-percent drop in the Australian bluefin tuna catch and improvements in the halibut and sable fish fishery of British Columbia, in conjunction with stabilizing investment returns and compensation for unem-ployed workers *(Fujita et al., 1996)*.

CHAPTER 8

PERVERSE SUBSIDIES: OVERVIEW ASSESSMENT

Perverse subsidies of $1.5 trillion are larger than all but the five largest national economies in the world. They are twice as large as global military spending per year, larger than the top twelve corporations' annual sales, and larger than the global fossil fuels industry or the global insurance industry.

We are now in a position to consider all subsidies in the six sectors reviewed, and hence all their perverse subsidies. The collective findings are set out in Table 8.1. Overall subsidies worldwide are estimated to be almost $1.9 trillion per year, and perverse subsidies almost $1.5 trillion per year. The subsidies total amounts to 6.8 percent of the global economy of $28 trillion, and the perverse subsidies total 5.3 percent. Were we to include other sectors on top of the six assessed in this report, the two totals and percentages would be so much higher.

Table 8. 1

SUBSIDIES: OVERALL TOTALS (billion $ per year)

Sector	Conventional Subsidies*	Environmental Externalities documented/ quantified	Total Subsidies (range)**	Perverse Subsidies (range)**
Agriculture	325	250	575	460 (390-520)
Fossil Fuels/Nuclear Energy	145	***	145	110
Road Transportation	558	359	917 (798-1041)	639
Water	60	175	235	220
Fisheries	22	—	22	22
Totals (rounded)	1,110	785	1,895	1,450

* *Subsidies of established and readily recognized sorts, including both direct financial transfers and indirect supports such as tax credits.*

** *Ranges: some of these estimates are supported by ranges: for details, see text. In some instances, estimates are not inserted because there is simply too little agreement even about ranges.*

*** *Regrettably it has not been possible to come up with even a reasonably agreed estimate for this value: the data are too patchy and disparate.*

These findings are to be compared with a couple of other recent studies. Roodman *(1996)* postulates select subsidies at more than $500 billion per year, and suggests that a good proportion of these can be categorized as perverse subsidies though without offering an estimate as to the share. De Moor *(1997)*, who covers the same four big sectors as in this report but does not deal with forestry or fisheries, comes up with a subsidy total of well over $700 billion per year (range, $707-887 billion), and suggests a perverse subsidy total somewhere between $250 and $550 billion. The present report's two totals are larger than the other studies' primarily because it considers more implicit subsidies in the form of environmental externalities. The two in Agriculture (soil erosion and pesticides) amount to $250 billion and the two in Water (water-related diseases and time costs of fetching water) amount to $175 billion, making $425 together. For reasons explained in Chapter 1, these are all considered to be perverse subsidies; there is no proportionate reduction as in the other estimates. These four instances alone constitute 54 percent of all environmental externalities and 29 percent of all perverse subsides. To reiterate a key point: many environmental externalities—including what could ultimately prove to be as big as the rest put together, global warming—are either underestimated or omitted from the final calculation through sheer lack of documentation of economic costs entailed.

There are further reasons to think that the total of perverse subsidies, approaching $1.5 trillion per year, is not unduly high. Environmental damaging subsidies in just one developed country, Britain, are estimated to be in the order of $33 billion per year *(Maddison et al., 1997)*, while environmental costs in just one developing country, China, are estimated to be $90 billion per year, possibly twice as much *(Smil, 1997)*. Total costs worldwide in the road transportation sector alone are roughly estimated at around $2 trillion per year, possibly more *(Delucci, 1997; Litman, 1996)*, of which environmental externalities could account for $1 trillion *(von Weizsacker et al., 1997)*.

The size of both subsidies and perverse subsidies means they exert exceptionally large impacts on the world's economies and environments. The subsidies total is almost as big as the GNP of Germany, and the perverse subsidies total is one fifth bigger than the GNP of France. The Rio Earth Summit proposed an Agenda 21 budget for sustainable development of $600 billion per year. The world's governments said they could not possibly countenance an annual budget of that size—it would be fiscally irresponsible and was completely unrealis-

---

Perverse subsidies totalling almost $1.5 trillion a year amount to funds going into unsustainable development. This is two and a half times the Rio Earth Summit's budget for sustainable development—a sum that governements dismissed as unthinkable.

The United States accounts for 21 percent of perverse subsidies worldwide.

---

tic for many other potent reasons. Yet there are almost two and a half times more funds in the perverse subsidies, these being funds that promote unsustainable development.

Perverse subsidies are large in other senses:

- They are almost twice as large as the annual growth in the world's economy.

- They are twice as large as global military spending per year.

- They are larger than the top twelve corporations' annual sales.

- They are three times as much as the annual cash incomes of the 1.3 billion poorest people.

- They are three times as much as the international narcotics industry.

- They are larger than the global fossil fuels industry or the global insurance industry.

In individual sectors too, they are large. Perverse subsidies for road transportation, $639 billion per year, are greater than the GNPs of all but the top 11 countries in the world. Perverse subsidies for agriculture, $460 billion, are almost as big as the GNPs of Spain or Indonesia (latter based on purchasing power parity). Perverse subsidies for road transportation subsidies in the United States alone, $232 billion, are as large as the GNP of Belgium or Pakistan (latter based on purchasing power parity).

Perverse Subsidies: the Leaders

Despite some progress in phasing out perverse subsidies, many egregious examples persist. The leaders could well include:

1. German coal is subsidized to the extent to $6.7 billion per year. It would be economically efficient (and would reduce coal pollution such as acid rain and global warming) for the government to close down all the mines and send the workers home on full pay for the rest of their lives.

2. The global ocean fisheries catch—well above sustainable yield—is annually worth around $100 billion at dockside, where it is sold for some $80 billion, the shortfall being made up with government subsidies. The result is depletion of many major fisheries to commercial extinction, plus bankruptcy of fishing businesses and sizeable unemployment.

3.   The Australian government subsidizes some of its most environmentally damaging industries to the tune of US$4.5 billion per year, and the environmental impact of those industries is expected to cost Australian taxpayers at least US$5.9 billion *(Department of the Environment, Sport and Territories, Government of Australia, 1996)*. The taxpayer ends up paying to damage the environment and then again to restore it.

4.   The European Union has subsidized excess food production until there have been milk and wine lakes and butter and beef mountains (not to mention a manure mountain in the Netherlands). In early 1993 cereal surpluses of 30 million tonnes would have been enough to provide an Italian-style diet to 75 million people for one year. Taxpayers footed the bill to supply the subsidies that boosted these crops in the first place, then they paid again to store the excess stockpiles.

5.   The Japanese government has dedicated four airports in the northern part of the country to transporting vegetables and flowers to consumers in the main part of the country. They are to be followed by another five airports in 1998 costing almost $30 million in subsidies. To fly onions from Ono in northeastern Kyushu Island to Tokyo costs nearly six times as much as to transport them by road. The airports, paid for entirely by taxpayers, have been built ostensibly to integrate isolated farming communities into the Japanese agro-economy. More realistically, they have served as a sop to the farming lobby after it made concessions to the Japanese government's negotiations for the 1993 Uruguay Round on world trade.

6.   Saudi Arabia spent $40 billion during the 1980s on developing its farming, thanks largely to extravagant subsidies for water. The country increased its wheat output from virtually nil in 1980 to more than 4 million tonnes in 1992, even producing an exportable surplus thanks to huge subsidies that reduced the price from a level 10 times that of American wheat. Following the recent decline in oil prices, however, the Saudi government has slashed its agricultural subsidies and wheat output has dropped by half.

7.   In the United States, one government agency heavily subsidizes irrigation for crops that another agency has paid farmers not to grow. Note the comment by an economist critic, Paul Hawken *(1997)*: "The government subsidizes energy costs so that farmers can deplete aquifers to grow alfalfa to feed cows that make milk that is stored in warehouses as surplus cheese that does not feed the hungry."

8.   Also in the United States, gasoline is now cheaper than bottled water, thanks to subsidies of many sorts. Despite the view of many Americans that gasoline is expensive, it now costs less in real terms than for 60 years. The same applies to many other aspects of United States road transportation, thanks to extensive subsidies. Well might it be said that Detroit and the oil

companies are on a kind of welfare. The unpaid costs of road transportation amount to $464 billion per year, which is equivalent to $1700 per American. Hidden subsidies for oil serve to create an energy policy by default—a policy that is actually the reverse of the government's stated priorities. Oil subsidies prolong the country's risky dependence on foreign supplies, especially from the Persian Gulf. Moreover, this de facto energy policy discourages private investments in new, cleaner technologies such as hyper-cars and other revolutionary forms of energy efficiency *(Heede, 1997; Lovins, 1996)*.

All in all, a typical American taxpayer is paying at least $2000 a year in perverse subsidies, and paying almost another $2000 more for consumer goods and services with their increased prices, or through environmental degradation.

Despite their irrationality, these subsidies persist virtually untouched. This is because subsidies tend to create special-interest groups and political lobbies, leaving the subsidies hard to remove long after they have served their original purpose. In all major capitals, there are swarms of lobbyists, sometimes 100 or more for each legislator. By definition, these lobbyists are bent on advancing narrow sectoral interests rather than the public good. For instance, the American Petroleum Institute spends for public relations and other forms of lobbying almost as much as the total budget of the top five United States environmental groups *(Gelbspan, 1997)*. In face of subsidy support of this scale and leverage, most efforts to cut back on even the most perverse subsidies amount to spectacular failure. In late 1997 during the run-up to the Kyoto Conference on Climate Change, a coalition of fossil-fuel interests in the United States mounted the Global Climate Information Project, being a $13 million ad campaign pushing a do-nothing agenda.

Nonetheless, the subsidies total has declined somewhat in recent years. New Zealand has all but eliminated its agriculture subsidies, while the United States and the European Union have ambitious plans to follow semi-suit. Russia, Eastern Europe, China and India have together slashed their fossil-fuel subsidies by 61 percent, or $43 billion, since 1990-91.

The Crux: Covert Costs of Perverse Subsidies

Perverse subsidies have several features in common:

- Economically they push up the costs of government, inducing higher taxes and prices for all. In turn, this means they aggravate budget deficits.

- They divert government funds from better options for fiscal support.

- They distort economies in numerous other ways. For instance, they undermine market decisions about investment, and they reduce the pressure for businesses to become more efficient.

- They tend to benefit the few at the expense of the many, and, worse, the rich at the expense of the poor.

- They can serve to pay the polluter.

- They foster many other forms of environmental degradation, which apart from their intrinsic harm, act as a further drag on economies.

For all these reasons, perverse subsidies militate against sustainable development. They are a no-no whether economically or environmentally or socially.

Consider just one factor, the increased tax burden, illustrated through a graphic analysis by Roodman *(1996; see also Erlandson et al., 1995)*. Of global taxes totalling $7.5 trillion each year, 90 percent is a burden on work and investment, thus slowing economic growth. If instead governments were to tax e.g., pollution more fully, they could raise at least $1 trillion a year worldwide, which could then be used to cut wage and profit taxes by as much as 15 percent. Furthermore, a phase-out of all perverse subsidies would allow governments to cut taxes worldwide by 5 percent or more.

The Double Dividend

If perverse subsidies were to be greatly reduced (while still leaving some subsidies to placate special interests—the political constraint cannot be ignored, however unpalatable it may be), there would actually be a double dividend:

1. There would be an end to the formidable obstacles imposed by perverse subsidies on sustainable development.

2. There would be a huge stock of funds available to give a new push to sustainable development—funds on a scale that would be unlikely to become available through any other source. In the case of the United States, for instance, they would amount to more than $300 billion. This is larger than the Pentagon budget, $240 billion, and more than twice as large as the federal deficit, $126 billion.

Compare the prospect to a car. Eliminating perverse subsides would be like, firstly, taking off the brakes and moving into high gear. Secondly it would be like giving the engine and all the other major mechanisms such a streamlining that the car would start to operate with undreamed of efficiency.

To grasp the scale of the opportunity, consider the prospect for the United States with $300 billion a year available. It could go at least half way to meet the country's great unmet needs: increased savings to support capital investment for growth, plus increased savings to finance retirement accounts; strengthening of both primary and secondary education; boosting of scientific and technological advance; rebuilding physical infrastructure; providing health care for perhaps 30 million uninsured; reducing the number of citizens, particularly children, in poverty; slowing the rate of environmental deterioration; and addressing endemic problems such as widespread drug abuse, rising crime levels, homelessness, and low level of foreign aid *(McNamara, 1997)*. To fix even half of these needs would rank among the finest advances in the country's history.

PART III

POLICY:

POTENTIAL AND PRACTICE

CHAPTER 9

POLICY OPTIONS AND RECOMMENDATIONS

Were just half of the perverse subsidies to be phased out, just half of the funds released would enable most governments to abolish their budget deficits at a stroke, to reorder their fiscal priorities in fundamental fashion, and to restore our environments more vigorously than through any other single measure.

This report demonstrates that perverse subsidies are abundant and entrenched. The better news is that we may have reached a propitious time to tackle them. Many governments are espousing the marketplace economy with reduced scope for government intervention. Many governments also face fiscal constraints that give them further incentive to reduce their activist roles in their economies. So the political climate for radical reform of subsidies is probably better than for decades. The transition economies in particular face an admirable opportunity thanks to their political and economic liberalization. At the same time, the OECD countries have a special responsibility to set the pace in that they account for roughly two thirds of all subsidies and even more of all perverse subsidies.

In addition, there is now a solid track record of countries that have greatly reduced or even abolished some of their subsidies. This should serve as a helpful precedent for other countries.

- New Zealand has eliminated virtually all its agricultural subsidies since the early 1980s, even though—or perhaps because—its economy is more dependent on agriculture than most OECD countries. Today there are more farmers in New Zealand than when the subsidy phase-out began. Several Latin American countries, notably Chile and Argentina, have recently taken to slashing their agricultural subsidies.

- Russia has reduced its fossil fuel subsidies from $29 billion in 1990-91 to $9 billion in 1995-96. Eastern Europe from $13 billion to just under $6 billion, China from $25 billion to $10 billion and India from $4 billion to $3 billion *(World Bank, 1997a)*.

- Brazil has gone far to cut back its subsidies for cattle ranching in Amazonia, thus reducing deforestation *(Browder and Godfrey, 1997)*.

- Since the mid-1980s, Bangladesh and several other Asian countries have recognized that excessive applications of nitrogenous fertilizers, stimulated by extravagant subsidies, are wasteful in economic terms and highly polluting in environmental terms (eutrophication of waterways, threats to drinking water supplies). Indonesia has reduced its fertilizer subsidies from $732 million to $96 million per year; Pakistan from $178 million to $2 million; Bangladesh from $56 million to zero; and Philippines from $48 million to zero *(World Bank, 1997a)*.

Thus a policy push to cut subsidies is apparent in countries of the OECD, countries in transition, and developing countries of several sorts and conditions. There are numerous other instances. Some are generalized, e.g., many developing countries are slowly (and occasionally rapidly) getting rid of their subsidies as governments loosen control of their economies and open up the marketplace. Other examples are of much smaller scale but show what can be accomplished at local level. Over the next several years New York City will spend $240 million on rebates to customers who replace old 6 gallons-per-flush toilets with 1.6-gallons-per-flush models. Cutting the municipal water flows will eliminate the need for $800 million in expansion of wastewater treatment plants. Obviously the best buy for New York is increasing water efficiency *(Pinkham et al., 1994)*.

Big-Picture Strategies

How shall we set about the challenge of eliminating perverse subsidies from the body politic? There are various policy openings available *(Gale and Barg, 1995; International Institute for Sustainable Development, 1994)*. One generalized option is to be opportunistic and to seize on emergent "windows" such as the recent strong political shift to marketplace-ism. The credo of the marketplace stands opposed to subsidies, let alone perverse subsidies, as a form of government intervention that ipso facto must be distortive and counter-productive (this applies especially to the economies in transition with their switch to market liberalism). Resistance to subsidies in general also stems from the privatization ethos which is becoming widespread. There can even be opportunity in economic crisis, such as the one which spurred New Zealand's move to drop agricultural subsidies: the public economy was finally over-burdened to breaking point. India's subsidies now total over 14 percent of GDP, yet the government wishes to bring down its fiscal deficit to under 4 percent of GDP, thus supplying marked motivation to cut subsidies drastically. (A similar situation reportedly prevails in Turkey.) There could be parallel scope in an environmental crisis such as another Chernobyl-type disaster.

India's subsidies total over 14 percent of GDP, yet the government wishes to bring down its fiscal deficit to under 4 percent of GDP, thus supplying marked motivation to cut subsidies drastically.

Special-interest groups often feel so addicted to their subsidy entitlements that they suffer severe withdrawal pangs at talk of cutting back any subsidies at all. They find allies in bureaucratic roadblocks and institutional inertia.

These formidable opportunities are matched by formidable obstacles *(de Moor, 1997; Roodman, 1997; see also Gale and Barg, 1995; International Institute for Sustainable Development, 1994).* We have already noted the problem of special-interest groups, which often feel so addicted to their "entitlements" that they suffer severe withdrawal pangs at talk of cutting back any subsidies, let alone perverse subsidies. They find allies in bureaucratic roadblocks and institutional inertia. Then there can be upsets to equity concerns, especially with regard to who no longer gets what. Finally there is uncertainty about how reduction of perverse subsidies, however rational in principle, will work out in nitty-gritty practice; for instance, will it mean losing a competitive edge to competitors abroad?

There are various ways to overcome these obstacles *(de Moor, 1997; Roodman, 1997; see also Gale and Barg, 1995; International Institute for Sustainable Development, 1994).* One is to formulate alternative policies that target the same subsidy objectives better, while also compensating losers. A related measure is to develop an economic-policy context that encourages subsidy removal through e.g., reducing government controls generally and freeing up of markets. A subsidiary measure is to introduce "sunset" provisions that require surviving subsidies to be re-justified periodically, thus avoiding the entrenchment problem. All these measures can be strongly reinforced by promoting transparency about perverse subsidies, especially about their impacts both economic and environmental, and their costs to both taxpayers and consumers.

Perhaps the most important way of all to overcome obstacles to reform is to build support constituencies, especially among the public. The more citizens know that their tax dollars and consumer payments are going down a rathole of perverse subsidies, the more there will be political support for reform. These constituencies—with an interest in the public good rather than sectoral benefit—can engage in information campaigns about the perversity of certain subsidies. Governments cannot deal with perverse subsidies without first learning about the nature and extent of these subsidies. Yet information, especially statistical data, is often incomplete and fragmented across agencies, if it exists at all. An information campaign stands a better chance of success when it stems from grassroots activism, i.e., from the taxpayers and consumers who are penalized by perverse subsidies *(Barg, 1996; see also Runge and Jones, 1996).*

There has been a success story on this front in the United States, where environmentalists (e.g., Friends of the Earth, the Sierra Club and the Wilderness

---

A U.S. coalition of 22 NGOs has highlighted subsidies worth $39 billion over five years, with items ranging from over-logging of the Tongass National Forest and price supports for cotton to a royalty holiday for deepwater oil drilling and aid to the Three Gorges Dam in China. The whistle blowing has done much to mobilize the social consensus and political will to tackle the offending subsidies.

Society) have made common cause with economic reformers (e.g., Citizens for Tax Justice, Taxpayers for Common $ense and the Public Interest Research Group). This coalition of 22 NGOs has highlighted perverse subsidies through their periodic "Green Scissors" reports. The most recent report *(Cuff et al., 1996; see also Erlandson et al., 1995)* fingers 47 government projects worth $39 billion over five years, with items ranging from over-logging of the Tongass National Forest and price supports for cotton to a royalty holiday for deepwater oil drilling and aid to the Three Gorges Dam in China. The whistle blowing has done much to mobilize the social consensus and political will to tackle the offending subsidies.

Supplementary Measures

All the above will help us along the road toward sustainable development as the over-arching context that should justify all our economic and environmental endeavors. While removal of perverse subsidies could well do more than any other single initiative, it will need to backed by supplementary measures.

a) Regulation

However well the free market eventually works, governments will still need to restrict certain activities. Means available include environmental standards, tradable quotas, limits to resource exploitation, the polluter pays principle and the precautionary principle.

b) User charges

Charges for goods and services—whether as concerns energy, transportation, water, timber, whatever—will encourage more careful use. These charges should be imposed equitably, with those enjoying higher incomes paying more or higher-value items carrying higher prices.

c) *Tradeable permits*

These offer much potential, yet they remain one of the rarest of all policy instruments. Outside the United States there are only half a dozen instances, while inside the United States there are not many more, the largest being the 1990 Clean Air Act that allows permits to emit sulphur dioxide *(Cairncross, 1995)*.

d) *Green taxes*

These are a prime mode to change people's behavior toward the environment *(Bernow et al., 1996; Barg, 1996; O'Riordan, 1996)*. Regrettably, few governments employ green taxes in this manner, preferring to use them to increase general revenues *(Burke, 1997)*.

Subsidies to Support the Environment

It can be legitimate in certain circumstances to devise subsidies to promote the environmental cause. The environment often features some of the characteristics of a public good, so subsidies in support are rational both economically and politically. The idea is occasionally put into practice. The United States government is spending $2.2 billion between 1996 and 2002 on agri-environmental measures such as soil conservation and wetland protection. The European Union is engaged on a suite of similar measures, costing $1.7 billion in 1995 alone *(Roodman, 1996)*. The Singapore government is supplying a $14 billion subsidy over 20 years to promote public transportation and to help reduce the use of private cars; this is a sizeable subsidy for a government with an annual budget of only some $40 billion.

But there are difficulties with environmental subsidies *(Barg, 1996)*:

- According to many experts, no subsidy can be a good subsidy. Any subsidy is inherently distortionary, and even subsidies in support of the environment confuse market choices. Counter to this, subsidies can occasionally help the market to work better, for example by smoothing the way for new energy technologies.

- Once a new subsidy, however well intentioned, is in place, it can prove difficult to remove at a later time when it has outlived its purpose.

- Because it is tough to choose among several worthy opportunities, it is best not to subsidize any at all, instead leaving the choice to the market.

- New subsidies are likely to contravene complex international trade rules.

- New subsidies are unlikely to achieve their goals in the fast-moving, complex situations of today *(Barg, 1996)*.

Measuring and Monitoring

When once we start to remove perverse subsidies, it will be essential to measure progress. To meet this purpose, a number of principles have been formulated *(Gale and Barg, 1995; International Institute for Sustainable Development, 1994)*. Performance assessment should:

- Be guided by a clear vision of sustainable development as the justifying framework for subsidy reform. In addition, the vision needs to be defined by a set of goals, which in turn can help to monitor success.

- Include a review of the entire economic sector (agriculture, road transportation, etc.) in question.

- Evaluate the economic, environmental and human subsystems at issue, covering all costs and benefits in both monetary and non-monetary terms.

- Consider equity factors within communities, also between present and future generations, with focus on such concerns as poverty and over-consumption, also human rights.

- Establish a monitoring process to keep a sharp eye on all aspects of the unfolding situation—perhaps a Subsidy Watch?

- Recognize the difference between the size of a perverse subsidy while it is in place and the gain in social well-being after it has gone. These two can be very far from the same thing "since it requires knowledge of the slopes of the demand and supply curves as well as the magnitude of the environmental damage" *(Maddison et al., 1997)*. As we have seen on many occasions in this book, the most harmful subsidies are not necessarily the largest financially. We must bear in mind, moreover, that the proposed subsidy reductions do not take account of their fiscal and economic contexts, especially the ways in which they would lead to changes in prices and other factors.

Taken together, these principles and practices—which accord with criteria established by the World Bank, the Organization for Economic Co-operation and Development, and the World Trade Organization—can constitute a "template" for measuring progress toward sustainable development *(Andersson et al., 1995; Gale and Barg, 1995)*.

Let us not underestimate the political problems of dismantling perverse subsidies. To cite President Jacques Chirac, "Politics is not about the art of the possible; it is about making what is necessary possible." To cite another political supremo, the one-time Mayor of New York, Fiorella LaGuardia, "A political leader shouldn't be so far ahead of the band that he can't hear the music." One could add: "Don't take too long a lead off second base." There can be almost an infinity of distance between a prophet and a politician.

A key question arises: Who is to do the monitoring and measuring? Answer: Governments in the first instance, provided they become persuaded of the virtues of subsidy reform, and even though it has often been their obfuscating practices that have allowed perverse subsidies to survive and prosper. They will need to come up with a consistent framework for statistical analysis of perverse subsidies in all salient sectors, through e.g., a radical revision of their national accounts. Thereafter they will need to standardize and disseminate their information as a routine practice *(Barg, 1996)*. In addition to the work done by governments, there could be even more vital work to be undertaken by NGOs. They often know at least as much if not more about perverse subsidies than do governments, and they are far more inclined to examine them. In many respects too, they have a sharper sense of the public interest. Fortunately there are large numbers of NGOs waiting for the "go". Thirdly, there should be a role for international agencies such as the World Bank group, and, in the case of developed countries, the Organization for Economic Co-operation and Development.

Finally, let us not underestimate the political problems of dismantling perverse subsidies. However irrational they may seem from economic and environmental standpoints, they are all supported by powerful special interests—otherwise they would not still exist. These patrons must be dealt with carefully. Special interests, however invalid, are not be dismissed as an excrescence on the body politic and hence to be eliminated without more ado. They are to be heeded and their needs—even if more akin to "needs"—are to be reckoned with (for instance, retraining for workers thrown out of jobs). To cite President Jacques Chirac, "Politics is not about the art of the possible; it is about making what is necessary possible." To cite another political supremo, the one-time Mayor of New York, Fiorella LaGuardia, "A political leader shouldn't be so far ahead of the band that he can't hear the music." One could also say: "Don't take too long a lead off second base." There can be almost an infinity of distance between a prophet and a politician.

REFERENCES

Abramovitz, J.N. 1998. Sustaining the World's Forests. In L.R. Brown et al., *State of the World 1998*. W.W. Norton, New York.

Adamowicz, W., P. Boxall, M. Luckert, W. Phillips and W. White, eds. 1996. *Forestry, Economics and the Environment*. CAB International, Wallingford, Oxon., U.K.

Adger, W.N., K. Brown, R. Cervigni and D. Moran. 1995. Total Economic Value of Forests in Mexico. *Ambio* 24: 286-296.

Ahmad, M. 1997. *Economic Rent in Indonesia's Timber Production*. Michigan State University, East Lansing, Michigan.

Alexeyev, V. 1991. *Human and Natural Impacts on the Health of Russian Forests*. Institute of Forest and Timber Research, Siberian Branch, USSR Academy of Sciences, Moscow.

Alkire, C. 1993. *Returns to the Treasury from National Forest Timber Programs, FY 1992*. The Wilderness Society, Washington DC.

Allan, J.A. 1995. Water in the Middle East and in Israel-Palestine: Some Local and Global Issues. In M. Haddad and E. Feitelson, eds. *Joint Management of Shared Aquifers:* 31-44. Palestine Consultancy Group and the Truman Research Institute of the Hebrew University, Jerusalem, Israel.

Alliance to Save Energy, American Council for an Energy Efficient Economy, Natural Resources Defense Council, Tellus Institute, and Union of Concerned Scientists. 1997. *Energy Innovations: A Prosperous Path to a Clean Environment*. Alliance to Save Energy, Washington DC.

Alverson, D.L., M. Freeberg, J. Pope and S. Murawski. 1994. *A Global Assessment of Fisheries By-Catch and Discards: A Summary Overview*. Food and Agriculture Organization, Rome, Italy.

American Automobile Manufacturers Association. 1996. *World Motor Vehicle Data, 1996*. American Automobile Manufacturers Association, Detroit, Michigan.

American Solar Energy Society. 1989. *Societal Costs of Energy*. American Solar Energy Society, Boulder, Colorado.

Andersen, L.E. 1996. *A Cost-Benefit Analysis of Deforestation in the Brazilian Amazon*. Institute for Applied Economics Research, Rio de Janeiro, Brazil.

Andersen, L.E. 1997. *Modelling the Relationship Between Government Policy, Economic Growth, and Deforestation in the Brazilian Amazon*. Department of Economics, University of Aarhus, Denmark.

Anderson, D. (former World Bank economist) 1997. Personal communication, telephone discussion of July 6th. 1997.

Anderson, D. and K. Ahmed. 1993. Where We Stand with Renewable Energy. *Finance and Development* 1. 40-42.

Anderson, K. 1995. The Political Economy of Coal Subsidies in Europe. Energy Policy 23: 485-496. See also Lobbying Incentives and the Pattern of Protection in Rich and Poor Countries. *Economic Development and Cultural Change* 43: 401-423.

Anderson, K. and R. Blackhurst, editors. 1992. *The Greening of World Trade Issues.* University of Michigan Press, Ann Arbor, Michigan.

Anderson, T.L., ed. 1983. *Water Rights: Scarce Resource Allocation, Bureaucracy, and the Environment.* Pacific Research Institute, San Francisco, California.

Anderson, T.L. 1995. Water, Water Everywhere, But Not a Drop to Sell. In J.L. Simon, ed., *The State of Humanity*: 425-433. Blackwell Scientific, Oxford, U.K.

Anderson, T.L. , ed. 1996. *Water Marketing: The Next Generation.* Rowan and Littlefield, London, U.K.

Anderson, T.L. and P. Snyder. 1997. *Water Markets: Priming the Invisible Pump.* The Cato Institute, Washington DC.

Andersson, T., C. Folke and S. Nystromm. 1995. *Trading with the Environment: Ecology, Economics, Institutions and Policy.* Earthscan, London, U.K.

Aplet, G., N. Johnson, J.T. Olson and V.A. Sample, eds. 1993. *Defining Sustainable Forestry.* Island Press, Washington DC.

Apps, M., ed. 1995. Boreal Forests and Global Climate. *Water, Air and Soil Pollution* 82: special issue.

Apps, M., J. Kurz, R.J. Luxmoore, L.O. Nielsson, R.A. Sedjo, R. Schmidt, L.G. Simpson and T.S. Vinson. *Water, Air and Soil Pollution* 70: 39-53.

Apps, M. and D. Price, eds. 1996 *Forest Ecosystems, Forest Management and the Global Carbon Cycle.* Springer-Verlag, New York.

Aral Sea Program Unit. 1994. *Aral Sea Program, Phase 1.* The World Bank, Washington DC.

Arima, E. 1996. *Assessing the Effects of Policies on Deforestation in the Brazilian Amazon.* Department of Agricultural Economics and Rural Sociology, Pennsylvania State University, Philadelphia.

Arima, E.Y. and C. Uhl. 1998. Ranching in the Brazilian Amazon in a National Context: Economics, Policy and Practice. *Society and Natural Resources* (in press).

Armstrong, G. 1996. Australia's Environmental Policy: The Ends and Means. In P. Sheehan, B. Grewal and M. Kumnick, eds. *Dialogues on Australia's Future:* 257-280. Victoria University of Technology, Melbourne, Australia.

Arnold, M. 1991. *Forestry Expansion—A Study of Technical, Economic and Ecological Factors: The Long-Term Global Demand and Supply of Wood.* U.K. Forestry Commission, Wrecclesham, Surrey, U.K.

Arnott, R. and K. Small. 1994. The Economics of Traffic Congestion. *American Scientist* 82: 446-455.

Ascher, W. 1993. *Political Economy and Problematic Forestry Policies in Indonesia: Obstacles to Incorporating Sound Economics and Science.* Center for International Development Research, Duke University, Durham, North Carolina.

ASTRA. 1982. Rural Energy Consumption Patterns: A Field Study. *Biomass* 2(4), September.

Auer, M.R. and X. Ye. 1997. Re-Evaluating Energy Efficiency in China. *The Environmentalist* 17: 21-25.

Bahatia, R. and M. Falkenmark. 1993. *Water Resource Policies and the Urban Poor: Innovative Approaches and Policy Imperatives.* The World Bank, Washington DC.

Baker, B. 1998. Rethinking Roads in the Nation's Forests. *BioScience* 48: 156.

Baldock, D. 1996. Environmental Impacts of Agro-Environmental Measures. In *Subsidies and Environment: Exploring the Linkages*: 123-137. Organisation for Economic Co-operation and Development, Paris, France.

Balick, M.J., W. Elisabetsky and S. Laird, eds. 1996. *Tropical Forest Medical Resources and the Conservation of Biodiversity.* Columbia University Press, New York.

Barber, C.V. 1997. *Case Study of Indonesia.* Committee on International Security Studies, American Academy of Arts and Sciences, Cambridge, Massachusetts.

Barber, C.V., N.C. Johnson, and E. Hafild. 1994. *Breaking the Logjam: Obstacles to Forest Policy Reform in Indonesia and the United States.* World Resources Institute, Washington DC.

Barbier, E.B. 1995. The Economics of Forestry and Conservation: Economic Values and Policies. *Commonwealth Forestry Review*: 26-34.

Barbier, E.B. and J.C. Burgess. 1993. *Timber Trade and Tropical Deforestation: Global Trends and Evidence from Indonesia.* Department of Environmental Economics and Environmental Management, University of York, York, U.K.

Barbier, E.B., J.T. Bishop, B.A. Aylward and J.C. Burgess. 1992. *The Economics of Tropical Forest Land Use Options: Methodology and Valuation Techniques*. London Environmental Economics Centre, London, U.K.

Barbier, E., J. Burgess and A. Markandya. 1991. The Economics of Tropical Deforestation. *Ambio* 20: 55-58.

Barbier, E.B., J.C. Burgess, J.T. Bishop and B.A. Aylward. 1994. *The Economics of the Tropical Timber Trade*. Earthscan, London, UK

Barg, S. 1996. Eliminating Perverse Subsidies: What's the Problem? In *Subsidies and Environment: Exploring the Linkages*: 23-41. Organisation for Economic Co-operation and Development, Paris, France.

Barrow, C.J. 1991. *Land Degradation: Development and Breakdown of Terrestrial Environments*. Cambridge University Press, New York.

Baskin, Y. 1997. *The Work of Nature*. Island Press, Washington DC.

Bates, R. and E. Moore. 1992. *Commercial Energy Efficiency and the Environment*. The World Bank, Washington DC.

Batie, S.S. 1995. *Developing Indicators for Environmental Sustainability: Nuts and Bolts*. Department of Agricultural Economics, Michigan State University, East Lansing, Michigan.

Batie, S.S. 1996. *Environmental Benefits Resulting from Agricultural Activities: The Case of Non-European OECD Countries*. Department of Agricultural Economics, Michigan State University, East Lansing, Michigan.

Beattie, R. 1994. Environmental Accounting: Including the Environment in Measures of Well-Being. In J. Sullivan, editor, *Environmental Policies: Implications for Agricultural Trade*: 6-12. Economic Research Service, U.S. Department of Agriculture, Washington DC.

Berger, J.J. 1997. *Charging Ahead: The Business of Renewable Energy and What it Means for America*. H. Holt and Co., New York.

Bernow, S. and 15 others. 1996. *Ecological Tax Reform*. Institute for Ecological Studies, University of Maryland, Solomons, Maryland.

Bhattacharyya, S.C. 1995. Estimation of Subsidies on Coal in India. *Natural Resources Forum* 19: 135-142.

Binswanger, H. 1989. *Brazilian Policies that Encourage Deforestation in the Amazon*. The World Bank, Washington DC.

Bochuan, H. 1991. *China on the Edge: The Crisis of Ecology and Development*. China Books and Periodicals Inc., San Francisco.

Body, R. 1991. *Our Food, Our Land: Why Contemporary Farming Practices Must Change.* Rider Publishers, London, U.K.

Bohringer, C. 1995. *Carbon Taxes and National Policy Constraints: The Case of German Coal Subsidies.* Institute for Energy Economics, University of Stuttgart, Stuttgart, Germany.

Bollard, A. 1992. *New Zealand: Economic Reforms 1984-1991.* International Center for Economic Growth, San Francisco, California.

Bonanno, A. et al. 1994. *From Columbus to ConAgra: The Globalization of Agriculture and Food.* University of Kansas Press, Lawrence, Kansas.

Bonino, E. 1996. Fishing for Ever. *Our Planet* 8(4): 13-15.

Bonnis, G. 1995. Farmers, Forestry and the Environment. *The OECD Observer* 196, October/November 1995.

Botsford, L.W., J.C. Castilla and C.H. Peterson. 1997. The Management of Fisheries and Marine Ecosystems. *Science* 277: 509-515.

Bousquet, F. and C. Queiroz. 1995. *Russian Road Financing System.* The World Bank, Washington DC.

Bovard, J. 1995. *Shakedown: How The Government Screws You from A to Z.* Viking, New York.

Bovard, J. 1996. *The Farm Fia$co.* Institute for Contemporary Studies, San Francisco, California.

Bovenberg, L. and S. Cnossen, eds. 1995. *Public Economics and the Environment in an Imperfect World.* Kluwer Academic Press, Dordrecht, Netherlands.

Boyce, J.K. 1993. *The Philippines: The Political Economy of Growth and Impoverishment in the Marcos Era.* Macmillan Press, New York.

Bradshaw, B. 1995. *Implications of Reduced Subsidies for Agriculture and Agro-Ecosystem Health.* Faculty of Environmental Sciences, University of Guelph, Guelph, Ontario, Canada.

Brechin, R. 1995. Assessing the Relationship Between Government Policy and Deforestation. *Journal of Environmental Economics and Management* 28: 1-18.

Briscoe, J. 1996. *Water as an Economic Good: The Idea and What It Means in Practice.* The World Bank, Washington DC.

Briscoe, J. and M. Garn. 1994. *Financing Agenda 21: Fresh Water.* The World Bank, Washington DC.

British Petroleum. 1997. *BP Statistical Review of World Energy 1997.* British Petroleum, London, U.K.

Broad, R. 1988. *Unequal Alliance: The World Bank, the International Monetary Fund, and the Philippines.* University of California Press, Berkeley, California.

Broad, R. 1995. The Political Economy of Natural Resources: Case Studies of the Indonesian and Philippine Forest Sectors. *Journal of Developing Areas* 29: 317-340.

Broadus, J.M. and R.V. Vartanov, eds. 1994. *The Oceans and Environmental Security.* Island Press, Washington DC.

Bromley, D.W. 1996. *The Environmental Implications of Agriculture.* Department of Agricultural Economics, University of Wisconsin, Madison, Wisconsin.

Brookfield, H. and Y. Byron, eds. 1993. *Southeast Asia's Environmental Future: The Search for Sustainability.* United Nations University Press, Tokyo, Japan.

Browder, J.O. 1988. Public Policy and Deforestation in the Brazilian Amazon. In R. Repetto and M. Gillis, eds., *Public Policies and the Misuse of Forest Resources*: 247-298. Cambridge University Press, Cambridge, U.K.

Browder, J.O., ed. 1989. *Fragile Lands of Latin America.* Westview Press, Boulder, Colorado.

Browder, J.O. 1990. The Social Costs of Rainforest Destruction: A Critique and Economic Analysis of the "Hamburger Debate". *Interciencia* 13: 115-120.

Browder, J.O. and B.J. Godfrey. 1997. *Rainforest Cities: Urbanization, Development, and Globalization of the Brazilian Amazon.* Columbia University Press, New York.

Brown, K. and W.N. Adger. 1994. Economic and Political Feasibility of International Carbon Offsets. *Forest Ecology and Management* 68: 217-229.

Brown, K. and D.W. Pearce. 1994. The Economic Value of Non-Marketed Benefits of Tropical Forests: Carbon Storage. In J. Weiss, ed., *The Economics of Project Appraisal and the Environment*: 102-123. Edward Elgar, London, U.K.

Brown, L.R. 1995. *Who Will Feed China?.* W.W Norton, New York.

Brown, L.R. and H. Kane, 1994. *Full House: Reassessing the Earth's Population Carrying Capacity.* W.W. Norton, New York.

Brown, L.R. and eleven others. 1993. *State of the World 1993.* W.W. Norton, New York.

Bruce, J., H.E. Lee and E.F. Haites, eds. 1996. *Climate Change 1995: Economics and Social Dimensions of Climate Change.* Cambridge University Press, Cambridge, U.K.

Buchmann, S. and G.P. Nabhan. 1996. *The Forgotten Pollinators.* Island Press, Washington DC.

Burgess, P.F. 1989. In D. Poore, P. Burgess, J. Parma, S. Rietbergen and T. Synnott, eds., *No Timber Without Trees: Sustainability in the Tropical Forest.* Earthscan Publications, London, U.K.

Burgess, J.C. 1990. The Contribution of Efficienct Energy Pricing to Reducing Carbon Dioxide Emissions. *Energy Policy* 18: 449-455.

Burniaux, J.-W., J. Martin and J. Oliveira-Martins. 1994. *The Effects of Existing Distortions in Energy Markets on the Cost of Policy to Reduce CO2 Emissions.* Organisation for Economic Co-operation and Development, Paris, France.

Burtraw, D. and A.J. Krupnick. 1996. The Second-best Use of Social Cost Estimates. *Resource and Energy Economics* 18: 467-489.

Button, K. J. 1993. *Transport Economics*, second edition. Edward Elgar Publishing Ltd., Aldershot, U.K.

Caccia, C. 1996. *Keeping a Promise: Towards a Sustainable Budget.* Report of the Standing Committee on Environment and Sustainable Development, Ottawa, Canada.

Cairncross, F. 1995. *Green Inc.: A Guide to Business and the Environment.* Earthscan, London, U.K.

Carnel, C. and G. Viatte. 1993. A Fallow Year for Agricultural Reform. *OECD Observer* 182: 4-6.

Castro, R. 1994. *The Economics Opportunity Costs of Wildlands Conservation Areas: The Case of Costa Rica.* Department of Economics, Harvard University, Cambridge, Massachusetts.

Cavallo, A.J. 1995. High-Capacity Factor Wind Energy Systems. *Journal of Solar Energy Engineering* 117: 137-143.

Cavallo, A. 1996. Security of Supply: A Major Neglected Fossil Fuel Subsidy. *Wind Engineering* 20: 47-52.

Center for Responsive Politics. 1995. *The Politics of Sugar.* Center for Responsible Politics, Washington DC.

Chalmers, M. 1997. Personal communication, letter of 3 June 1997. Peace Research Institute, University of Bradford, Bradford, U.K.

Chamberlin, B. 1996. *Farming and Subsidies: Debunking the Myths.* Government Printer, Wellington, New Zealand.

Chan, N.W. 1986. Drought Trends in Northwestern Peninsular Malaysia. *Wallaceana* 44: 8-9.

Chichilnisky, G. and G. Heal. 1998. Economic Returns on the Biosphere. *Nature* 391: 629-630.

Chopra, K. 1993. The Value of Non-Timber Forest Products: An Estimation for Tropical Deciduous Forests in India. *Economic Botany* 47: 251-257.

Christmas, J. and C. Rooy. 1991. The Water Decade and Beyond. *Water International* 16: 127-134.

Ciais, P., P.P. Tans, M. Trolier, J.W.C. White and R.J. Francey. 1995. A Large Northern Hemisphere Terrestrial CO_2 Sink. *Science* 269: 1098-1102.

Cline, W.R. 1992. *The Economics of Global Warming.* Institute for International Economics, Washington DC.

Clugston, R.M. and T.J. Rogers. 1995. Sustainable Livelihoods in North America. *Journal of the Society of International Development* 3: 60-63.

Cobb, C.W. and J.B. Cobb, eds. 1994. *Green National Product: A Proposed Index of Sustainable Economic Welfare.* University Press of America, Lanham, Maryland.

Cobb, C., T. Halstead and J. Rowe. 1995. *The Genuine Progress Indicator: Summary of Data and Methodology.* Redefining Progress, San Francisco, California.

Cohen, H.A. and S. Plaut.1995. Quenching the Levant's Thirst. *Middle East Quarterly* March 1995: 37-44.

Commission of the European Communities. 1991. *The Agricultural Situation in the European Community: 1991 Report.* Commission of the European Communities, Brussels, Belgium.

Commonwealth of Australia. 1996. *Subsidies to the Use of Natural Resources.* Department of the Environment, Sport and Territories, Commonwealth of Australia, Canberra, Australia.

Constantino, L. and N. Kishor. 1993. *Forest Management and Competing Land Uses: An Economic Analysis for Costa Rica.* The World Bank, Washington DC.

Conway, G.R. and J.M. Pretty. 1991. *Unwelcome Harvest: Agriculture and Pollution.* Earthscan, London, U.K.

Conway, D., M. Krol, J. Alcamo and M. Holme. 1996. Future Availability of Water in Egypt: The Interaction of Global, Regional, and Basin-Scale Driving Forces in the Nile Basin. *Ambio* 25: 336-342.

Cookson, W.O.C.M. and M. F. Moffatt. 1997. Asthma: An Epidemic in the Absence of Infection? *Science* 275: 41-42.

Cortner, H.J. and D.L. Schweitzer. 1993. Below-Cost Timber Sales and the Political Marketplace. *Environmental Management* 17: 7-14.

Costanza, R. and 12 others. 1997. The Value of the World's Ecosystem Services and Natural Capital. *Nature* 387: 253-260.

Crews, K.A. and C.L. Stouffer. 1997. *World Population and the Environment.* Population Reference Bureau, Washington DC.

Cruz, W. and R. Repetto. 1992. *The Environmental Effects of Stabilization and Structural Adjustment Programs: The Philippine Case.* World Resources Institute, Washington DC.

Cuff, C., R. de Gennaro and G. Kripke. 1996. *The Green Scissors Report: Cutting Wasteful and Environmentally Harmful Spending and Subsidies.* Friends of the Earth and the National Taxpayers Union Foundation, Washington DC.

Cullinane, S.L. and K.P.B. Cullinane. 1995. Increasing Car Ownership and Use in Egypt: The Straw that Breaks the Camel's Back? *International Journal of Transport Economics* 22: 35-63.

Daily, G.C. 1995. Restoring Productivity to the World's Degraded Lands. *Science* 269: 350-354.

Daily, G.C., ed. 1997. *Nature's Services: Societal Dependence on Natural Ecosystems.* Island Press, Washington DC.

Dankmeyer, I. and K. Johnson. 1992. *Building Forest Wealth.* The Northwest Policy Center, Seattle, Washington.

Dasgupta, P. 1994. *An Inquiry into Well-Being and Destitution.* Clarendon Press, Oxford, U.K.

Data Resources Inc. 1993. *Transportation Sector Subsidies: U.S. Case Study Results.* Organisation for Economic Co-operation and Development, Paris, France.

Data Resources Inc. 1994. *The Energy, Environment and Economic Effect of Phasing Out Coal Subsidies in OECD Countries.* Organisation for Economic Co-operation and Development, Paris, France.

Dauvergne, P. 1993. The Politics of Deforestation in Indonesia. *Pacific Affairs* 66: 497-518.

Dauvergne, P. 1997. *Shadows in the Forest: Japan and the Political Economy of Deforestation in Southeast Asia*. MIT Press, Cambridge, Massachusetts.

Davis, S.C,. and D.N. McFarlin. 1996. *Transportation Energy Data Book*; Edition 16. Oak Ridge National Laboratory, Oak Ridge, Tennessee

Day, B. 1997. *Economic Distortions and Their Influence on Forests*. Centre for Social and Economic Research on the Global Environment, University College London, London, U.K.

de Almeida, A.L.O. 1992. *The Colonization of the Amazon*. University of Texas Press, Austin, Texas.

de Almeida, O.T. and C. Uhl. 1995. Brazil's Rural Land Tax: Tool for Stimulating Productive and Sustainable Land Uses in the Eastern Amazon. *Land Use Policy* 12: 105-114.

DeCanio, S.J. 1995. *The Energy Paradox: Bureaucratic and Organizational Barriers to Profitable Energy-Saving Investments*. Department of Economics, University of California, Santa Barbara, California.

deCanio, S. et al. (over 2500 economists). 1997. *Economists Statement on Climate Change*. Redefining Progress, San Francisco, California.

Decision Focus Inc. 1995. *Impact of Removing Energy Subsidies on Greenhouse Gas Emissions*. Decision Focus Inc.

Delucchi, M.A. 1995. *Summary of Non-Monetary Externalities of Motor Vehicle Use*. Institute of Transportation Studies, University of California, Davis, California.

Delucchi, M. 1996. Total Cost of Motor-Vehicle Use. *ACCESS* 8: 7-13.

Delucchi, M.A. 1997. *The Annualized Social Cost of Motor-Vehicle Use in the U.S., 1990-1991: Summary of Theory, Data, Methods, and Results*. Institute of Transportation Studies, University of California, Davis, California.

Delucchi, M.A. and J. Murphy. 1995. *Government Expenditures Related to the Use of Motor Vehicles*. Institute of Transportation Studies, University of California, Davis, California.

de Moor, A.P.G. 1997. *Perverse Incentives: Hundreds of Billions of Dollars in Subsidies Now Harm the Economy, the Environment, Equity and Trade*. The Earth Council, San Jose, Costa Rica.

de Moor, A.P.G. and P. Calamai. 1997. *Subsidizing Unsustainable Development: Undermining the Earth with Public Funds*. The Earth Council, San Jose, Costa Rica.

Denno, R.F. and T.J. Perfect, eds. 1994. *Plant Hoppers: Their Ecology and Management*. Chapman and Hall, New York.

Department of the Environment, Sport and Territories, Government of Australia. 1996. *Subsidies to the Use of Natural Resources.* Department of the Environment, Sport and Territories, Government of Australia, Canberra, Australia.

Department of Water Resources, State of California. 1994. *California Water Plan Update*, Vol. I. Department of Water Resources, State of California, Sacramento, California.

DeSai, A.V. 1992. Alternative Energy in the Third World: A Reappraisal of Subsidies. *World Development* 20: 959-965.

Devall, W., ed. 1994. *Clear Cut: The Tragedy of Industrial Forestry.* Island Press, Washington DC.

Diefenbacher, H. 1994. The Index of Sustainable Economic Welfare: A Case Study of the Federal Republic of Germany. In C.W. Cobb and J.B. Cobb, eds., *The Green National Product: A Proposed Index of Sustainable Economic Welfare.* University Press of America, Lanham, Maryland.

Dinhem, B. 1996. Getting off the Pesticide Treadmill. *Our Planet* 8 (4): 27-28.

Dixon, R.K., S. Brown, R.A. Houghton, A.M. Solomon, M.C. Trexler and J. Wisniewski. 1994. Carbon Pools and Flux of Global Forest Ecosystems. *Science* 263: 185-190.

Doering, O. 1992. Federal Policies as Incentives or Disincentives to Ecologically Sustainable Agricultural Systems. *Journal of Sustainable Agriculture* 2: 21-36.

Dower, R. et al. 1996. *A Sustainable Future for the United States.* World Resources Institute, Washington DC.

Downing, T.E. 1998. *Confidence in Climate Change, Impact Assessment and Economic Evaluation.* International Energy Agency, Paris, France (in press).

Downing, T.E. and M.L. Parry. 1994. Climate Change and World Food Security. *Food Policy* 19: 99-104.

Downing, T., S. Hecht, H. Pearson and C.G. Downing, eds. 1992. *Development or Destruction: The Conversion of Tropical Forests to Pasture in Latin America.* Westview Press, Boulder, Colorado.

Downing, T.E., R. Hoekstra, N. Eyre, D. Blackwell and R. Greener. 1997a. *Evaluation of Climate Damages: Sensitivity of the Open Framework to Emissions of Carbon Dioxide, Methane and Nitrous Oxide.* Environmental Change Unit, Oxford, U.K.

Downing, T.E., R.S.J. Tol and X. Olsthoorn, eds. 1997b. *Climate Change and Risk*. Routledge, London, U.K.

Dragun, A.K. 1995. *The Subsidisation of Logging in Victoria*. Department of Economics, LaTrobe University, Melbourne, Australia.

DRI/McGraw-Hill. 1994. *The Energy, Environment and Economic Effects of Phasing Out Coal Subsidies in OECD Countries*. Organisation for Economic Co-operation and Development, Paris, France.

Duchin, F., C. Hamilton and G.-M. Lange. 1993. *Environment and Development in Indonesia: An Input-Output Analysis of Natural Resource Issues*. Natural Resources Management Project, Jakarta, Indonesia.

Dudek, D.J., J. Goffman, D. Salon and S. Wade. 1997. *More Clean Air for the Buck: Lessons from U.S. Acid Rain Emissioms Trading Program*. Environmental Defense Fund, New York.

Dudley, N.J. 1992. Water Allocation By Markets, Common Property and Capacity Sharing: Companions or Competitors? *Natural Resources Journal* 32: 757-778.

Dudley, N., J.-P. Jeanrenaud and F. Sullivan, 1995. *Bad Harvest: The Timber Trade and the Degradation of the World's Forests*. Earthscan, London, U.K.

Dudley, N. 1997. *The Year the World Caught Fire*. World Wide Fund for Nature, Gland, Switzerland.

DuPont, P. and K. Egan. 1997. Solving Bangkok's Transport Woes: The Need to Ask the Right Questions. *World Transport and Policy Practice* 3 (1): 25-37.

Durning, A.T. 1994. Redesigning the Forest Economy. In L.R. Brown et al., eds. *State of the World 1994*: 22-40. W.W. Norton, New York.

Durning, A.T. and H.B. Brough. 1991. *Taking Stock: Animal Farming and the Environment*. Worldwatch Institute, Washington DC.

Earle, S.A. 1995. *Sea Change: A Message of the Oceans*. G.P. Putnam's Sons, New York.

Ebert, J.D. 1997. *Toward a Sustainable Future: Addressing the Long-Term Effects of Motor Vehicle Transportation on Climate and Ecology*. U.S. National Research Council, Washington DC.

EcoPlan. 1992. *Damage Costs of Air Pollution: A Survey of Existing Estimates*. European Federation for Transport and Environment, Brussels, Belgium.

ECOTEC. 1994. *An Evaluation of the Benefits of Reduced Sulphur Dioxide Emissions*. Department of the Environment, London, U.K.

Ehrlich, A.H. 1995. Implications of Population Pressure on on Agriculture and Ecosystems. *Advances in Botanical Research* 21: 79-103.

Ehrlich P.R. and A.H. Ehrlich. 1996. *Betrayal of Science and Reason*. Island Press, Washington DC.

Ehrlich, P.R., A.H. Ehrlich and G.C. Daily. 1993. Food Security, Population, and Environment. *Population and Development Review* 19 (1): 1-32.

Ekins, P. 1996. The Secondary Benefits of CO2 Abatement: How Much Emission Reductions Do They Justify? *Ecological Economics* 16: 13-24.

Ellerman, D. 1995. The World Price of Coal. *Energy Policy* 23: 499-500.

El Serafy, S. 1997. Green Accounting and Economic Policy. *Ecological Economics* 21: 217-229.

Elvik, R. 1995. The External Costs of Traffic Injury: Definition, Estimation, and Possibilities for Internalization. *Accident Analysis and Prevention* 26: 719-732.

Energy Information Administration, U.S. Department of Energy. 1997. *Annual Energy Review 1996*. Energy Information Administration, U.S. Department of Energy, Washington DC.

Engelman, R. and P. LeRoy. 1993. *Sustaining Water: Population and the Future of Renewable Water Supplies*. Population Action International, Washington DC.

Engelman, R. and P. LeRoy. 1995a. *Conserving Land: Population and Sustainable Food Production*. Population Action International, Washington DC.

Engelman, R. and P. LeRoy. 1995b. *Sustaining Water: An Update*. Population Action International, Washington DC.

Engelman, R. and P. LeRoy. 1995c. *Catching the Limit: Population and the Decline of Fisheries*. Population Action International, Washington DC.

Erlandson, D., J. Few and G. Kripke. 1995. *Dirty Little Secrets: Polluters Save While People Pay*. Friends of the Earth, Washington DC.

Ervin, D. 1996. *Agriculture, Trade and the Environment: Anticipating the Policy Challenges*. Organisation for Economic Co-operation and Development, Paris, France.

Erwin, T.L. 1988. The Tropical Forest Canopy: the Heart of Biotic Diversity. In E.O. Wilson, ed., *Biodiversity*: 123-129. National Academy Press, Washington DC.

Estes, R. 1996. *The Tyranny of the Bottom Line and Corporate Social Accounting* (not available for checking).

Evanson, R.E. 1991. Genetic Resources: Assessing Economic Value. In J.R. Vincent, E.W. Crawford and J. Hoehn, eds., *Valuing Environmental Benefits in Developing Economies*:169-181. Michigan State University Press, East Lansing, Michigan.

Evanson, R.E. and M.W. Rosegrant. 1995. *Developing Productivity (Non- Price Yield and Area) Projections for Commodity Market Modeling.* International Food Policy Research Institute, Washington DC.

Eyre, N., T. Downing, R. Hoekstra, R. Tol, K. Rennings and O. Hohneyer. 1997. *Global Warming Damages.* Report of the Global Warming Sub-Task Group for the ExternE project. The European Commission, Brussels, Belgium.

Faeth, P., ed. 1993. *Agricultural Policy and Sustainability: Case Studies from India, Chile, the Philippines and the United States.* World Resources Institute, Washington DC.

Faeth, P. 1995. *Growing Green: Enhancing the Economic and Environmental Performance of U.S. Agriculture.* World Resources Institute, Washington DC.

Faeth, P., R. Repetto, K. Kroll, Q. Dai and G. Helmers. 1991. *Paying the Farm Bill: U.S. Agricultural Policy and the Transition to Sustainable Agriculture.* World Resources Institute, Washington DC.

Falkenmark, M. 1994. Landscape as Life Support Provider: Water-Related Limitations. In F. Graham-Smith, ed., *Population—The Complex Reality*: 103-116. The Royal Society, London, U.K., and North American Press, Golden, Colorado.

Falkenmark, M. and R.A. Suprapto. 1992. Population-Landscape Interactions in Development: A Water Perspective to Environmental Sustainability. *Ambio* 11: 31-36.

Falkenmark, M. and C. Widstrand. 1992. Population and Water Resources: A Delicate Balance. *Population Bulletin* 47 (3).

Fankhauser, S. 1994. The Social Costs of Greenhouse Gas Emissions—An Expected Value Approach. *The Energy Journal* 15: 157-184.

Fankhauser, S. 1995. *Valuing Climate Change: The Economics of the Greenhouse.* Earthscan, London, U.K.

Fankhauser, S. and D.W. Pearce. 1994. The Social Costs of Greenhouse Gas Emissions. In *The Economics of Climate Change.* Organisation for Economic Co-operation and Development, Paris, France.

Farah, J. 1994. *Pesticide Policies in Developing Countries: Do They Encourage Excessive Use?* The World Bank, Washington DC.

Fearnside, P.M. 1993. Deforestation in Brazilian Amazonia: The Effect of Population and Land Tenure. *Ambio* 22: 537-545.

Figuera, J. 1992. *Dimensions of Parking.* Federal Transit Administration, Washington DC.

Fitzgerald, B. 1986. *An Analysis of Indonesian Trade Policies.* The World Bank, Washington DC.

Flavin, C. 1994. Storm Warmings: Climate Change Hits the Insurance Industry. *World Watch* 7: 10-20.

Flavin, C. and S. Dunn. 1997. *Rising Sun, Gathering Winds: Policies to Stabilize the Climate and Strengthen Economies.* Worldwatch Institute, Washington DC.

Flavin, C. and M. Lenssen. 1994. *Power Surge: Guide to the Coming Energy Revolution.* W.W. Norton, New York.

Flavin, C. and N. Lenssen. 1995. *Powering the Future: Blueprint for a Sustainable Electricity Industry.* Worldwatch Institute, Washington DC.

Food and Agriculture Organization. 1990. *Situation and Outlook of the Forestry Sector in Indonesia.* Food and Agriculture Organization, Jakarta, Indonesia.

Food and Agriculture Organization. 1992. *Third Interim Report on the State of Tropical Forests.* Food and Agriculture Organization (Forest Resources Assessment Project), Rome.

Food and Agriculture Organization. 1993a. *Marine Fisheries and the Law of the Sea: A Decade of Change.* Food and Agriculture Organization, Rome, Italy.

Food and Agriculture Organization. 1993b. *Forest Resources Assessment 1990.* Food and Agriculture Organization, Rome, Italy.

Food and Agriculture Organization. 1994. *The Oceans' Most Valuable Commercial Species are Fished to Capacity.* Food and Agriculture Organization, Rome, Italy.

Food and Agriculture Organization. 1995. *State of World Fisheries and Aquaculture 1995.* Food and Agriculture Organization, Rome, Italy.

Food and Agriculture Organization. 1996. *State of World Fisheries and Aquaculture 1996.* Food and Agriculture Organisation, Rome, Italy.

Food and Agriculture Organization and The Government of Indonesia. 1990. *Situation and Outlook of the Forestry Sector in Indonesia.* Food and Agriculture Organization, Rome, Italy, and Government of Indonesia, Jakarta, Indonesia.

Francis, M.A. 1994. *Below-Cost Timber Sales.* The Wilderness Society, Washington DC.

Fraser, A.I. 1997. Personal communication, letters of 15 May and 2 June 1997. Indonesia-U.K. Tropical Forest Management Programme, Jakarta, Indonesia.

Frederiksen, H.D. 1996. Water Crisis in the Developing World: Misconceptions About Solutions. *Journal of Water Resources Planning and Management* March/April: 79-87.

Frederiksen, H.D. 1997. Personal communication, letter of 28 December, 1997. Harald D. Frederiksen Associates,Eugene, Oregon.

Frederiksen, H.D. and C. Perry. 1995. *Needs and Priorities in Water-Related Research.* International Irrigation Management Institute, Colombo, Sri Lanka.

Freeman, A.M. 1996. Estimating the Environmental Costs of Electricity: An Overview and Review of the Issues. *Resource and Energy Economice* 18: 347-362.

Fujita, R.M. and D.D. Hopkins. 1994. *Individual Transferable Quotas for Fish Harvest Privileges.* Environmental Defense Fund, Oakland, California.

Fujita, R.M. and I. Zebos. 1996. *Innovative Approaches for Fostering Conservation in Marine Fisheries.* Environmental Defense Fund, Oakland, California.

Fujita, R.M., D.D. Hopkins and W.R.Z. Willey. 1996. Creating Incentives to Curb Overfishing. *Forum for Applied Research and Public Policy* 11: 29-34.

Fujita, R.M., J. Philip and D.D. Hopkins. 1996. *The Conservation Benefits of Individual Transferable Quotas.* Environmental Defense Fund, Oakland, California.

Gadgil, A., A.H. Rosenfeld and L. Price. 1991. *Making the Market Right for Environmentally Sound Energy-Efficient Technology: U.S. Buildings Sector Successes That Must Work in Developing Countries and Eastern Europe.* International Symposium on Environmentally Sound Energy Technologies and Their Transfer to Developing Countries and European Economies in Transition, Milan, October 21-25 1991. Cited in Roodman and Lenssen, 1995.

Gaffney, M. 1992. The Taxable Surplus in Water Resources. *Contemporary Policy Issues* 10: 74-82.

Gale, R.J.P. and S.R. Barg, eds. 1995. *Green Budget Reform: An International Casebook of Leading Practices*. Earthscan Publications, London, U.K.

Gale, R.J.P. and S.R. Barg. 1995. The Greening of Budgets: The Choice of Governing Instrument. In R. Gale, S. Barg and A. Gillis, eds. *Green Budget Reform: An International Case Book of Leading Practices*: 1-29. Earthscan Publications, London, U.K. and International Institute for Sustainable Development, Winnipeg, Manitoba, Canada.

Gannon, E., K.A. Cook and C. Williams. 1995. *Faking Takings: Farm Subsidies and Private Property in Perspective*. Environmental Working Group, Washington DC.

Garcia, J.R. 1984. Waterfalls, Hydropower, and Water for Industry: Contributions from Canaima National Park, Venezuela. In J.A. McNeely and K.R. Miller, eds., *National Parks, Conservation and Development: The Role of Protected Areas in Sustaining Society*. 588-591. Smithsonian Institution Press, Washington DC.

Garcia, S.M. and C. Newton. 1995. *Current Situation, Trends, and Prospects in World Capture Fisheries*. Food and Agriculture Organization, Rome, Italy.

Gardener, B.D. 1995. *Plowing Ground in Washington: The Political Economy of U.S. Agriculture*. Pacific Research Institute for Public Policy, San Francisco, California.

Gardener, B.D. 1997. Some Implications of Federal Grazing, Timber, Irrigation, and Recreation Subsidies. *Choices* 12 (3): 9-14.

Gardner, B.L. 1994. Liberalization in New Zealand Agriculture. *American Journal of Agricultural Economics* 76: 1053-1054.

Gardner, G. 1996. *Shrinking Fields: Cropland Loss in a World of Eight Billion*. Worldwatch Institute, Washington DC.

Gardner-Outlaw, T. and R. Engelman. 1997. *Sustaining Water, Easing Scarcity: A Second Update*. Population Action International, Washington DC.

Gates, J., D. Holland and E. Gudmundsson. 1997. Theory and Practice of Fishing Vessel Buyback Programs. In World Wide Fund for Nature International, *Subsidies and Depletion of World Fisheries*: 71-117. World Wide Fund for Nature International, Gland, Switzerland.

Gelbspan, R. 1997. *The Heat is On*. Addison-Wesley, Reading, Massachusetts.

Geller, H. and R.N. Elliott. 1994. *Industrial Energy Efficiency: Trends, Savings Potential and Policy Options*. American Council for an Energy- Efficient Economy, Washington DC.

Gentry, A. 1993. Tropical Forest Biodiversity and the Potential for New Medicinal Plants. In A.D. Kinghorn and M.F. Balandrin, eds., *Human Medicinal Agents from Plants*: 13-24. American Chemical Society, Washington DC.

Ghassemi, F., A.J. Jakeman and H.A. Nix. 1995. *Salinization of Land and Water Resources: Human Causes, Extent, Management and Case Studies*. University of New South Wales Press, Sydney, Australia.

Gibbs, W.W. 1997, Transportation's Perennial Problems. *Scientific American* 277 (4)October: 32-35.

Gillis, M., 1988. In R. Repetto and M. Gillis, editors, *Public Policies and the Misuse of Forest Resources*. Cambridge University Press, New York.

Gillis, M. 1991. Economics, Ecology and Ethics: Mending the Broken Circle for Tropical Forests. In F. Bormann and S. Kellert, eds., *Ecology, Economics, Ethics: The Broken Circle*. Yale University Press, New Haven, Connecticut.

Gillis, M. 1992. Forest Concession Management and Revenue Policies. In N. Sharma, editor, *Managing the World's Forests*. Kendall/Hunt Publishers, Dubuque, Iowa.

Gillis, M. 1994. *Forest Incentive Policies*. The World Bank, Washington DC.

Gimbel, K.L., ed. 1994. *Limiting Access to Marine Fisheries: Keeping the Focus on Conservation*. Center for Marine Conservation and World Wildlife Fund, Washington DC.

Gitlitz, J.S. 1993. *The Relationship Between Primary Aluminum Production and the Damming of World Rivers*. International Rivers Network, Berkeley, California, USA (cited in Koplow, 1996).

Gladstone, J. 1992. *Water Efficiency for Today and Tomorrow*. Water Department, City of Seattle, Washington.

Glantz, M.H., ed. 1994. *Drought Follows the Plow: Cultivating Marginal Areas*. Cambridge University Press, Cambridge, U.K.

Glazovsky, N.F. 1995. The Aral Sea Basin. In J.X. Kasperson, R.E. Kasperson and B.L. Turner, eds., *Regions at Risk: Comparisons of Threatened Environments*: 92-139. United Nations University Press, Tokyo, Japan.

Gleick P.H. 1989. The Implications of Global Climatic Changes for International Security. *Climatic Change* 15: 309-325.

Gleick, P.H., ed. 1993. *Water in Crisis: A Guide to the World's Fresh Water Resources*. Oxford University Press, Oxford, U.K.

Gleick, P.H. 1996. Basic Water Requirements for Human Activities: Meeting Basic Needs. *Water International* 21: 83-92.

Gleick, P. 1997. *Water 2050: Moving Toward A Sustainable Vision for the Earth's Fresh Water*. Pacific Institute for Studies in Development, Environment and Security, Oakland, California.

Gleick, P.H., P. Loh, S.V. Gomez and J. Morrison. 1995. *California Water 2020: A Sustainable Vision*. The Pacific Institute for Studies in Development, Environment and Security, Oakland, California.

Goldemberg, J. 1996. *Energy, Environment and Development*. Earthscan, London, U.K.

Goldstone, J.A. 1995. The Coming Chinese Collapse. *Foreign Policy* 99: 35-52.

Goodland, R. and H. Daly. 1996. If Tropical Log Export Bans are so Perverse, Why are There So Many? *Ecological Economics* 18: 189-196.

Goriz, C.M., A. Subramanian and J. Simas. 1995. *Irrigation Management Transfer in Mexico*. The World Bank, Washington DC.

Gorte, R.W. 1993. *Timber Sales Cost Accounting: The Forest Service and TSPIRS*. Congressional Research Service, Washington DC.

Government of India. 1997. *Government Subsidies in India*. Dept. of Economic Affairs, Ministry of Finance, Delhi, India.

Government of Indonesia. 1991. *Indonesia Forestry Action Program*. Government of Indonesia, Jakarta, Indonesia.

Grainger, R.J.R. and S.M. Garcia. 1996. *Chronicles of Marine Fishery Landings (1950-1994): Trend Analysis and Fisheries Potential*. Food and Agriculture Organisation, Rome, Italy.

Greene, D.L. 1995. *Evaluating Energy Subsidies in Transportation: Lessons from Full Social Cost Accounting*. Oak Ridge National Laboratory, Oak Ridge, Tennessee.

Greenland, D.J., G.D. Bowen, H. Eswaran, R. Rhodes and C. Valentin. 1994. *Soil, Water and Nutrient Management Research: A New Agenda*. International Board for Soil Research and Management, Bangkok, Thailand.

Griffiths, A. and S. Wall. 1993. *Applied Economics*. Longman, London, UK.

Grubb, M. 1996. *Renewable Energy Strategies for Europe*. Earthscan, London, U.K.

Grubb, M., T. Chapuis and M. Ha Duong. 1995. The Economics of Changing Course—Implications of Adaptability and Inertia for Optimal Climate Policy. *Energy Policy* 23: 417-432.

Gudmundsson, H. and M. Hojer. 1996. Sustainable Development Principles and Their Implications for Transport. *Ecological Economics* 19: 269-282.

Gulati, A. 1989. Input Subsidies in Indian Agriculture—A Statewise Analysis. *Economic and Political Weekly* June 24: A-57-65.

Gupta, S., K. Miranda and I. Parry. 1995. Public Expenditure Policy and the Environment: A Review and Synthesis. *World Development* 23: 515-528.

Gurney, K. 1997. *The Economics of Mitigating Climate Change: Boom or Bust?* School of Environmental Science and Management, University of California, Santa Barbara, California.

Gurvich, E. and G. Hughes. 1996. *The Environmental Impact of Energy Subsidies: A Case Study of Russia.* Pollution Management and Environmental Economics Division, the World Bank, Washington DC.

Gurvich, E., A. Golub, A. Mukhin, M. Uzyakov and M. Ksenofontov. 1997. Impacts of Russian Energy Subsidies on Greenhouse Gas Emissions. In Organisation for Economic Co-operation and Development, *Reforming Energy and Transport Subsidies: Environmental and Economic Implications.* Organisation for Economic Co-operation and Development, Paris, France .

Hall, J. et al. 1989. *Economic Assessment of the Health Benefits from Improvements in Air Quality in the South Coast Air Basin, Los Angeles.* South Coast Air Quality Management District, Los Angeles, California.

Hall, J.P. 1995. Forest Health Monitoring in Canada: How Healthy is the Boreal Forest? *Water, Air and Soil Pollution* 82: 77-85.

Haltmaier, S. 1997. Transport Subsidies: U.S. Case Study. In Organisation for Economic Co-operation and Development *Reforming Energy and Transpost Subsidies: Environmental and Economic Implications.* Organisation for Economic Co-operation and Development, Paris, France.

Hamilton, C. 1995. The Economics of Logging High Conservation Value Native Forests. *Economic and Labour Relations Review* 6: 159-179.

Hamilton, C. 1997. The Sustainability of Logging in Indonesia's Tropical Forests: A Dynamic Input-Output Analysis. *Ecological Economics* 21: 183-195.

Hanna, S.S. 1997. The New Frontier of American Fisheries Governance. *Ecological Economics* 20: 221-233.

Hardin, G. 1968. The Tragedy of the Commons. *Science* 162: 1243-1248.

Hardin, G. 1995. Second Thoughts on "The Tragedy of the Commons". In H.E. Daly and K.N. Townsend, eds. *Valuing the Earth—Economics, Ecology, Ethics*: 145-151.

Hardjono, J., ed. 1991. *Indonesia: Resources, Ecology, and Environment*. Oxford University Press, Singapore.

Harvey, G. 1996. *The Killing of the Countryside*. Jonathan Cape, London, U.K.

Hawken, P. 1997. Natural Capitalism. *Mother Jones* March/April 1997: 40-54.

Hawken, P., A. Lovins and H. Lovins. 1998. *Natural Capitalism: The Coming Efficiency Revolution*. Hyperian Press, New York.

Heath, J. and H. Binswanger. 1996. Natural Resource Degradation Effects of Poverty and Population Growth are Largely Policy Induced: The Case of Colombia. *Environment and Development Economics* 1: 65-84.

Hecht, S.B. 1985. Environment, Development and Politics: Capital Accumulation and the Livestock Sector in Eastern Amazonia. *World Development* 13: 663-684.

Hecht, S.B. 1992. Logics of Livestock and Deforestation: The Case of Amazonia. In T. Downing et al., eds., *Development or Destruction: The Conversion of Tropical Forests to Pasture in Latin America*: 7-25. Westview Press, Boulder, Colorado.

Heede, R. 1997. Personal communication, letters of 23 July and 22 August, 1997. Rocky Mountain Institute, Snowmass, Colorado.

Heede, R. 1998. Personal communication, letter of 21 January, 1998. Rocky Mountain Institute, Snowmass, Colorado.

Heede, H.R. and A.B. Lovins. 1985. Hiding the True Costs of Energy Sources. *The Wall Street Journal* 17 July: 28.

Heede, R., R. Morgan and S. Ridley. 1985. *The Hidden Costs of Energy: How Taxpayers Subsidize Energy Development*. Center for Renewable Resources, Washington DC.

Heggie, I.G. 1995. *Management and Financing of Roads: An Agenda for Reform*. The World Bank, Washington DC.

Heinrichs, E.A., ed. 1994. *Biology and Management of Rice Insects*. John Wiley and Sons, Chichester, U.K.

Helmberger, P.G. 1991. *Economic Analysis of Farm Programs*. McGraw-Hill, New York.

175

Hendrison, J. 1992. *Recommendations for Controlled Timber Harvesting in the SBK Forest Concession*. Natural Resources Management Programme, Jakarta, Indonesia.

Hepher, T. 1997. *OECD Says Drop in Farm Subsidies May Not Last.* Communications Division, Organisation for Economic Co-operation and Development, Paris, France.

Hermach, T. 1996. *Trees Restore the Earth*. Native Forests Council, Eugene, Oregon.

Hill, R., P. O'Keefe and C. Snape. 1995. *The Future of Energy Use*. Earthscan, London, U.K.

Hilliard, T.J. 1994. *Golden Patents, Empty Pockets: A 19th Century Law Gives Miners Billions, The Public Pennies*. Mineral Policy Center, Washington DC.

Hird, V. and A. Paxton. 1994. *The Food Miles Report: The Dangers of Long-Distance Food Transport*. The SAFE Alliance, London, U.K.

Holden, M. 1994. *The Common Fisheries Policy: Origin, Evaluation and Future*. Blackwells Science, Oxford, U.K.

Holdren, J.P. 1989. Energy in Transition. *Scientific American* 263 (3): 109-112.

Hongliang, Liu. 1997. Personal communication, letter of December 24th, 1997. Chinese Research Academy of Environmental Sciences, Beijing, P.R. China.

Hope, E. and B. Singh. 1995. *Energy Price Increases in Developing Countries: Case Studies of Colombia, Ghana, Indonesia, Malaysia, Turkey and Zimbabwe*. The World Bank, Washington DC.

Houghton, J.T., G.J. Jenkins and J.J. Ephramus, eds. 1990. *Climate Change: The IPCC Scientific Assessment (Final Report of Working Group 1)*. Cambridge University Press, New York.

Houghton, J.T. and five others, eds. 1996. *The Science of Climate Change: The Second Assessment Report of the Intergovernmental Panel on Climate Change*. Cambridge University Press, New York.

Howe, C.W. 1996. Sharing Water Fairly. *Our Planet* 8 (3): 15-17.

Hubbard, H.N. 1991. The Real Cost of Energy. *Scientific American* 264: 18-23.

Humphries, M., L. Parker and J. Blodgett. 1989. *Acid Rain Legislation and the Domestic Aluminum Industry*. Congressional Research Service, Washington DC (cited in Koplow, 1996).

Hulme, M. and D. Viner. 1995 *A Climate Change Scenario for Assessing the Impact of Climate Change on Tropical Rain Forests*. World Wildlife Fund-US, Washington DC.

Hurst P. 1990. *Rainforest Politics: Ecological Destruction in Southeast Asia*. Zed Books, London.

Hwang, R. 1995. *Money Down the Pipeline: Uncovering the Hidden Subsidies to the Oil Industry*. Union of Concerned Scientists, Cambridge, Massachusetts.

Hyde, W.F. and D.H. Newman. 1991. *Forest Economics and Policy Analysis: An Overview*. The World Bank, Washington DC.

Hyde, W.F., G.S. Amacher, and W. Magrath. 1993. *Deforestation, Scarce Forest Resources, and Forest Land Use: Theory, Empirical Evidence, and Policy Implications*. The World Bank, Washington DC.

Indian National Institute of Public Finance and Policy. 1997. *Government Subsidies in India*. Indian National Institute of Public Finance and Policy, New Delhi, India.

Ingram, G.K. and M. Fay. 1994. *Valuing Infrastructure Stocks and Gains from Improved Performance*. The World Bank, Washington DC.

International Energy Agency. 1992. *Energy Policies of IEA Countries: 1992 Review*. International Energy Agency, Paris, France.

International Energy Agency. 1993. *Cars and Climate Change*. International Energy Agency, Paris, France.

International Energy Agency. 1994. *Coal Information*. Organisation for Economic Co-operation and Development, Paris, France.

International Energy Agency. 1995. *Energy Policies of IEA Countries, 1994 Review*. Organisation for Economic Co-operation and Development, Vienna, Austria.

International Energy Agency. 1996. *Energy Policies of IEA Countries*. International Energy Agency, Paris, France.

International Institute for Sustainable Development. 1994. *Making Budgets Green: Leading Practices in Taxation and Subsidy Reform*. International Institute for Sustainable Development, Winnipeg, Canada.

Jackson, T. and S. Stymne. 1996. *Sustainable Economic Welfare in Sweden: A Pilot Index 1950-1992*. Stockholm Environment Institute, Stockholm, Sweden.

Jackson, T., F. Laing, A. MacGillivray, N. Marks, J. Rolls and S. Stymne. 1997. *An Index of Sustainable Economic Welfare for the United Kingdom 1950-1996.* Centre for Environmental Strategy, University of Surrey, U.K.

Jardine, K. 1994. *The Carbon Bomb: Climate Change and the Fate of the Northern Boreal Forests.* Stichting Greenpeace Council, Amsterdam.

Johansson, T.B. et al., 1993. *Renewable Energy.* Island Press, Washington DC.

Johnson, D.G. 1991. *World Agriculture in Disarray,* second edition. Macmillan, London, U.K.

Johnson, N. and B. Cabarle, 1993. *Surviving the Cut: Natural Forest Management in the Humid Tropics.* World Resources Institute, Washington DC.

Jones, P. M. 1992. The Real Costs of Nuclear Power. *OECD Observer* 178: 8-11.

Jones, W. 1995. *The World Bank and Irrigation.* The World Bank, Washington DC.

Jones, A. and J. Dyer. 1995. *The Water Efficiency Revolution.* Rocky Mountain Institute, Snowmass, Colorado.

Jones, T. and J. Short. 1994. The Economics of Transport Costs. *OECD Observer* 188: 11-14.

Jordan, C.F. 1985. *Nutrient Cycling in Tropical Forest Ecosystems.* John Wiley, Chichester, U.K.

Jorgenson, D.W. Associates. 1994. *The Elimination of Federal Energy Subsidies: Environmental Gains, Tax Considerations and Economic Consequences.* Organisation for Economic Co-operation and Development, Paris, France.

Just, R.E. and N. Bockstael, eds. 1991. *Commodity and Resource Policies in Agricultural Systems.* Springer Verlag, New York.

Kaczynski, V.M. 1992. *Market Conditions and Sustainable Development of Fishery Resources.* United Nations Conference on Trade and Development, New York.

Kageson, P. 1992. *External Costs of Air Pollution: The Case of European Transport.* European Federation for Transport and Environment, Stockholm, Sweden.

Kageson, P. 1993. *Getting the Prices Right: A European Scheme for Making Transport Pay Its True Costs.* European Federation for Transport and Environment, Stockholm, Sweden.

Kaimowitz, D. 1995. *Livestock and Deforestation in Central America in the 1980s and 1990s: A Policy Perspective*. Centre for International Forestry Research, Jakarta, Indonesia.

Kane, H. 1996. Shifting to Sustainable Industries. In L.R. Brown and 20 others, *State of the World 1996*: 152-167. W.W Norton, New York.

Kane, H. 1997. Coal Use Up Slightly. In L.R. Brown, C. Flavin and H. Kane, eds. *Vital Signs 1996*: 52-53. W.W. Norton, new York.

Kay, J.H. 1997. *Asphalt Nation*. Crown Publishers, New York.

Kaya, Y. 1993. *Energy Conservation in Japan, Past, Present and Future. In International Conference on Energy Efficiency in Asian Countries*: 71- 80. Organisation for Economic Co-operation and Development, Paris, France.

Keller, A. and J. Keller. 1995. *Effective Efficiency: A Water Use Efficiency Concept for Allocating Freshwater Resources*. Winrock International, Arlington, Virginia.

Keller, A., J. Keller and D. Seckler. 1995. *Integrated Water Resource Systems: Theory and Policy Implications*. International Irrigation Management Institute, Colombo, Sri Lanka.

Kendall, H.W. and D. Pimentel. 1994. Constraints on the Expansion of the Global Food Supply. *Ambio* 23: 198-205.

Keppler, J. 1995. *Public Goods, Infrastructure, Externalities and Subsidies*. Organisation for Economic Co-operation and Development, Paris, France.

Ketcham, B. 1992. *Price It Right! End Roadway Entitlements*. Konheim and Ketcham, Brooklyn, New York.

Ketcham, B. and C. Komanoff. 1993. *Win-Win Transportation: A No-Losers Approach to Financing Transport in New York City and the Region*. Konheim and Ketcham, Brooklyn, New York.

Keyfitz, N. 1991. Population and Development within the Ecosphere: One View of the Literature. *Population Index* 57(1): 5-22.

Kishor, N.M. and L.F. Constantino. 1993. *Forest Management and Competing Land Uses: An Economic Analysis for Costa Rica*. The World Bank, Washington DC.

Kolchugina, T.P. and T.S. Vinson. 1995. Role of Russian Forests in the Global Carbon Balance. *Ambio* 24: 258-264.

Komanoff, C. 1994. *Pollution Taxes for Roadway Transportation*. Konheim and Ketcham, Brooklyn, New York.

Koplow, D. 1993. *Federal Energy Subsidies: Energy, Environmental and Fiscal Impacts*. Alliance to Save Energy, Washington DC.

Koplow, D. 1995. *Energy Subsidies and the Environment*. Industrial Economics Inc., Cambridge, Massachusetts.

Koplow, D. 1996. Energy Subsidies and the Environment. In *Subsidies and Environment: Exploring the Linkages*: 201-218. Organisation for Economic Co-operation and Development, Paris, France.

Koplow, D. and A. Martin. 1997. *Federal and Alaskan Subsidies to Oil Exploration, Development and Transport*. Industrial Economics Inc., Cambridge, Massachusetts.

Kosmo, M. 1989. Commercial Energy Subsidies in Developing Countries. *Energy Policy* 17: 244-253.

Kovda, V.A. 1983. Loss of Productive Land due to Salinization. *Ambio* 12: 91-92.

Kozloff, K. and O. Shobowale. 1994. *Rethinking Development Assistance for Renewable Electricity*. World Resources Institute, Washington DC.

Krause, F. 1997. *The Costs and Benefits of Cutting U.S. Carbon Emissions: A Critical Review of the Economic Arguments of the Fossil Fuel Lobby*. International Project for Sustainable Energy Paths, El Cerrito, California.

Krautkraemer, J.A. 1995. Incentives, Development and Population: A Growth-Theoretic Perspective. In T.M. Swanson, ed., *The Economics and Ecology of Biodiversity Decline*: 13-24. Cambridge University Press, Cambridge, UK

Kreith, M. 1991. *Water Inputs in California Food Production*. Water Education Foundation, Sacramento, California.

Krueger, A.O. 1988. *The Political Economy of Control: American Sugar. Program in International Political Economy*. Duke University, Durham, North Carolina.

Krugman, P.R. 1996. The Tax Reform Obsession. *New York Times* Magazine, April 7th 2-3.

Krupnick, A. 1990. *The Environmental Costs of Energy Supply: A Framework for Estimation*. Resources for the Future Inc., Washington DC.

Krupnick, A.J. and D. Bertraw. 1997. The Social Costs of Electricity: Do The Numbers Add Up? *Energy and Resource Economics* 18: 423-466.

Krupnick, A., M. Walls and H. Hood. 1993. *The Distributional and Environmental Implications of an Increase in the Federal Gasoline Tax*. Resources for the Future Inc., Washington DC.

Kumar, S.K. and D. Hotchkiss. 1988. *Consequences of Deforestation for Women's Time Allocation, Agricultural Production and Nutrition in Hill Areas of Nepal*. International Food Policy Research Institute, Washington DC.

Kumar, P., M. Rosegrant and P. Hazell. 1995. *Cereals Prospects in India to 2020: Implications for Policy*. International Food Policy Research Institute, Washington DC.

Kurz, W.A. and M.J. Apps. 1995. An Analysis of Future Carbon Budgets of Canadian Boreal Forests. *Water, Air and Soil Pollution* 82: 321-331.

Lampietti, J.A. and J.A. Dixon. 1995. *To See the Forest for the Trees: A Guide to Non-Timber Forest Benefits*. The World Bank, Washington DC.

Lapp, D. 1993. Federal Subsidies for Nuclear Power. *Environmental Action* 25 (1): 12-16.

Larsen, B. 1994. *World Fossil Fuel Subsidies and Global Carbon Emissions in a Model with Interfuel Substitution*. The World Bank, Washington DC.

Larsen, B. and A. Shah. 1992. *World Fossil Fuel Subsidies and Global Carbon Emissions*. The World Bank, Washington DC.

Larsen, B. and A. Shah. 1993. Global Climate Change, Energy Subsidies and National Carbon Taxes. In L. Bovenberg and S. Cnossen, eds., *Public Economics and the Environment in an Imperfect World*: 113-132. Kluwer Academic Publishers, Dordrecht, Netherlands.

Larsen, B. and A. Shah. 1994. *Global Climate Change, Economic Policy Instruments and Developing Countries*. The World Bank, Washington DC.

Larsen, B. and A. Shah. 1995. Global Climate Change, Energy Subsidies and National Carbon Taxes. In L. Bovenberg and S. Cnossen, eds. *Public Economics and the Environment in an Imperfect World*: 113-132. Kluwer Academic Press, Boston, Massachusetts.

LaVeen, E.P. and L.B. King. 1985. *Turning Off the Tap on Federal Water Subsidies, Vol. I: The Central Valley Project—The $3.5 Billion Giveaway*. Natural Resources Defense Council and California Rural Legal Assistance Foundation, San Francisco, California.

Legg, W. 1993. Direct Payments for Farmers? *OECD Observer* 185: 26-29.

Legg, W. 1996. Agricultural Subsidies and the Environment. In *Subsidies and Environment: Exploring the Linkages*: 117-121. Organisation for Economic Co-operation and Development, Paris, France.

Legg, W. 1997. Ecological Agriculture. *OECD Observer*, No. 206, June 1997: 41-43.

Legg, W. and L. Portugal. 1997. How Agriculture Benefits the Environment. *OECD Observer* 205.

Leggett, J., ed. 1996. *Climate Change and the Financial Sector: The Emerging Threat and the Solar Solution.* Gerling Akademie Verlag, Munich, Germany.

Lenney, W. et al., 1994. The Burden of Paediatric Asthma. *European Respiratory Review* 4: 49-62.

Lennsen, M. and C. Flavin. 1996. Meltdown. *World Watch* 9(3): 23-31.

Lichtenberg, E. and D. Zilberman. 1986. The Welfare Economics of Price Supports in U.S. Agriculture. *American Economic Review* 76: 1121-1142.

Litman, T. 1996. *Transportation Cost Analysis: Techniques, Estimates and Implications.* Victoria Transport Policy Institute, Victoria, Canada.

Litman, T. 1997. Personal communication, letter of 11 June 1997.

Loper, J.W. 1994. *State and Local Taxation: Energy Policy by Accident.* Alliance to Save Energy, Washington DC.

Losos, E., J. Hayes, A. Phillips, D. Wilcove and C. Alkire. 1995. Taxpayer-Subsidized Resource Extraction Harms Species. *BioScience* 45: 446-455.

Lovins, A.B. 1996. Negawatts: Twelve Transitions, Eight Improvements and One Distraction. *Energy Policy* April.

Lovins, A.B. 1997. Letter in *The Economist*, Dec. 20th, 1997: 8.

Lovins, A.B. and L.H. Lovins. 1997. *Climate: Making Sense and Making Money.* Rocky Mountain Institute, Snowmass, Colorado.

Lovins, A.B., L.H. Lovins and R.A. Heede. 1992. Energy Policy. In M. Green, ed., *Changing America: Blueprints for a New Administration*: 671- 686. Newmarket Press, New York.

Lowe, M.D. 1994. Reinventing Transport. In L.R. Brown et al., eds. *State of the World 1994*: 81-98. W.W. Norton, New York.

Lynch, S., ed. 1994. *Designing Green Support Programs.* Henry A. Wallace Institute, Greenbelt, Maryland.

MacKenzie, J.J., R.C. Dower, and D.T. Chen. 1992. *The Going Rate: What It Really Costs to Drive.* World Resources Institute, Washington DC.

MacKenzie, J.J. 1997. *Climate Protection and the National Interest: The Links Among Climate Change, Air Pollution, and Energy Security.* World Resources Institute, Washington DC.

MacNeill, J. 1994. *Changing Land Tenure and Sustainable Development.* MacNeill and Associates, Ottawa, Canada.

MacNeill, J., P. Winsemius and T. Yakushiji. 1991. *Beyond Interdependence: The Meshing of the World's Economy and the Earth's Ecology.* Oxford University Press, New York.

Maddison, D. D.W. Pearce, O, Johansson, E. Calthrop, T. Litman and E. Verhoef. 1996. *Blueprint 5: The True Cost of Road Transport.* Earthscan, London.

Maddison, D., D. Pearce, N. Adger and H. McCloud. 1997. Environmentally Damaging Subsidies in the United Kingdom. *European Environment* 7: 110-117.

Magrath, W. & P. Arens. 1989. *The Costs of Soil Erosion on Java: A Natural Resource Accounting Approach.* The World Bank, Washington DC.

Mahar, D. 1989. *Government Policies and Deforestation in Brazil's Amazon Region.* World Bank, Washington DC.

Mahar, D. and R. Schneider. 1994. Incentives for Tropical Deforestation: Some Examples from Latin America. In K. Brown and D.W. Pearce, eds., *The Causes of Tropical Deforestation*: 159-171. University College London Press, London, U.K.

Mahmood, K. 1987. *Reservoir Sedimentation: Impact, Extent and Mitigation.* The World Bank, Washington DC.

Maier, L. 1997. Letting the Land Rest. *The OECD Observer* 203: 12-15.

Maier, L. and R. Steenblik. 1995. Towards Sustainable Agriculture. *The OECD Observer* 196, October/November 1995.

Manurung, E.G.T. and J. Buongiorno. 1997. The Effects of the Ban on Tropical Log Exports on the Forestry Sector of Indonesia. *Journal of World Forest Resources Management* 8: 21-49.

Maskus, K. 1989. Large Costs and Small Benefits of the American Sugar Programme. *World Economy* 12: 85-104.

Matson, P.A., W.J. Parton, A.G. Power and M.J. Swift. 1997. Agricultural Intensification and Ecosystem Properties. *Science* 277: 504-508.

Matthiasson, T. 1996. Why Fishing Fleets Tend to be Too Big. *Marine Resource Economics* 11: 173-179.

Mattos, M. and C. Uhl. 1994. Economic and Ecological Perspectives on Ranching in the Eastern Amazon. *World Development* 22: 145-158.

McCalla, A.F. 1994. *Agriculture and Food Needs to 2025: Why We Should be Concerned.* Consultative Group on International Agricultural Research, The World Bank, Washington DC.

McGinn, A.P. 1998. *Promoting Sustainable Fisheries*. Worldwatch Institute, Washington DC.

McGoodwin, J.R. 1995. *Crisis in the World's Fisheries: People, Problems, and Policies*. Stanford University Press, Stanford, California.

McKenna, M. 1994. Power Failure: Let's Pull the Plug on The Federal Energy Program. *Policy Review* 81-86.

McKenzie, K.J. 1995. *An Approach for Measuring Industrial Tax/Subsidy Rates, With a View to Assessing Their Environmental Implications*. Department of Economics, University of Calgary, Calgary, Canada.

McMorran, R.T. and D.C.L. Nellor. 1994. *Tax Policy and the Environment: Theory and Practice*. International Monetary Fund, Washington DC.

McNamara, R.S. 1997. A Vision for Our Nation and the World in the Twenty-First Century. In N.R. Goodwin, F. Ackerman and D. Kiron, eds., *The Consumer Society*. Earthscan, London, U.K.

McPherson, Ch. P. 1996. Policy Reform in Russia's Oil Sector. *Finance and Development* 33(2): 6-9.

McShane, C. 1994. *Down the Asphalt Path: The Automobile and the American City*. Columbia University Press, New York.

Meadows, D.H. 1995. *Home, Home, on the Underpriced, Overgrazed Range*. Department of Environmental Studies, Dartmouth College, Hanover, New Hampshire.

Meher-Homji, V.M. 1992. Probable Impact of Deforestation on Hydrological Processes. In N. Myers, ed., *Tropical Forests and Climate*: 163-174. Kluwer Academic Publishers, Dordrecht, Netherlands.

Mendelsohn, R. and M.J. Balick. 1995. The Value of Undiscovered Pharmaceuticals in Tropical Forests. *Economic Botany* 49: 223-228.

Michaelis, L. 1995. *Environmental Implications of Subsidies to Energy and Transport: Project Summary and Conclusions*. Organisation for Economic Co-operation and Development, Paris, France.

Michaelis, L. 1996. The Environmental Implications of Energy and Transport Subsidies. In *Subsidies and Environment: Exploring the Linkages*: 175-191. Organisation for Economic Co-operation and Development, Paris, France.

Midgley , P. 1994. *Urban Transport in Asia: An Operational Agenda for the 1990s*. The World Bank, Washington DC.

Milazzo, M.J. 1997. *Re-examining Subsidies in World Fisheries*. National Marine Fisheries Service, Washington DC.

Miller, G. (Chairman of Committee). 1994. *Taking from the Taxpayer: Public Subsidies for Natural Resource Development.* Committee on Natural Resources, U.S. House of Representatives, Washington DC.

Miller, P. and J. Moffet. 1993. *The Price of Mobility: Uncovering the Hidden Costs of Transportation.* Natural Resources Defense Council, San Francisco, California.

Ministry of Agriculture, Government of New Zealand. 1995. *Farming for the Market: The New Zealand Experience.* Ministry of Agriculture, Wellington, New Zealand.

Ministry of Agriculture, Government of New Zealand. 1996. *Situation and Outlook for New Zealand Agriculture.* Ministry of Agriculture, Wellington, New Zealand.

Ministry of Defence, Government of the United Kingdom. 1996. *Defence Estimates 1996.* Ministry of Defence, London, U.K.

Moore, M. 1995. *Redefining Integrated Pest Management: Farmer Empowerment and Pesticide Reduction in the Conext of Sustainable Agriculture.* Pesticide Action Network, San Francisco, California.

Moos, E. 1996. *Priorities for Agricultural Trade.* U.S. Department of Agriculture, Washington DC.

Morgan, R. 1994. *Planet Gauge: The Real Facts of Life.* Earthscan, London, U.K.

Morisugi, H. 1997. The Social Costs of Motor Vehicle Use in Japan. In Organisation for Economic Co-operation and Development, *Reforming Energy and Transport Subsidies: Environmental and Economic Implications.* Organisation for Economic Co-operation and Development, Paris, France.

Muller, F. 1997. *Will the Climate Change Convention Shift U.S. Jobs to Developing Countries?* Economic Policy Institute, Washington DC.

Mundle, S. and M.G. Rao. 1991. Volume and Composition of Government Subsidies in India, 1987-88. *Economic and Political Weekly* May 4: 1157-1172.

Murray, D. 1994. *Cultivating Crisis: The Human Cost of Pesticides in Latin America.* University of Texas Press, Austin, Texas.

Murty, J.V.S. 1994. *Watershed Management in India.* Wiley Eastern, New Delhi.

Mussared, D. 1995. Waterworks. *Ecos* 85: 13-16.

Myers, J.H., C. Higgins and E. Kovacs. 1989. How Many Insect Species are Necessary for the Biological Control of Insects? *Environmental Entomology* 18: 541-547.

Myers, N. 1981. The Hamburger Connection: How Central America's Forests Became North America's Hamburgers. *Ambio* 10: 3-8.

Myers, N. 1987. Linking Environment and Security, *Bulletin of the Atomic Scientists* 4 (8): 46-47.

Myers, N. 1992 Tropical Forests: The Policy Challenge. *The Environmentalist* 12: 15-27.

Myers, N. 1993. Tropical Forests: The Main Deforestation Fronts. *Environmental Conservation* 20: 9-16.

Myers, N. 1994. Tropical Deforestation: Rates and Patterns. In K. Brown and D.W. Pearce, eds., *The Causes of Tropical Deforestation*: 27-40. University College London Press, London, UK.

Myers, N. 1995. The World's Forests: Need for a Policy Appraisal. *Science* 268: 823-824.

Myers, N. 1996. Environmental Services of Biodiversity. *Proceedings of U.S. National Academy of Sciences* 93: 2764-2769.

Myers, N. 1997. The World's Forests and Their Ecosystem Services. In G.C. Daily, ed., *Nature's Services: Societal Dependence on Natural Ecosystems*: 215-235. Island Press, Washington DC.

Nadis, S. and J.J. MacKenzie. 1993. *Car Trouble*. World Resources Institute, Washington DC.

Naiman, R.J., J.J. Magnuson, D.M. McKnight and J.A. Stanford. 1995. *The Freshwater Imperative*. Island Press, Washington DC.

Naylor, R.L. and P.R. Ehrlich. 1997. The Value of Natural Pest Control Services in Agriculture. In G.C. Daily, ed., *Nature's Services: Societal Dependence on Natural Ecosystems*: 151-174. Island Press, Washington DC.

Newbury, D.M. 1995. Removing Coal Subsidies: Implications for European Electricity Markets. *Energy Policy* 23: 523-533.

Nilsson, S. 1994. Air Pollution and European Forests. In J. Rose, ed., *Acid Rain: Current Situation and Remedies*. Gordon and Breach Science Publishers, Amsterdam, Netherlands.

Noble, I.R. and R. Dirzo. 1997. Forests and Human-Dominated Ecosystems. *Science* 277: 522-525.

Nordhaus, W.D. 1994. *Managing the Global Commons: The Economics of Climate Change*. MIT Press, Cambridge, Massachusetts.

Norse, E.A., ed. 1993. *Global Marine Biological Diversity Strategy*. Island Press, Washington DC.

Northridge, S. 1991. *The Environmental Impacts of Fisheries in the European Community Waters*. M.R.A.G., Brussels, Belgium.

Northwest Area Foundation. 1994. *A Better Row to Hoe: The Economic, Environmental and Social Impact of Sustainable Agriculture*. Northwest Area Foundation, St. Paul, Minnesota.

Oldeman, L.R., R.T.A. Hakkeling and W.G. Sombroek. 1990. *World Map of the Status of Human-Induced Soil Degradation*. International Soil Reference and Information Centre, Wageningen, Netherlands, and United Nations Environment Programme, Nairobi, Kenya.

Olivecrona, C. 1995. Wind Energy in Denmark. In R. Gale and S. Barg, eds., *Green Budget Reform: An International Casebook of Leading Practices*: 30-54. Earthscan Publications Ltd., London, U.K.

Oppenheimer, T. 1996. The Rancher Subsidy. *The Atlantic Monthly* January 1996: 26-28, 36-38.

Orfeuil, J.-P. 1996. Transport Subsidies and the Environment. In *Subsidies and Environment: Exploring the Linkages*: 163-173. Organisation for Economic Co-operation and Development, Paris, France.

Organisation for Economic Co-operation and Development. 1992. *The Economic Costs of Reducing Carbon Dioxide Emissions*. Organisation for Economic Co-operation and Development, Paris, France.

Organisation for Economic Co-operation and Development. 1993. *Agricultural Policies, Markets and Trade: Monitoring and Outlook, 1993*. Organisation for Economic Co-operation and Development, Paris, France.

Organisation for Economic Co-operation and Development. 1994. *Agricultural Policies, Markets and Trade: Monitoring and Outlook, 1994*. Organisation for Economic Co-operation and Development, Paris, France.

Organisation for Economic Co-operation and Development. 1995. *Sustainable Agriculture: Concepts, Issues and Policies in OECD Countries*. Organisation for Economic Co-operation and Development, Paris, France.

Organisation for Economic Co-operation and Development. 1996. *Subsidies and Environment: Exploring the Linkages*. Organisation for Economic Co-operation and Development, Paris, France.

Organisation for Economic Co-operation and Development. 1997a. *Agricultural Policies in OECD Countries: Monitoring and Evaluation.* Organisation for Economic Co-operation and Development, Paris, France.

Organisation for Economic Co-operation and Development. 1997b. *Reforming Energy and Transport Subsidies: Environmental and Economic Implications.* Organisation for Economic Co-operation and Development, Paris, France.

Organisation for Economic Co-operation and Development, U.S. Environment Protection Agency, and the World Bank. 1995. *The Impact of Russian Energy Subsidies on Greenhouse Gas Emissions.* Organisation for Economic Co-operation and Development, Paris, France.

Ostro, B. 1996. *A Methodology for Estimating Air Pollution Health Effects.* World Health Organization, Geneva, Switzerland.

Ostrom, E,. 1990. *Governing the Commons: The Evolution of Institutions for Collective Action.* Cambridge University Press, Cambridge, U.K.

O'Toole, R. 1993. *1992 TSPIRS Recalculations.* Cascade Holistic Economic Consultants, Oak Grove, Oregon.

O'Toole, R. 1995. *Timber Sale Subsidies, But Who Gets Them?* Thoreau Institute, Oak Grove, Oregon.

Paarlberg, R. 1989. The Farm Policy Agenda: It's Time to Change it. *Choice* 4 (2): 22-23.

Paarlberg, R.L. 1996. Caring for the Future: Minimizing Change or Maximizing Choice, In N.R. Goodwin, ed. *As If the Future Mattered*: 186-207. University of Michigan Press, Ann Arbor, Michigan.

Paarlberg, R. and D. Orden. 1996. Explaining U.S. Farm Policy in 1996 and Beyond. *American Journal of Agricultural Economics* 78: 1305-1313.

Pachauri, R.K. 1994. *The Energy Scene in India—Last Two Decades.* Tata Energy Research Institute, Delhi, India, for the World Resources Institute, Washington DC.

Pagiola, S., J. Kellenberg, L. Vidaeus and J. Srivastava. 1997. Mainstreaming Biodiversity in Agricultural Development: Toward Good Practice, cited in World Bank, 1997, *Expanding the Measure of Wealth.* The World Bank, Washington DC.

Panayotou, T. 1993. *Green Markets.* Institute for Contemporary Studies Press, San Francisco, California.

Panayotou, T. 1995. *Matrix of Financial Instruments and Policy Options: A New Approach to Financing Sustainable Development.* Harvard Institute for International Development, Cambridge, Massachusetts.

Panayotou, T. 1997. Win-Win Finance. *Our Planet* (publication of the United Nations Environment Programme) 9(1): 15-18.

Panayotou, T. and P.S. Ashton. 1992. *Not by Timber Alone.* Island Press, Washington DC.

Papendick, R.I., L.F. Elliott and R.B. Dahlgren. 1986. Environmental Consequences of Modern Production Agriculture: How Can Alternative Agriculture Address These Issues and Concerns? *American Journal of Alternative Agriculture* 1: 3-10.

Paris, R. and I. Ruzicka. 1991. *Barking Up the Wrong Tree: The Role of Rent Appropriation in Sustainable Forest Management.* Asian Development Bank, Manila, Philippines.

Parris, K. 1997. Environmental Indicators for Agriculture. *OECD Observer* 203:

Parris, K. and J. Melanie. 1993. Japan's Agriculture and Environmental Policies: Time to Change. *Agriculture and Resources Quarterly* 5: 386- 399.

Parry, I.W.H. 1993. Some Estimates of the Insurance Value Against Climate Change from Reducing Greenhouse Gas Emissions. *Resources and Energy Economics* 15: 99-115.

Pauly, D., V. Christensen, J. Dalsgaard, R. Froese, and F. Torres Jr. 1998. Fishing Down Marine Food Webs. *Science* 279: 860-863.

Pearce, D.W. 1993. *Economic Values and the Natural World.* Earthscan, London, U.K.

Pearce, D.W. 1995. *Blueprint 4: Capturing Global Environmental Values.* Earthscan, London, U.K.

Pearce, D.W. and G. Atkinson. 1992. *Are National Economies Sustainable? Measuring Sustainable Development.* CSERGE, University College, London, U.K.

Pearce, D. and S. Puroshothaman. 1993. *Protecting Biological Diversity: The Economic Value of Pharmaceutical Plants.* Centre for Social and Economic Research into the Global Environment, University College London, London, U.K.

Pearce, D.W. and J.J. Warford. 1993. *World Without End: Economics, Environment, and Sustainable Development.* Oxford University Press, New York.

Pearce, D., D. Maddison, N. Adger and H. McLeod. 1996. *Government Subsidies with Unintended Environmental Effects.* Centre for Social and Economic Research on the Global Environment, University College, London, U.K.

Pearce, D.W., W.R. Cline, A.N. Achanta, S. Fankhauser, R.K. Pachauri, R.S.J. Tol and P. Vellinga. 1996. The Social Costs of Climate Change: Greenhouse Damage and the Benefits of Control. In *The Science of Climate Change: The Second Assessment Report of the Intergovernmental Panel on Climate Change, 3rd vol*: 183-189. Cambridge University Press, Cambridge, U.K.

Perlack, R., M. Russell and Z. Shen. 1993. Reducing Greenhouse Gas Emissions in China. *Global Environmental Change* 3: 78-100

Pigou, A.C. 1920. *The Economics of Welfare.* Macmillan, London, U.K.

Pigou, A.C. 1950. *The Economics of Welfare* second edition. Macmillan, London, U.K.

Pimentel, D. 1991. Ethanol Fuels: Energy Security, Economics, and the Environment. *Journal of Agricultural and Environmental Ethics.* 1-13

Pimentel, D., ed. 1991. *Handbook of Pest Management In Agriculture*, second edition. C.R.C. Press, Boca Raton, Florida.

Pimentel, D. 1992. Diversification of Biological Control Strategies in Agriculture. *Cr p Protection* 10: 243-253.

Pimentel, D.M., ed. 1997. *Techniques for Reducing Pesticide Use: Economic and Environmental Benefits.* John Wiley, Chichester, U.K.

Pimentel, D. et al., 1992. Conserving Biological Diversity in Agricultural/Forestry Systems. *BioScience* 42: 354-362.

Pimentel, D. and A. Grinier. 1997. Environmental and Socio-Economic Costs of Pesticide Use. In D. Pimentel, ed., *Techniques for Reducing Pesticide Use: Economic and Environmental Benefits*: 51-78. John Wiley, Chichester, U.K.

Pimentel, D. and H. Lehman, eds. 1993. *The Pesticide Question: Environment, Economics, Ethics.* Chapman and Hall, London, U.K.

Pimentel, D. and M. Pimentel, eds. 1996. *Food, Energy and Society* (revised edition). University Press of Colorado, Boulder, Colorado.

Pimentel, D. and ten others. 1995. Environmental and Economic Costs of Soil Erosion and Conservation Benefits. *Science* 267: 1117-1122

Pimentel, D. and eight others. 1997a. Economic and Environmental Benefits of Biodiversity. *BioScience* 47: 747-757.

Pimentel, D. X. Huang, A. Cordova and M. Pimentel. 1997b. Impact of Population Growth on Food Supplies and Environment. *Population and Development Review.*

Pimentel, D. and ten others. 1997c. Water Resources: Agriculture, The Environment and Society. *BioScience* 47: 97-106.

Pimentel, D., M. McNair, L. Buck, M. Pimentel and J. Kamil. 1997d. The Value of Forests to World Food Security. *Human Ecology* 25: 91-120.

Pinkham, R. and S. Chaplin. 1996. *Water 2010: Four Scenarios for 21st Century Water Systems.* Rocky Mountain Institute, Snowmass, Colorado.

Pinkham, R., A.B. Lovins and L.H. Lovins. 1994. *Let's Tap Water Efficiency Before Spending on Treatment.* Rocky Mountain Institute, Snowmass, Colorado.

Pinstrup-Andersen, P. 1988. *Food Subsidies in Developing Countries: Costs, Benefits, and Policy Options.* Johns Hopkins University Press, Baltime, Maryland.

Pinstrup-Andersen, P. 1994. *World Food Trends and Future Food Security.* International Food Policy Research Institute, Washington DC.

Pinstrup-Andersen, P. and R. Pandya-Lorch. 1995. *The Future Food and Agricultural Situation in Developing Countries, and the Role of Research and Training.* International Food Policy Research Institute, Washington DC.

Pittman, P., D. Katz and J. Lancelot. 1997. *Clearcutting Virgin Rainforest on the Tongass: $100 Million.* Natural Resources Defense Council and Taxpayers for Commonsense, Washington DC.

Poboon, C., J. Kenworthy, P. Newman and P. Barter, 1994. *Bangkok: Anatomoy of a Traffic Disaster.* Institute for Science and Technology Policy, Murdoch University, Perth, Australia.

Poore, D., P. Burgess, J. Palmer, S. Rietbergen and T. Synott. 1989. *No Timber Without Trees.* Earthscan, London, U.K.

Pope, C., M. Thun, M. Namboodin, D. Dokery, J. Evans, F. Speizer and C. Heath. 1995. Particulate Air Pollution as Predictor of Mortality in a Perspective Study of U.S. Adults. *American Journal of Respiratory and Critical Care Medicine* 151: 669-674.

Porter, G. 1997. *Fisheries Subsidies, Overfishing and Trade.* Center for International Environmental Law, Washington DC.

Postel, S. 1996. *Dividing the Waters: Food Security, Ecosystem Health and the New Politics of Scarcity.* Worldwatch Institute, Washington DC.

Postel, S. 1997a. Dividing the Waters. *Technology Review* April 1997: 54- 62.

Postel, S. 1997b. *Last Oasis* (revised edition). W.W. Norton, New York.

Postel, S. and S. Carpenter. 1997. Freshwater Ecosystem Services. In G.C. Daily, ed., *Nature's Services: Societal Dependence on Natural Ecosystems*: 195-214. Island Press, Washington DC.

Potter, C. 1997. *Against the Grain: Agri-Environmental Reform in the United States and the European Union.* CAB International, Wallingford, U.K.

Power, T.M. 1996. *Lost Landscapes and Failed Economies.* Island Press, Washington DC.

Praveen, J. 1994. The Short-Run Trade-Off Between Food Subsidies and Agricultural Production Subsidies in Developing Countries. *Journal of Developing Studies* 31: 265-278.

Pretty, J.N. 1995. *Regenerating Agriculture: Policies and Practices for Sustainability and Self-Reliance.* Earthscan, London, U.K.

Pretty, J.N. 1996. Sustainability Works. *Our Planet* 8(4): 19-22.

Princeton, M.L. 1996b. Conditionality and Logging Reforms in the Tropics. In R.O. Keohane and M.A. Levy, eds. *Institutions for Environmental Aid— Pitfalls and Promises*: 176-197. MIT Press, Cambridge, Massachusetts.

Principe, P. 1996. Monetizing the Pharmacological Benefits of Plants. In M.J. Balick, W. Elisabetsky and S. Laird, eds., *Tropical Forest Medical Resources and the Conservation of Biodiversity*: 191-218. Columbia University Press, New York.

Proxmire, W. 1997. *Japan Gets the Logs and the United States Get Rolled.* Office of Senator William Proxmire, Senate Office Building, Washington DC.

Radetski, M. 1995. Elimination of West European Coal Subsidies: Implications for Coal Produoduction and Coal Imports. *Energy Policy* 23: 509-518.

Rajkumar, A.S. 1996. *Energy Subsidies.* The World Bank, Washington DC.

Reddy, A.K.N., R.H. Williams and T.B. Johansson. 1997. *Energy After Rio: Prospects and Challenges.* United Nations Development Programme, New York.

Reed Sturgess and Associates. 1994. *Economic Evaluation of Wood and Water from the Thomson Catchment.* Melbourne Water and the Department of Conservation and Natural Resources, Melbourne, Australia.

Reisner, M. 1996. *Cadillac Desert: The American West and Its Disappearing Water.* Viking, New York.

Repetto, R. 1985. *Paying the Price: Pesticide Subsidies in Developing Countries.* World Resources Institute, Washington DC.

Repetto, R. 1986. *Skimming the Water: Rent Seeking and the Performance of Public Irrigation Systems.* World Resources Institute, Washington DC.

Repetto, R. 1987. Population, Resources, Environment: An Uncertain Future. *Population Bulletin* 42(2). Population Reference Bureau, Washington DC.

Repetto, R. 1988. *The Forest For the Trees? Government Policies and the Misuse of Forest Resources.* World Resources Institute, Washington DC.

Repetto, R. 1990. *Macroeconomic Policies and Deforestation.* United Nations University, Tokyo, Japan, and WIDER, Helsinki, Finland.

Repetto, R. 1994. *The "Second India" Revisited: Population, Poverty, and Environmental Stress Over Two Decades.* World Resources Institute, Washington DC.

Repetto, R. 1995. *Jobs, Competitiveness, and Environmental Regulation: What are the Real Issues?* World Resources Institute, Washington DC.

Repetto, R. and D. Austin. 1997. *The Costs of Climate Protection: A Guide for the Perplexed.* World Resources Institute, Washington DC.

Repetto, R. and S.S. Baliga. 1996. *Pesticides and the Immune System: Public Health Risks.* World Resources Institute, Washington DC.

Repetto, R. and T. Bradley. 1997. *Fiscal Reform for Sustainable Development.* World Resources Institute, Washington DC.

Repetto, R. and M. Gillis. 1988. *Public Policies and the Misuse of Forest Resources.* Cambridge University Press, Cambridge, U.K.

Repetto, R. and J. Lash. 1997. Planetary Roulette: Gambling with the Climate. *Foreign Policy* 108: 84-98.

Repetto, R., W. Magrath, M. Wells, C. Beer and F. Rossini. 1989. *Wasting Assets: Natural Resources in the National Income Accounts.* World Resources Institute, Washington DC.

Reynolds, R., W. Moore, M.A. Worsop and M. Storey. 1993. *Impacts on the Environment of Reduced Agricultural Subsidies: A Case Study of New Zealand.* Ministry of Agriculture and Fisheries, Wellington, New Zealand.

Richardson, S.D. 1990. *Forests and Forestry in China: Changing Patterns of Resource Development.* Island Press, Washington DC.

Rind, D., R. Goldberg, J. Hansen, C. Rosenzweig and R. Ruedy. 1990. Potential Evapotranspiration and the Likelihood of Future Drought. *Journal of Geophysical Research* 95: 9983-10,004.

Ritson, C. and D. Harvey, eds. 1995. *The CAP and the World Economy*. CAB International, Wallingford, U.K.

Rocky Mountain Institute. 1992. *Farm Subsidies: Consequences and Alternatives*. Rocky Mountain Institute, Old Snowmass, Colorado.

Rodhe, H., J. Galloway and D. Zhao. 1992. Acidification in South-East Asia—Prospects for the Coming Decades. *Ambio* 21: 148-150.

Roelofs, C. and C. Komanoff. 1994. *Subsidies for Traffic: How Taxpayer Dollars Underwrite Driving in New York State*. Konheim and Ketcham, Brooklyn, New York.

Rogers, P. 1992. *Economic and Institutional Issues: International River Basins*. The World Bank, Washington DC.

Roodman, D.M. 1995. Public Money and Human Purpose: The Future of Taxes. *World Watch* 8 (5): 10-19.

Roodman, D.M. 1996. *Paying the Piper: Subsidies, Politics and the Environment*. Worldwatch Institute, Washington DC.

Roodman, D.M. 1996. Harnessing the Market for the Environment. In L.R. Brown et al., eds. *State of the World 1996*: 168-187. W.W. Norton, New York.

Roodman, D.M. 1997. *Getting the Signals Right: Tax Reform to Protect the Environment and the Economy*. Worldwatch Institute, Washington DC.

Roodman, D.M. and N. Lenssen. 1995. *A Building Revolution: How Ecology and Health Concerns are Transforming Construction*. The Worldwatch Institute, Washington DC.

Rosegrant, M.W. 1995. *Dealing with Water Scarcity in the Next Century*. International Food Policy Research Institute, Washington DC.

Rosegrant, M.W. 1997. *Water Resources in the Twenty-First Century: Challenges and Implications for Action*. International Food Policy Research Institute, Washington DC.

Rosegrant, M.W. and P.L. Pingall. 1991. *Sustaining Rice Productivity Growth in Asia: A Policy Perspective*. International Rice Research Institute, Manila, Philippines.

Rosegrant, M.W. and R. Gazmuri-Schleyer. 1995. *Reforming Water Allocation Policy through Markets in Tradeable Water Rights*. International Food Policy Research Institute, Washington DC.

Rosegrant, M. and R. Gazmuri-Schleyer. 1996. Establishing Tradeable Water Rights: Implementation of the Mexican Water Law. *Irrigation and Drainage Systems* 10: 263-279.

Rosegrant, M., R. Gazmuri-Schleyer and S. Yadav. 1995. Water Policy for Efficient Agricultural Diversification: Market-Based Approaches. *Food Policy* 20: 203-223.

Rosegrant, M.W., C. Ringler and R.V. Gerpacio. 1997. *Water and Land Resources and Global Food Supply.* International Food Policy Research Institute, Washington DC.

Ross, M.L. 1996a. *The Political Economy of Boom and Bust Logging in Indonesia, the Philippines, and East Malaysia 1950-1994.* Ph. D. dissertation, Dept. of Political Science, Princeton University, Princeton, New Jersey.

Ross, M. 1996b. Conditionality and Logging Reforms in the Tropics. In R.O., Keohane and M.A. Levy, eds. *Institutions for Environmental Aid: Pitfalls and Promise*: 176-197. MIT Press, Cambridge, Massachusetts.

Rothengatter, W. and S. Mauch. 1994. *External Effects of Transport.* Union Internationale des Chemin de Fers, Paris, France.

Ruijgrok, E. and F. Oosterhuis. 1997. *Energy Subsidies in Western Europe.* Institute of Environmental Studies, Free University of Amsterdam, Amsterdam, Netherlands (for Greenpeace International, Amsterdam, Netherlands).

Runge, C.F. 1994. The Environmental Effects of Trade on the Agricultural Sector. In *The Environmental Effects of Trade*: 19-54. Organisation for Economic Co-operation and Development, Paris, France.

Runge, C.F. 1996. Environmental Impacts of Agriculture and Forestry Subsidies. In *Subsidies and the Environment: Exploring the Linkages*: 139- 161. Organisation for Economic Co-operation and Development, Paris, France.

Runge, C.F. and T. Jones. 1996. *Subsidies, Tax Disincentives and the Environment: An Overview and Synthesis. Subsidies and Environment: Exploring the Linkages:* 7-21. Organisation for Economic Co-operation and Development, Paris, France.

Ryan, J.C. 1995. *Hazardous Handouts: Taxpayer Subsidies to Environmental Degradation.* Northwest Environment Watch, Seattle, Washington.

Ryan, M. and C. Flavin. 1995. Facing China's Limits. In L.R. Brown and 12 others *State of the World 1995*: 113-131. W.W. Norton, New York.

Rylander, J.C. 1996. Accounting for Nature: A Look at Attempts to Fashion a "Green GDP". *Renewable Resources Journal* (summer).

Safina, C. 1994. Where Have All The Fishes Gone? *Issues in Science and Technology* 10 (3): 37-43.

Safina, C. 1995. The World's Imperiled Fish. *Scientific American* 273 (5): 30-37.

Safina, C. 1998. *Song for the Blue Ocean*. Henry Holt Publishers, New York.

Salati, E. and C.A. Nobre. 1992. Possible Climatic Impacts of Tropical Deforestation. In N. Myers, ed., *Tropical Forests and Climate*: 177-196. Kluwer Academic Publishers, Dordrecht, Netherlands.

Sampath, R.K. 1992. Issues in Irrigation Pricing in Developing Countries. *World Development* 20: 967-977.

Sandrey, R. and R. Reynolds, eds. 1990. *Farming Without Subsidies: New Zealand's Recent Experience*. GP Books, Wellington, New Zealand.

Schiff, M. and A. Valdes. 1992. *The Plundering of Agriculture in Developing Countries*. The World Bank, Washington DC.

Schlesinger, A.M., Jr. 1986. *The Cycles of American History* (not available for checking).

Schneider, R. 1992. *Brazil: An Anlysis of Environmental Problems in the Amazon*. The World Bank, Washington DC.

Schneider, R. 1995. *Government and the Economy on the Amazon Frontier*. The World Bank, Washington DC.

Schoonmaker, P.K., B. von Hagen and E.C. Wolf, eds. 1996. *The Rain Forests of Home: Profile of a North American Bioregion*. Island Press, Washington DC.

Schrank, W.E. 1997. The Newfoundland Fishery: Past, Present and Future. In World Wide Fund for Nature International, *Subsidies and Depletion of World Fisheries*: 35-70. World Wide Fund for Nature International, Gland, Switzerland.

Seckler, D. 1993. *Designing Water Resources Strategies for the Twenty-First Century*. Winrock International, Arlington, Virginia.

Seckler, D. 1996. The New Era of Water Resources Management: From "Dry" to "Wet" Water Savings. *Issues in Agriculture* 8, Consultative Group on International Agricultural Research, The World Bank, Washington DC.

Serageldin, I. 1993. *Toward Sustainable Management of Water Resources*. The World Bank, Washington DC.

Serageldin, I. 1994. *Water Supply, Sanitation, and Environmental Sustainability: The Financing Challenge*. The World Bank, Washington DC.

Serageldin, I. 1995. *Sustainability and the Wealth of Nations: First Steps in an On-Going Journey*. The World Bank, Washington DC.

Serageldin, I. 1996. Beating the Water Crisis. *Our Planet* 8(3): 4-7.

Shaefer, A. and D. Victor. 1997. The Past and Future of Global Mobility. *Scientific American* 277 (4): 58-63.

Shah, T. 1993. *Groundwater Markets and Irrigation Development—Political Economy and Practical Policy*. Oxford University Press, Bombay, India.

Shapiro, R.J. and C.J. Soares. 1997. *Cut and Invest to Grow: How to Expand Public Investment Whilst Cutting the Deficit*. Progressive Policy Institute, Washington DC.

Sharma, N., ed. 1992 *Managing the World's Forests: Looking for Balance Betweeen Conservation and Development*. Kendall/Hunt Publishers, Dubuque.

Shelby, M.A., A. Cristofaro, B. Shackleton and B. Schillo. 1994. *The Climate Implications of Eliminating U.S. Energy and Related Subsidies*. Organisation for Economic Co-operation and Development, Paris, France.

Shelby, M. et al. 1995. *The Climate Change Implications of Eliminating US Energy and Related Subsidies*. U.S. Environmental Protection Agency, Washington DC.

Shepherd, A.A. 1996. *New Zealand: The Environmental Effects of Removing Agricultural Subsidies*. Organisation for Economic Co-operation and Development, Paris, France.

Shoup, D. 1992. *Cashing Out Employer Paid Parking*. Federal Transit Administration, Washington DC.

Shoup, D. 1994. *Curbing Gridlock: Peak-Period Fees to Relieve Traffic Congestion*. National Research Council, Washington DC.

Shoup, D. and Wilson. 1990. cited in Nadis and MazKenzie, 1993.

Shprentz, D.S., G.C. Bryner and J.S. Shprentz. 1996. *Breath Taking: Premature Mortality Due to Particle Air Pollution in 239 American Cities*. Natural Resources Defense Council, New York.

Shukla, J., C. Nobre and P. Sellers. 1990. Amazon Deforestation and Climate Change. *Science* 247: 1322-1325.

Shuldiner, A. and T. Raymond. 1998. *Who's in the Lobby?* Center for Responsive Politics, Washington DC.

Shvidenko, A.Z. and S. Nilsson. 1994. What do we Know About the Siberian Forests? *Ambio* 23: 396-404.

Sinclair, D. 1987. Government Irrigation Subsidies Result in Huge Economic and Environmental Losses Worldwide. *Ambio* 16: 149-151.

Sinner, J., I. Cairns, M. Storey and B. Warmington. 1995. *Agri-Environmental Programmes in New Zealand: A Report to the OECD*. Ministry of Agriculture, Wellington, New Zealand.

Sissenwine, M.P. and A.A. Rosenberg. 1993. Marine Fisheries at a Critical Juncture. *Fisheries* 18 (10): 6-14.

Small, K.A. and C. Kazimi. 1995. On the Costs of Air Pollution from Motor Vehicles. *Journal of Transport Economics and Policy* 29: 7-32.

Smil, V. 1992. *Environmental Change as a Source of Conflict and Economic Loss in China*. American Academy of Arts and Sciences, Cambridge, Massachusetts.

Smil, V. 1997. China Shoulders the Cost of Environmental Change. *Environment* 39 (6).

Smil, V. 1997. Global Population and the Nitrogen Cycle. *Scientific American* 277 (1): 76-81.

Smil, V. and M. Yushi, 1998. *The Economic Costs of China's Environmental Degradation*. American Academy of Arts and Sciences, Cambridge, Massachusetts.

Smith, N. 1996. *Floods of Fortune: Ecology and Economy Along the Amazon River*. Columbia University Press, New York.

Smith, T.M. and H.H. Shugart. 1993. The Transient Response of Terrestrial Carbon Storage to a Perturbed Climate. *Nature* 361: 523-526.

Snape, R. H. 1991. International Regulation of Subsidies. *The World Economy* 14: 139-164.

Soden, K. 1988. *United States Farm Subsidies*. Rocky Mountain Institute, Old Snowmass, Colorado.

Sopuck, R.D. 1993. *Canada's Agricultural and Trade Policies: Implications for Rural Renewal and Biodiversity*. National Round Table on the Environment and the Economy, Ottawa, Canada.

Soule, J.D. and J.K. Piper. 1992. *Farming in Nature's Image: An Ecological Approach to Agriculture*. Island Press, Washington DC.

Southgate, D. 1995. Economic Progress and Habitat Conservation in Latin America. In T.M. Swanson, editor, *The Economics and Ecology of Biodiversity Decline: The Forces Driving Global Change*: 91-98. Cambridge University Press, Cambridge, U.K.

Southgate, D., ed. 1997. *Alternatives to Tropical Deforestation*. Oxford University Press, New York.

Spinelli, F. 1994. *Farming without Subsidies in New Zealand.* U.S. Department of Agriculture, Washington DC.

Steenblik, R.P. 1995. A Note on the Concept of 'Subsidy'. *Energy Policy* 23: 483-484.

Steenblik, R. 1997. When Farmers Fend for the Environment. *The OECD Observer* 203: 16-17.

Steenblik, R.P. and P. Coroyannakis. 1995. Reform of Coal Policies in Western and Central Europe: Implication for the Environment. *Energy Policy* 537-553.

Steenblik, R.P. and K.J. Wigley. 1990. Coal Policies and Trade Barriers. *Energy Policy* 18: 351-367.

Sterner, T. 1989. Oil Products in Latin America: The Politics of Energy Pricing. *Energy Journal* 10 (2) 25-45.

Sterner, T. 1996. Tax Expenditures and the Environment. In *Subsidies and Environment: Exploring the Linkages*: 81-97. Organisation for Economic Co-operation and Development, Paris, France.

Stevens, G. 1997. The Pros and Cons of Nuclear Energy. *OECD Observer* 206: 38-40.

Stoeckel, A.B., D. Vincent and S. Cuthbertson, eds. 1989. *Macroeconomic Consequences of Farm Support Policies*. Duke University Press, Durham, North Carolina.

Strachan, L. et al., 1994. A National Survey of Asthms Prevalence, Severity and Treatment in Great Britain. *Archives of Disease in Childhood* 70: 174-178.

Sumner, D.A. 1995. *Agricultural Policy Reform in the United States*. American Enterprise Institute Press, Washington DC.

Sutton, M. 1996. *A New Paradigm for Managing Marine Fisheries in the Next Milennium*. World Wide Fund for Nature, Godalming, U.K.

Swaminathan, M.S. 1996. *Sustainable Agriculture: Towards Food Security*. Konark Publishers Ltd., Delhi, India.

Swinnen, J. and F.A. Van der Zee. 1993. The Political Economy of Agricultural Policies: A Survey. *European Review of Agricultural Economics* 20: 261-290.

Swiss Re. 1995. *Global Warming: Element of Risk*. Swiss Re, Zurich, Switzerland.

Templet, P.H. 1995. Grazing the Commons: An Empirical Analysis of Externalities, Subsidies and Sustainability. *Ecological Economics* 12: 141-159.

Thorne-Miller, B. and J. Catena. 1991. *The Living Ocean*. Island Press, Washington DC.

Thorpe, J., G. Graham, J. Lanna and C. Nash. 1995. *Conservation of Fish and Shellfish*. Academic Press, London, U.K.

Thrupp, L.A. 1995. *Institutional and Policy Factors in Pest Management Reforms*. World Resources Institute, Washington DC.

Thrupp, A. 1996. *Partnerships for Safe and Sustainable Agriculture*. World Resources Institute, Washington DC.

Thurman, W.N. 1995. *Assessing the Environmental Impact of Farm Policies*. American Enterprise Institute, Washington DC.

Tinker, I. 1990. The Real Rural Energy Crisis: Womens' Time. In A.V. DeSai, ed. *Human Energy*. Wiley, New Delhi, India.

Titus, J. 1992. The Cost of Climate Change in the United States. In S.K. Majumdamdar et al., eds., *Global Climate Change: Implications, Challenges and Mitigation Measures*. Pennsylvania Academy of Sciences, Philadalephia, Pa.

Tol, R.S.J. 1995. The Damage Costs of Climate Change: Towards More Comprehensive Calculations. *Environmental and Resource Economics* 5: 353-374.

Tolman, J. 1996. *Federal Agricultural Policy: A Harvest of Environmental Abuse*. Competitive Enterprise Institute, Washington DC.

Toman, M. 1995. *Analyzing the Environmental Impacts of Subsidies: Issues and Research Directions*. Resources for the Future, Washington DC.

Toman, M. 1996. Analysing the Environmental Impacts of Subsidies: Issues and Research Directions. In *Subsidies and Environment: Exploring the Linkages*: 43-51. Organisation for Economic Co-operation and Development, Paris, France.

Transportation Research Board. 1997. *Toward a Sustainable Future: Addressing the Long-Term Effects of Motor Vehicle Transportation on Climate and Ecology*. National Academy Press, Washington DC.

Tsuar, R. and A. Dinar. 1995. *Efficiency and Equity Considerations in Pricing and Allocating Irrigation Water*. The World Bank, Washington DC.

Tucker, M. 1997. Climate Change and The Insurance Industry: The Cost of Increased Risk and the Impetus for Action. *Ecological Economics* 22: 85- 96.

Tweeten, L. 1992. The Economics of an Environmentally Sound Agriculture. *Research in Domestic and International Agribusiness Management* 10: 39- 83.

Tweeten, L. and C. Zulauf. 1997. Pubic Policy for Agriculture After Commodity Programs. *Review of Agricultural Economics* 19: 263-280.

Uhl, C., P. Barreto, A. Verissimo and E. Vidal. 1997. Natural Resource Management in the Brazilian Amazon: An Integrated Research Approach. *BioScience* 47: 160-168.

U.K. Department of Health. 1995. *Asthma: An Epediomological Overview*. Her Majesty's Stationery Office, London, U.K.

U.K. Royal Commission on Environmental Pollution. 1994. *Transport and the Environment*. Her Majesty's Stationery Office, London, U.K.

Umali, D.L. 1993. *Irrigation Induced Salinity*. The World Bank, Washington DC.

United Nations. 1992. *AGENDA 21 of the United Nations Conference on Environment and Development*. United Nations, New York.

United Nations. 1995. *Energy Statistics Yearbook*. United Nations, New York.

United Nations. 1997. *Comprehensive Assessment of Freshwater Resources of the World*. The United Nations, New York.

U.N. Commission on Sustainable Development. 1994. *Financial Resources and Mechanisms for Sustainable Development: Overview of Current Issues and Development*. U.N. Commission on Sustainable Development, United Nations, New York.

United Nations Development Programme. 1994. *Human Development Report 1994*. Oxford University Press, New York.

United Nations Development Programme. 1997. *Human Development Report 1997*. Oxford University Press, New York.

U.S. Congressional Research Service. 1992. *The External Costs of Oil Used in Transport*. U.S. Congressional Research Service, Washington DC.

U.S. Department of Agriculture. 1994a. *Agricultural Resources and Environmental Indicators*. Economic Research Service, U.S. Department of Agriculture, Washington DC.

U.S. Department of Agriculture. 1994b. *Estimates of Producer and Consumer Subsidy Equivalents: Government Intervention in Agriculture, 1982-92*. Economic Research Service, U.S. Department of Agriculture, Washington DC.

U.S. Department of Agriculture. 1995. *Agricultural Income and Finance*. Economic Research Service, U.S. Department of Agriculture, Washington DC.

U.S. Department of Energy. 1992. *Federal Energy Subsidies: Direct and Indirect Interventions in Energy Markets.* Government Printing Office, Washington DC.

U.S. Department of Energy. 1995. *The United States Energy Profile.* U.S. Department of Energy, Washington DC.

U.S. Department of Energy. 1996. *Annual Energy Review 1995.* Energy Information Administration, U.S. Department of Energy, Washington DC.

U.S. Energy Information Administration. 1992. *Federal Energy Subsidies: Direct and Indirect Interventions in Energy Markets.* Energy Information Administration, Washington DC.

U.S. Environmental Protection Agency. 1997. *The Benefits and Costs of the Clean Air Act, 1970-1990.* U.S. Environmental Protection Agency, Washington DC.

U.S. Forest Service. 1993. *Timber Sale Program Annual Report: Fiscal Year 1992.* U.S. Department of Agriculture, Washington DC.

U.S. Geological Survey. 1990. *National Water Summary, 1987.* Government Printing Office, Washington DC.

U.S. National Fish and Wildlife Foundation. 1992. *FY 1993 Fisheries and Wildlife Assessment.* National Oceanic and Atmospheric Administration, Washington DC.

U.S. National Fish and Wildlife Foundation. 1995. *FY 1996 Fisheries and Wildlife Assessment.* U.S. National Fish and Wildlife Foundation, Washington DC.

U.S. National Marine Fisheries Service. 1992. *Our Living Oceans: Second Annual Report on the Status of U.S. Living Marine Resources.* U.S. Department of Commerce, Washington DC.

U.S. National Oceanic and Atmospheric Administration/National Marine Fisheries Service. 1994. *Report of the 17th Northeast Regional Stock Assessment Workshop.* U.S. Department of Commerce, Washington DC.

U.S. National Research Council. 1989. *Alternative Agriculture.* National Academy of Sciences Press, Washington DC.

U.S. National Research Council. 1994. *Curbing Gridlock: Peak-Period Fees to Relieve Traffic Congestion.* National Academy of Sciences, Washington DC.

U.S. National Research Council. 1995a. *Ecologically Based Pest Management: New Solutions for a New Century.* National Research Council, Washington DC.

U.S. National Research Council. 1995b. *Understanding Marine Biodiversity.* National Academy Press, Washington DC.

Vaidyanathan, A. 1993. *Second India Series Revisited: Food and Agriculture.* Madras Institute of Development Studies, Madras, India, for The World Resources Institute, Washington DC.

van der Leeden, F., F.L. Troise and D.K. Todd. 1990. *The Water Encyclopedia,* 2nd edition. Lewis Publishers, Chelsea, Michigan

van der Voet, E., R. Kleijn and U. de Haes. 1996. Nitrogen Pollution in the European Union: Origins and Proposed Solutions. *Environmental Conservation* 23: 120-132.

van Dyke, J.N., D. Zaelke and G. Hewison. 1994. *Freedom for the Seas in the 21st Century: Ocean Governance and Environmental Harmony.* Earthscan, London, U.K.

Verissimo, A., et a.. 1992. Logging Impacts and Prospects for Sustainable Forest Management in an Old Amazonian Frontier: The Case of Paragominas. *Forest Ecology and Management* 55: 169-199.

Verplaneke, E.B.A., DeStooper and M.F.L. de Boot. 1992. *Water Saving Techniques for Plant Growth.* Kluwer, Dordrecht, Netherlands.

Vincent, J.R., 1990, Don't Boycott Tropical Timber. *Journal of Forestry* 88 (4): 56

Vincent, J.R. 1992. The Tropical Timber Trade and Sustainable Development. *Science* 256: 1651-1655.

Vincent, J.R. 1995. Timber Trade, Economics, and Tropical Forest Management. In R.B. Primack and T.E. Lovejoy, eds., *Ecology, Conservation and Management of Southeast Asian Rainforests:* 241-262. Yale University Press, New Haven, Connecticut.

Vincent, J.R. and D. Fairman. 1995. *Multilateral Consultations for Promoting Sustainable Development Through Domestic Policy Changes.* Harvard Institute for International Development, Cambridge, Massachusetts.

Vincent, J.R., A.N.A. Ghani and H. Yusuf. 1993. *Economics of Timber Fees and Logging in Tropical Forest Concessions.* Harvard Institute for International Development, Cambridge, Massachusetts.

Vitousek, P.M. 1994. Beyond Global Warming: Ecology and Global Change. *Ecology* 75: 1861-1876.

von Amsberg, J. 1994. *Economic Parameters of Deforestation.* The World Bank, Washington DC.

von Weizsacker, E.U. and J. Jesinghous. 1992. *Ecological Tax Reform: A Policy Proposal for Sustainable Development*. Zed Books, London, U.K.

von Weizsacker, E.U., A.B. Lovins and L.H. Lovins. 1997. *Factor Four: Doubling Wealth, Halving Resource Use*. Earthscan, London, U.K.

Vorley, B. and D. Keeney, eds. 1997. *Bugs in the System: Reinventing the Pesticide Industry for Sustainable Agriculture*. Earthscan, London, U.K.

Walker, A. and B. Bell. 1994. *Aspects of New Zealand's Experience in Agricultural Reform Since 1984*. Ministry of Agriculture, Wellington, New Zealand.

Wallace, B. 1997. The Multidimensional Nature of Population/ Environmental Problems. *Politics and the Life Sciences* 16: 224-226.

Wang, X. 1996. *China's Coal Sector: Moving to a Market Economy*. The World Bank, Washington DC.

Ward, J. et al., 1989. *Reaping the Revenue Code: Why We Need Sensible Tax Reform for Sustainable Agriculture*. Natural Resources Defense Council, New York.

Watkins, K. ed. 1995. *The Oxfam Poverty Report*. Oxfam, Oxford, U.K.

Watson, R.T., M.C. Zinyowera et al., eds. 1996. *Climate Change 1995: Impacts, Adaptations and Mitigation of Climate Change*. Cambridge University Press, Cambridge, U.K.

Weber, P. 1993. *Abandoned Seas: Reversing the Decline of the Oceans*. Worldwatch Institute, Washington DC.

Weber, P. 1994. *Net Loss: Fish, Jobs and the Marine Environment*. Worldwatch Institute, Washington DC.

Weber, M.L. 1995. *A History of Federal Fisheries Management: 1940-1995*. U.S. National Marine Fisheries Service, Washington DC.

Weber, M.L. and J.A. Gradwohl. 1995. *The Wealth of Oceans: Environment and Development on Our Ocean Plant*. W.W. Norton, New York.

Whitehouse, E. 1996. Tax Expenditures and Environmental Policy. In *Subsidies and Environment: Exploring the Linkages*: 67-79. Organisation for Economic Co-operation and Development, Paris, France.

Wilderness Society. 1986. *America's Vanishing Rain Forest: A Report on Federal Timber Management in Southeast Alaska*. The Wilderness Society, Washington DC.

Willey, Z. 1992. Behind Schedule and Over Budget: The Case of Markets, Water and Environment. *Harvard Journal of Law and Public Policy* 15: 391-425.

Wilson, E.O. 1992. *The Diversity of Life*. Harvard University Press, Cambridge, Massachusetts.

Wilson, R. and J. Spengler. 1996. Conclusion: Policy Implications: National Dilemma. In R. Wilson and J. Spengler, eds., *Particles in Our Air: Concentrations and Health Effects*: 205-216. Harvard University Press, Cambridge, Massachusetts.

Wise, J.A. 1991. *Federal Conservation and Management of Marine Fisheries in the United States*. Center for Marine Conservation, Washington DC.

Wolfson, D. 1996. Tax Differentiation, Subsidies and the Environment. In *Subsidies and Environment: Exploring the Linkages*: 53-65. Organisation for Economic Co-operation and Development, Paris, France.

Woodwell, G.M. 1993. Forests: What in the World are They For? In G.M. Woodwell and K. Ramakrishna, eds., *World Forests for the Future: Their Use and Conservation*: 1-20. Yale University Press, New Haven, Connecticut.

Woodwell, G.M. and F.T. Mackenzie, eds. 1995. *Biotic Feedbacks in the Global Climatic System*. Oxford University Press, New York.

Working Group on Public Health and Fossil-Fuel Combustion. 1997. Short-Term Improvements in Public Health from Global-Climate Policies on Fossil-Fuel Combusion: An Interim Report. *The Lancet* November 8th.

World Bank. 1990. *Indonesia: Sustainable Development of Forests, Land and Water*. The World Bank, Washington DC.

World Bank. 1992. *World Development Report 1992*. Oxford University Press, New York.

World Bank. 1993a. *Water Resources Management: A World Bank Policy Study*. The World Bank, Washington DC.

World Bank, 1993b. *Indonesia Forestry Sector Review*. World Bank, Jakarta, Indonesia.

World Bank. 1994. *Indonesia: Environment and Development: Challenges for the Future*. World Bank, Washington DC.

World Bank. 1995. *Monitoring Environmental Progress*. The World Bank, Washington DC.

World Bank. 1996. *World Development Report 1996*. Oxford University Press, New York.

World Bank. 1997a. *Expanding the Measure of Wealth: Indicators of Environmentally Sustainable Development.* The World Bank, Washington DC.

World Bank. 1997b. *Clear Water, Blue Skies: China's Environment in the New Century.* The World Bank, Washington DC.

World Bank. 1997c. *Particulate Emissions Affecting Health in China.* The World Bank, Washington DC.

World Energy Council. 1992. *Renewable Energy Resources: Opportunities and Constraints 1990-2020.* World Energy Council, London, U.K.

World Energy Council. 1994. *New Renewable Energy Resources: A Guide to the Future.* Kogan Page, London, U.K.

World Health Organization. 1992. *Our Planet, Our Health.* World Health Organisation, Geneva, Switzerland.

World Resources Institute. 1990. *World Resources 1990-1991.* Oxford University Press, New York.

World Resources Institute, 1996. *World Resources 1996-97.* Oxford University Press, New York.

Wysham, D. 1997. *The World Bank and the G-7: Changing the Earth's Climate for Business.* Institute for Policy Studies, Washington DC.

Xie, J. 1996. *Water Subsidies, Water Use, and the Environment.* The World Bank, Washington DC.

Yablokov, A. 1997. Pers. comm. from the Senior Environmental Adviser to President Yeltsin, during stay at author's home in Oxford, U.K., April 9th, 1997.

Yep, G. 1995. *Reduction of Unaccounted For Water: The Job Can Be Better Done.* The World Bank, Washington DC.

Zak, D. 1995. Response of Terrestrial Ecosystems to Carbon Dioxide Fertilization. In S.J. Hassol and J. Katzenberger, eds., *Elements of Change 1994*: 202-204. Aspen Global Change Institute, Aspen, Colorado.

Zegras, C. and T. Litman. 1997. *An Analysis of the Full Costs and Impacts of Transportation in Santiago de Chile.* International Institute for Energy Conservation, Washington DC.

Zhou Fengqi. 1997. *Energy Consumption and Sustainable Development in China.* Office of the Director-General, Energy Research Institute, State Planning Commission, Beijing, People's Republic of China.

APPENDICES

APPENDIX 1.1

SUBSIDIES: THEIR TECHNICALITIES

Subsidies are not new. They include direct payments, low-interest loans, tax concessions and reliefs, supported services, tax-funded laboratories, research and development grants to industry, and training programs. There are more generalized types of subsidy too: assumption of liability by government (e.g., loan guarantees and site clean-ups such as the U.S. Superfund), provision of a good or service at less than market price or full economic cost, and financial support to maintain a product price above full cost. In addition to these direct subsidies, government interventions can include price controls, import tariffs and quotas, and infrastructure financing, among many other modes of supporting individual sectors.

Some of these interventions, notably direct subsidies, tax exemptions and infrastructure financing, can be viewed as conventional subsidies whereby governments provide direct financial support for a given activity. Others, such as price controls, are effectively "cross-subsidies", whereby the customer is paying either more or less than the uncontrolled market price for a good, so that the transfer is between consumers and producers (for example, electricity market regulation). Then there are covert or implicit subsidies, which can include the failure of governments to internalize environmental costs, e.g., pollution costs, in those prices faced by suppliers and users of energy *(Michaelis, 1995)*.

A formal and textbook definition *(Putnam and Bartlett, 1993)* states that "A subsidy is a transfer of economic resources by the government to the buyer or seller of a good or service that has the effect of reducing the price paid, increasing the price received, or reducing the cost of production of the good and service". This definition should include not only cash transfers but opportunity costs.

According to the same subsidies experts *(Putnam and Bartlett (1993)* (and for a more recent classification, see Organisation for Economic Cooperation and Development, 1997a), a thorough taxonomy of subsidies would include:

"1. Policies that transfer resources through market prices, e.g., price regulations, government procurement policies, import tariffs and non-tariff trade barriers.

2. Direct transfers, e.g., direct grants or payments to consumers or producers, or the provision of inputs at below-market prices.

3. Tax policies, e.g., tax credits, exemptions, deferrals, exclusions and deductions, investment expensing, accelerated depreciation, and other preferential tax treatment.

4. Policies that reduce input costs, e.g., preferential loans, loan or liability guarantees, indirect expenditures such as research and development.

5. Provision of infrastructure and subsidies to so-called "complementary goods."

There are further distinctions. For instance, an economic definition views a subsidy as "a government-directed, market-distorting intervention which decreases the cost of producing a specific good or service or increases the price which may be charged for it. A fiscal definition sees it as a government expenditure, exemption from general taxation provision, or assumption of liability that decreases the cost of producing a specific good or service, or increases the price which may be charged for it" *(Barg, 1995)*. Alternatively stated, an economic subsidy measures the difference between the opportunity-cost value of, say, an energy source and its actual price, whereas a financial measure indicates the difference between the price charged and the cost of production. The financial measure addresses the direct financial cost to the country of subsidizing energy, while an economic measure reveals what the country could secure if it adopted a full shadow-pricing approach. According to this approach, the economic definition is a more appropriate indicator of the true cost *(Pearce and Warford, 1993)*. These two perspectives are not mutually exclusive, and each can easily be expressed in terms of the other. For instance, uncompensated environmental damages distort marketplace prices *(Runge and Jones 1996)*.

It is apparent from the above that subsidies support various collective interests, known in the trade as public goods. Examples include sectors of strategic importance, notably agriculture, health, education and defence. But this raises further questions. Which public good is being supported by a particular subsidy, and is it a valid policy objective anyway? How large are the efficiency losses from taxes raised to finance the subsidy, and are there more productive ways of achieving the same public good? How large are the negative externalities created by the subsidy? How far does a subsidy serve to transfer wealth from public property to private profit, from natural capital to consumption, from the many to the few, and from the poor to the rich?

APPENDIX 1.2

FORESTRY

Forestry subsidies are not remotely on the scale of those in agriculture, fossil fuels, road transportation and other leading sectors considered in this report. Totalling $6 billion per year, they are only 27 percent as much as those of the next lowest, fisheries. They are significant nonetheless, for two reasons. First, until the start of the 1990s they were a good deal larger than they are today. Secondly, they reveal how exploitation of a natural resource that should be eminently renewable can quickly become nonrenewable, thanks to their distortive impact.

Forestry worldwide features subsidies of many sorts. They include tax breaks, low-interest loans, reduced royalties and under-pricing for commercial loggers, government outlays on forestland infrastructure (roads, etc.), on-going losses in state-owned enterprises, and inducements for agriculturalists to settle in tropical forests. When forestry subsidies were first introduced in e.g., the western United States, they helped to foster settlement of extensive territories and they thus served a valid purpose. In developing countries too, when subsidies started to be set up in the mid-1960s, they played a constructive role in promoting investment. But in both regions, most original subsidies have long out-lived their purpose. They persist in part because certain governments remain unaware of the all-round and enduring values of their forests, and hence they tend to view the forests as capital to be liquidated *(Barbier et al., 1992; Gillis, 1994; Repetto, 1990)*. Most such subsidies are implicit rather than direct, and are not intended to foster deforestation. Rather they support activities that inadvertently lead to deforestation. Moreover, many forestry subsidies are partially concealed, making them difficult to recognize.

Forestry in the sense of commercial logging is worth well over $400 billion per year, or 1.5 percent of the global economy. International trade in timber and other wood products is worth rather more than $100 billion (three percent of all international trade), four-fifths of it on the part of developed countries *(Food and Agriculture Organisation, 1994; Vincent, 1992; see also Devall, 1994; Dudley et al., 1995)*. Just three countries—Canada, Russia and the United States—account for more than half of all commercial timber worldwide (Food and Agriculture Organization, 1995). More importantly, forests supply many non-wood products and an array of environmental services, some of them much more valuable than commercial timber *(Myers, 1992)*. We shall come back to these diverse outputs toward the end of this chapter.

Regrettably there is much over-cutting of forests, often fostered by a plethora of subsidies. In turn again, this will be adverse for demand-and-supply patterns of timber in the foreseeable future (not to mention the abundant environmental services). In fact, there are already signs of timber shortages ahead in certain areas. The 1993 demand is projected to increase as early as the year 2010 by a full 56 percent *(Arnold, 1991; see also Apsey and Reed, 1994)*. In particular, there is a growing shortage of specialist hardwoods from the tropics. Tropical forest nations used to earn as much from timber exports as from cotton and twice as much as from rubber. Due to over-harvesting of timber stocks, however, this income is falling away steeply, imposing a severe economic limitation on those many tropical forest countries where timber revenues have made a sizeable contribution to GNP *(Sharma, 1992; see also Barbier and Burgess, 1993)*.

As a measure of burgeoning timber demand, consider the situation in China. A nation-wide construction boom has brought on a severe timber shortage for a country with 21 percent of the world's population, 13 percent of the global economy, but only three percent of the world's forests. Timber imports doubled during the decade 1984-93, reaching more than 10 million cubic meters of roundwood equivalent—a figure that is predicted to soar to 60 million cubic meters by shortly after the year 2000 *(Food and Agriculture Organization, 1993)*. Per-capita consumption of two main timber products, sawnwood and panels, amounts to less than two-thirds as much as Asia's average, and less than two-fifths as much as Indonesia's. Were China to increase its consumption to match Indonesia's, its share would amount to almost 60 percent of Asia's total—and if it ever matched Japan's, then 280 percent of Asia's total *(Bochuan, 1991; Richardson, 1990; Ryan and Flavin, 1995; Spears, 1995)*. In short, China seems poised to become the world's leading importer of wood.

This brief introduction highlights the role of subsidies that foster over-exploitation of forests. The great majority of the world's forests are state-owned. In theory, the state should be a better owner of forests than the private individual or company, since its time horizon can and should be longer than that of the private owner. But in practice a forest may be managed by political appointees whose time horizon is no longer than the tenure of their job, and who may therefore be inclined to turn a blind eye to deforestation that will not impose its full penalties until the longer-term future *(Cairncross, 1995)*. As a result, logging fees in countries such as Indonesia, Malaysia and Philippines are often set too low to reflect the full costs of replanting. Such "stumpage" fees, being only a share of replacement costs, cover less than 15 percent of total costs in Ivory Coast and Kenya *(World Bank, 1992)*. In the United States, the federal government has long sold logging rights in National Forests for sums that not only fail to reflect the environmental cost of such activities but even underestimate their commercial value. *(For some overviews of forestry economics and the role of subsidies, see Amsberg, 1994; Day, 1997; Hyde and Newman, 1991; Hyde et al., 1993; and Vincent et al., 1993.)*

Example of Over-Logging: Indonesia

To illustrate logging subsidies in tropical forests, consider Indonesia, a country with 10 percent of the world's remaining tropical forests and experiencing a deforestation rate of 1.4 percent per year *(Myers, 1993)*. The timber industry accounted for 7 percent of GDP in 1993, and exports of forest products totalled $7 billion in 1995, second only to oil and gas as a foreign exchange earner *(Hamilton, 1997; World Bank, 1994)*. But also in 1993, timber concessions covered more than 600,000 square kilometers or well over half of remaining forests. Worse, logging rates were around 44 million cubic meters of wood per year, far beyond the government's calculation of the maximum sustainable yield, viz. 31 million cubic meters *(Food and Agriculture Organization and Government of Indonesia, 1992)* and the World Bank's estimate (1993b) of 22 million cubic meters. So widespread was over-logging (in the sense of over-heavy and destructive logging that eliminates the bulk of the woody biomass *(Myers, 1989 and 1996)* that it directly caused as much as 15-20 percent of deforestation *(World Bank, 1994)*—though Indonesian officials insisted the amount was less than 10 percent. Some observers, e.g., Hamilton *(1997)* and Myers *(1993)* believe that if present trends persist, Indonesia could be obliged to import a large proportion of its timber needs within two decades—a period much shorter than the time since the "logging boom" began.

Over-logging in Indonesia has been greatly stimulated by subsidies both direct and indirect. True, the situation is somewhat improved today as compared with the 1980s. So pervasive were subsidies a decade ago that it is instructive to look in a little detail at the impacts of fiscal and other incentives prompting over-logging. The prime repercussion of subsidies was that they caused the government to extract less than one quarter of the taxes and royalties that should have been charged in terms of the natural resource rent, viz. the value of the trees before they were cut. This encouraged logging companies to heavily over-exploit the forests. In addition, under-pricing (another covert subsidy) induced loggers to take trees that would otherwise have been uneconomical to cut *(Barbier et al., 1994; Gillis, 1992; Johnson and Cabarle, 1993)*. During the early 1980s, the rate of rent capture, i.e., the government's performance as a percentage of the actual rent from logging, was no more than 37 percent *(Gillis, 1988 and 1994; see also Ascher, 1993; Barbier and Burgess, 1993)*. Moreover, if unreported timber harvests for 1980-85 had been subjected to the relatively low 1980 tax, the actual revenues of $1.55 billion would have increased by an additional $1.2 billion, or an average of $200 million per year *(World Bank, 1993b; see also Abramovitz, 1998; Broad, 1995; Dauvergne, 1993)*.

During the period 1970-84, timber enterprises—many of them foreign, notably Japanese and American—harvested 285 million cubic meters of raw logs in Indonesia's forests, taken from some 7000 square kilometers a year by the end of the period. The logging operations cost the companies an average of $49 per cubic meter, including a reasonable profit margin. Yet the companies charged $116 per cubic meter of raw log, most of which they pocketed. During just the four years 1979-82 they picked up an extra $8.8 billion, of which only $3 billion went to the government in taxes. The other $5.8 billion—almost exactly what Indonesia was receiving in foreign aid per year during that period—was taken out of the country to enrich shareholders elsewhere, notably in developed countries *(Roodman, 1995; see also Barbier and Burgess, 1993; Gillis, 1994; Vincent, 1995).*

On top of all this, there are inefficiencies in wood processing industries, this being a further reflection of subsidies. In Indonesia (also in African nations such as Ghana and Ivory Coast), many processing mills have been established in response to fiscal incentives among other subsidies; and Indonesia now controls at least 90 percent of the world's tropical plywood market *(Hamilton, 1997).* As a result of subsidies, however, its processing mills have tended to be small and inefficient, with conversion rates of logs into sawn lumber and plywood only about two-thirds of industry standards *(Barber et al., 1994).* Largely because of processing inefficiencies, during just the two years 1981-82 the Indonesian economy lost over $400 million in potential revenues, equivalent to 27 percent of the timber rent *(Gillis, 1988; Manurung and Buongiorno, 1997).* Moreover, for every one dollar gained in plywood exports, four dollars were sacrificed in log exports *(Fitzgerald, 1986; Goodland and Daly, 1996).* During the 1980s overall, while the government was subsidizing the sawnwood and plywood industries, log production fell by 20 percent and timber exports by 14 percent, while fewer jobs were created (net) *(Manurung and Buongiorno, 1997).* It was not until 1988 that the value of plywood exports exceeded the 1979 log export earnings of $2.1 billion *(Barber et al., 1994).*

How far have forestry subsidies been maintained on this scale? While there has been some drop-off since the heights of the early and mid-1980s (tax credits were abandoned in 1988), there is still a plethora of supports of one sort or another, many of them hard to identify. Despite a lengthy list of fine publications on Indonesian forestry in recent years *(Ahmad, 1997; Barber et al., 1994; Barbier et al., 1994; Brookfield and Byron, 1993; Dauvergne, 1997; Hardjono, 1991; Johnson and Cabarle, 1993; Ross, 1996a and b),* there is next to no specific indication of how much is being spent on subsidies in the mid-1990s. Certainly in 1988 there was a documented revenue loss of $400 million *(Gillis, 1992),* and if rent capture on just logs had matched that for oil in 1990 the government would have gained an additional $2.1 billion *(Barber et al., 1994; Roodman, 1996).* Conversely, rent capture increased from a mere 5 percent in 1986 and only 17 percent in 1990 to at least 30-40 percent in 1995 and possibly as high as 65 percent in 1996—even though there is little reason in principle why the amount should not be nearer 100 percent *(Fraser, 1997; Gray and Hadi, 1997; see also Ahmad, 1997; Ross, 1996a).* For a brief indication of how rent capture and hence covert subsidies can be calculated, see Box A.1.2.

Box A.1.2

INDONESIAN FORESTRY: RENT CAPTURE
AND COVERT SUBSIDIES

Research for the period 1993-96 shows that the proportion of economic rent captured by the government, and conversely the size of the covert subsidy, varies with final-product prices, since levies and royalties are a fixed amount rather than a percentage of market price. This means that when prices are high, the proportion of economic rent captured is low, and vice versa. The timber industry can generally afford to pay $200 per cubic meter of log while still making a reasonable profit; and we can accept a figure of $95 as a price at which a timber concessionnaire would have to sell logs in order to make an acceptable profit. Then the economic rent constitutes the difference between these two prices, or roughly $105 per cubic meter. Current levies and other government receipts total around $25 per cubic meter, or roughly one quarter of the economic rent. So government revenues fail to capture some 75 percent of the economic rent—and this figure can thus be taken as the size of the covert subsidy. The figure of 25 percent compares with other studies, viz. 17-40 percent *(Fraser, 1997)*.

Then there is the price of the processed wood product. If, as is usual, this is plywood, it would have to sell for more than $365 per cubic meter (against a log price of $95) if industry is to show a profit of 20 percent. The export price of plywood from Indonesia has ranged from $540 to $730 per cubic meter. This suggests that the industry could afford to pay much higher prices for its raw materials; and in turn, this means that the wood-processing industry is effectively and heavily subsidized. Fortunately the government has recently increased its levies twice over in real terms *(Fraser, 1997)*.

This recent advance notwithstanding, timber corporations still enjoy large if not excessive profits. To cite a British forestry expert, Alastair Fraser *(1997)*, "This is in effect a huge subsidy to the wood processing industry, which is very wasteful, using only the best logs and a limited number of tree species. It also means the wood processors can sell their products on the world market at low prices, which then means that large volumes can be sold, meaning in turn again that large areas of forest are logged to supply the raw materials. [The heavy wood-processing subsidies arise] primarily as a consequence of lack of data and analytic tools to monitor what is going on. In addition, the unintended subsidy has the effect of undervaluing the forest timber resource, and this in turn reduces the apparent impact on the economy of clearing forest for other land uses, which look so much more economically attractive as a consequence. It is difficult for the Forest Department to resist pressure to release forest for agriculture. It also results in waste all along the chain from tree stump to plywood mill. At the same time, it takes the attraction out of investment to minimize logging damage and foster regeneration."

What shall we make of this account of Indonesian forestry and its subsidies? While a good number of studies have been undertaken of the timber industry, notably by the World Bank, the Asian Development Bank, the Food and Agriculture Organization, the World Resources Institute, and several Indonesian NGOs, they differ widely in their findings on subsidies, mainly because of differences in analytic methods and base-line assumptions. But the World Bank *(1994)* feels able to conclude that fully two-thirds of deforestation in Indonesia, now amounting to 10,000 square kilometers per year, have been due to programs either sponsored or encouraged by government supports, primarily subsidies.

What level of subsidies shall we suppose for 1996? It could be anywhere between, say, $200 million and $750 million—possibly less still, conceivably even more. It is most unsatisfactory to end this Indonesia review in such imprecise manner. The author proposes a cautious estimate of $300 million. Admittedly, this is very much of a best-judgement assessment, and it is advanced solely in order to come up with an indication of any sort, however rough and ready. If no estimate were offered at all, some observers might suppose that implies subsides are effectively nil.

A figure of $300 million may not sound much in relation to subsidies for agriculture in Japan, $77 billion per year, or fossil fuels in the United States, $20 billion per year. In relation to the forestry future in Indonesia, however, it is certainly significant. It is also significant in relation to Indonesia's economy, where forestry products are the top export earner after oil and natural gas, and where Indonesia leads the world in exports of plywood and other processed wood products.

In addition to its logging subsidies, the Indonesian government has spent large amounts on inducements to smallscale farmers in over-populated Java, Bali and Madura, to migrate to the "outer islands" of Sumatra, Kalimantan (Borneo), Sulawesi and elsewhere. The Transmigration Programme was once so heavily subsidized that the government costs of moving just a single family were as high as $10,000 in 1986 dollars —and that in a country with a per-capita GNP of little over $600 *(Repetto, 1996; see also Barber et al., 1994; Repetto and Gillis,*

1988). All in all the programme resettled some 8 million people in 17,000 square kilometers of state forestlands *(Hamilton, 1997)*. Even though the programme added significantly to Indonesia's deforestation, it was not due to forestry subsidies, so it is not counted as part of the overall calculus for this report.

Example of Cattle Ranching: Brazil

Most of the extensive deforestation of Brazilian Amazonia can be traced directly to government-financed subsidies. Starting in the early 1970s, hefty subsidies became available for entrepreneurs wanting to ranch cattle in cleared forestlands. Generous tax and credit incentives created over 120,000 square kilometers of large cattle ranches in Amazonia, with the typical ranch covering more than half its costs through the subsidies. By supplying funds on exceptionally easy terms, the Brazilian government invited investors to acquire and clear large tracts of forests. During the period 1979-84, a typical ranch in Amazonia incurred costs of $415 per hectare and earned revenues of only $113 per hectare or little over one quarter of the costs. Yet it stayed in business, in fact it made a commercial killing, thanks to the many subsidies at work *(Browder, 1988; see also Hecht, 1992; Repetto, 1990 and 1996)*.

All in all, the Brazilian government spent $2.5 billion in subsidizing ranchers' investments through long-term loans, tax credits and other fiscal incentives, monetary inducements, and duty-free imports of capital equipment *(Repetto, 1996; Schneider, 1995)*. This support meant that many ranches, no matter how inefficient, made a vast profit, even to the extent that hardly any ranchers bothered to sell the timber felled to make way for the pasturelands. Virtually every ranch proved a financial success for the individual entrepreneur, while an economic setback for the national economy. An activity that was privately profitable was socially unprofitable. The combined costs of tax credits, subsidized credit, and timber revenues foregone from a forest destroyed totalled $4.8 billion during the period 1966-1983, or an average of $266 million per year *(Browder, 1988 and 1989; see also Binswanger, 1989; Schneider, 1995)*.

Government subsidies were also the driving force behind other forms of large private-investment ventures in Amazonia, with focus on crop agriculture or mixed cropping/ranching enterprises *(Arima and Uhl, 1997; Heath and Binswanger, 1996; Schneider, 1995; Southgate, 1997 and 1998)*. In the state of Rondonia alone, settlers received an implicit subsidy of $3200 per person, making an aggregate of $163 million by 1990. Subsidized settlers cleared 25 percent more forests than those not benefitting directly from government programs *(Repetto, 1988)*. Overall, the net value of future income available from unlogged and otherwise undisturbed forests may be 50-200 percent higher than the net present value of income from forest conversion through cattle ranching among other forms of agricultural settlement *(Gillis, 1992; see also Browder, 1988; Hyde et al., 1993; Mattos and Uhl, 1994; Schneider, 1992; Southgate, 1997; von Amsberg, 1994).*

In recent years, deforestation subsidies in Brazilian Amazonia have become "largely a thing of the past" *(Southgate, 1995 and 1997; see also Andersen, 1996; Schneider, 1995; Uhl et al., 1997).* This is especially the case for cattle ranching and some other forms of agricultural settlement. Now that it has been stripped of most of its subsidies, ranching offers a net annual return of only $6 and sometimes a mere $2 per head of cattle *(Arima and Uhl, 1997; Mattos and Uhl, 1994).* There is one prime reason for this recent shift: deforestation has long been seen to be a massive drain on government coffers.

A reduction in deforestation was eventually recognized in Brazil's interests as well as in the interests of the rest of the world *(Barbier et al., 1991; Binswanger, 1989; Krautkraemer, 1995; Schneider, 1994; Uhl et al., 1997).* Way back in 1987, many rural-credit subsidies were abolished, and today the degree of subsidization is far from what it was *(Andersen, 1997; Barber et al., 1994; Uhl et al., 1997).* The government has decided there will be no more subsidies for new ranches, though such supports continue for established ranches covering 120,000 square kilometers, these being ranches that have already cost the Brazilian treasury more than $2.5 billion in revenues foregone *(Repetto, 1990; Southgate, 1997).*

Other Examples of Subsidized Deforestation in the Humid Tropics

Deforestation has been fostered by multiple subsidies in tropical forest countries and regions as diverse as Colombia, Ecuador, Peru, Bolivia, Central America, Mexico, West Africa, Myanmar, Thailand and Malaysia. Few of these countries capture more than half the economic rent of their timber resources *(Barbier et al., 1994; Durning, 1994; Grut et al., 1990; Hyde et al., 1993; Repetto and Gillis, 1988; Southgate, 1997; Vincent, 1995; von Amsberg, 1994).* In Costa Rica, forests have been widely cleared for agriculture, especially cattle ranching. Consider just a single calculation of costs. If we subtract the loss of forests from the gain in secondary forests in order to determine a net change in timber, we find that in 1984 the net value of forests eliminated was $167 million, or $69 for each Costa Rican citizen—in a country with a per-capita GNP of only $1280 *(Beattie, 1994; see also Kishor and Constantino, 1993; Repetto et al., 1989).*

Costa Rica demonstrates how subsidized deforestation often reflects the unintended impact of policies outside the forestry sector—particularly road development and land distribution, as well as subsidized credit and fiscal incentives for cattle ranching and crop cultivation. As a result, deforestation can proceed at a rate way more than socially optimal—which, according to many observers, should surely be zero, given that most of Costa Rica's forests have already disappeared *(Peuker, 1992)*. At the same time, successive governments in Costa Rica have made exemplary efforts to set aside as much as 25 percent of the country's territory, mostly forests, under some form of protected status—a uniquely successful achievement among tropical forest countries of Latin America. The parallel deforestation in Costa Rica demonstrates how an enlightened government can ostensibly tolerate measure that undercut its conservation measures. When subsidies are indirect and covert, they can be specially insidious.

Total Subsidies in Tropical Forestry

What, finally, is the scale of subsidies promoting deforestation in the humid tropics? It is worthwhile attempting some sort of estimate, even an "informed guesstimate", insofar as no estimate at all might be construed in some quarters as meaning there are no subsidies of any consequence. Despite the extreme paucity of recent data, the author hazards the best-judgement assessment that logging subsidies throughout the humid tropics may now be in the order of $1 billion a year—a figure that reflects the various statistical analyses presented above. In reality, the subsidies could be somewhat less, and they could also be rather more. Cattle ranching subsidies are assumed to be only small as compared with logging subsidies. If both sets total only around $1 billion a year altogether, this is very little by contrast with the other types of subsidies addressed in this report. But they are significant for the economies of countries concerned *(Aplet et al., 1993; Dudley et al., 1995; Hyde and Newman, 1991; Hyde et al., 1993; Vincent, 1990; von Amsberg, 1994)*. In light of their adverse impact all round, they are all considered perverse.

Tropical deforestation has ranked high as an environmental and development concern since the late 1970s, yet the forests are declining faster than ever. A 1987 survey of 17 countries with over 70 percent of all tropical forests found fewer than 10,000 square kilometers being "sustainably" logged, or less than 0.2 percent of the forest area surveyed *(Poore et al., 1989)*. Two main reasons were adduced. First, government policies often help establish or perpetuate unsound logging practices. Second, governments collect only a small fraction of the rents (especially windfall profits) accrued by loggers, which both fosters corruption and deprives the government of a large stream of revenues. These government policies often have a political basis. Almost all tropical forests are government owned, enabling public officials to preside over the distribution of logging permits, which, in turn, assume a form of political patronage by public officials who thereafter under-tax and under-regulate the clients gaining these permits. Hence government leaders rarely have much concern about unsustainable logging *(Ross, 1996a and b)*.

Fortunately there are a few efforts to tackle the problems of tropical deforestation in a manner that should counter perverse subsidies to some extent. The Asian Development Bank, for instance, plans to use its forestry loans as leverage to give logging rights to whichever concern offers to post the highest guarantee bond. The bond will be invested for the life of a logging project, and will become forfeit if the logger fails to protect the forest. Another option advanced by the Bank is to award perpetual leases for an annual rent to be reviewed every five years and revoked if the holder fails to adhere to his agreement. Making the leases tradeable will offer an incentive for timber concessionaires to maintain the value of their concessions *(Cairncross, 1995)*.

Example of Over-Logging: the United States

Perverse subsidies apply to forestry in developed countries too. Remarkably enough, we encounter the same problem of inadequate data—out-of-date data, inconsistent data, even no data at all in certain instances.

In the United States, the Forest Service supports logging with an array of subsidies, many of them indirect or otherwise semi-concealed and hence hard to track down. Many if not most of these subsidies qualify as perverse. They promote logging in more than 400,000 square kilometers of National Forests even though virtually all the areas in question are regarded as economically unsuitable for sustained timber production. The Forest Service subsidizes the logging by selling timber at prices well below its own costs of road building, tree harvesting and timber marketing, and at a cost to American taxpayers of at least $100 million a year (some estimates suggest several times as much) *(O'Toole, 1993; see also Cortner and Schweitzer, 1993; Frances, 1994; Gardner, 1997; Miller, 1994)*.

In fact, timber sales in most National Forests lose money every year. In 1992 alone, 95 of the 120 National Forests operated at a loss totalling $175 million because the Forest Service spent more money on administering timber sales than it received in revenue from those sales *(O'Toole, 1995; see also Runge and Jones, 1996)*. In 1993, government subsidies for below-cost timber sales amounted to $323 million, including $35 million for the Tongass National Forest in Alaska *(Devall, 1994; see also O'Toole, 1995)*. The annual losses would have been even higher had they reflected transfer payments to states and long-term capital expenditures for road construction *(Alkire, 1993; Gorte, 1993; Losos et al., 1995; Roodman, 1996; U.S. Forest Service, 1993)*. One recent estimate *(O'Toole, 1995)* suggests that when we combine all subsidies identifiable and quantifiable, we find the total for 1992 represented a loss to U.S. taxpayers of $499 million.

So extensive is government road building in the National Forests, that 10 years ago the network already covered more than 575,000 kilometers of roads or eight times as much as the Interstate Highway System *(Wilderness Society, 1986)*. Over a recent seven-year period, the Forest Service ran its timber program at a $1.9 billion loss, in large part because of road-construction costs. The resulting deforestation contributed to widespread soil erosion and loss of wildlife habitats, which constituted further subsidization in the form of environmental externalities. In 1994 the government spent over $100 million on building and maintaining roads in the National Forests, largely for the use of timber companies that contributed nothing to the cost. By eliminating the construction of new forest roads, the government could save $475 million *(O'Toole, 1993)*. Fortunately it looks as if the roads budget is being reduced somewhat *(Baker, 1998)*.

The key question of whether the Forest Service makes a reasonable profit or actually loses money is beset by the curious accounting procedures adopted by the agency. It ignores many costs while counting certain receipts that never make their way into the Treasury. During 1989-94, the Service lost an annual average on timber sales of $282 million; and during the same period, it claimed average annual profits of $510 million, while ignoring the costs of road building and reforestation which thus amounted to large subsidies to the timber industry *(Roodman, 1996)*. During the shorter period 1992-94, when the agency claimed to make a $1.1 billion profit, the Government Accounting Office showed a loss of nearly $1.0 billion. Yet as the agency sells more timber and the Treasury loses more money on logging operations, the more the Service's budget grows. As some critics argue, it would be cheaper to pay loggers directly out of the Treasury than to continue subsidizing the depletion of an increasingly scarce asset. For an extended exposition of this theme, see O'Toole, 1995, and Roodman, 1996.

The subsidies problem is exemplified especially by the Tongass rainforest in Alaska, this being the biggest forest and the biggest money loser in the National Forest system. With 68,000 square kilometers (the size of West Virginia), it is the most extensive temperate rainforest on Earth, home to the world's greatest concentration of grizzly bears and bald eagles, with rivers supporting spawning grounds for all five species of Pacific salmon (a fishery with more wild salmon than in all the "lower 48" and vital to the Alaskan economy). It contains groves of spruce that were 30 meters tall and well over half a meter thick when George Washington was an infant. They still haven't stopped growing. Some of the nation's best trees, many of them are exported to Asia for rough building materials or even for chopsticks, are sold by the Forest Service at a fraction of their full economic worth.

The Tongass rainforest is being depleted through over-logging more rapidly than most rainforests in Amazonia or Borneo. During 1992-94, its timber program outlays exceeded revenues by $102 million, more than twice as much as for any other National Forest, the deficit being made up by the American taxpayer *(Pittman et al., 1997)*. Whether from the standpoint of the environment or the economy, the management (sic) of the Tongass does not make sense. Commercial loggers regularly buy trees for a few dollars each when the management costs to the Forest Service have been dozens of times as much, most of the costs going toward logging-road construction (the Forest Service is the largest road-building agency in the world) *(Proxmire, 1997)*. In fact, logging is so heavily subsidized that the Forest Service loses 98 cents for every $1 of taxpayer money spent. Timber sales cannot even accomplish their stated goal of safeguarding timber industry jobs, even though each job created costs taxpayers an average of $12,000 *(Pittman et al., 1997; Schoonmaker et al., 1996; see also Rehmke, 1989; Wilderness Society, 1986)*. Fortunately the Forests Service looks as if it may now be coming to grips with this outsize problem.

For purposes of this report, and reflecting the partial documentation presented above, perverse subsidies in U.S. forestry are estimated to be in the region of $500 million per year. It might seem strange that the United States does not have more precise and accurate figures. The gaps and inconsistencies in the review above reflect the curious fact that the Forest Service employs several different methods for making its calculations, which to this observer look like a convoluted accounting system that overlooks many costs, while counting certain revenues that never actually accrue to the government.

A still more regrettable situation is occurring in Russia, where the government has been supplying exceptionally large subsidies for timber transportation, notably from Siberia. Logs have been shipped by train either to ports in eastern Russia or to Europe, with very little charge to logging concerns for this substantial service *(Kolchugina and Vinson, 1995; Shvidenko and Nilsson, 1994; Yablakov, 1997)*. No statistical details are available on these subsidies. Fortunately it appears that they have been sharply reduced in the last two years or so *(Day, 1997)*, though little information is to hand. Meantime, logging in Siberia (often clear-cut logging) together with fires, has already destroyed 40,000 square kilometers of forests per year, while another 65,000 square kilometers have been depleted through the factors listed plus industrial pollution *(Alexeyev, 1991; Kolchugina and Vinson, 1995; Kolchugina et al., 1992; Shvidenko and Nilsson, 1994)*. This amount is twice as much as recent annual deforestation in Brazilian Amazonia, and four times as much as the area logged each year in the boreal forests of Canada *(Hall, 1995; Kurz and Apps, 1995; Li and Apps, 1995)*.

In Australia too, subsidies abound. Victoria's state government spends A$2.25 on logging subsidy to obtain A$1 of timber royalty, for a total net outlay of A$170 million per year *(Dragun, 1995)*. In the Thomson River catchment, being the main water supply for Melbourne, subsidies promote the logging of old growth forests to the detriment of the watershed, even though the water supplies are worth ten times more than the timber harvested and the water yield loss is estimated at A$65 million per year *(Hamilton, 1995; Read Sturgess and*

Associates, 1994). Total environmental externalities of logging in Victoria are estimated to be in the order of A$160 million per year *(Dragun, 1995).*

Subsidies Worldwide

This short review shows that subsidies are a frequent feature of forestry in all three main forest zones, viz. tropical, temperate and boreal. They are characteristic of developed and developing countries alike. They exert a sizeable influence on the nature and scope of forestry operations, and they contribute markedly to over-exploitation and other forms of forest mis-use. In fact, were these subsidies to be phased out, that measure alone would probably do more to slow deforestation in many countries than any other single initiative. Of course, subsidies can theoretically contribute to rational forest management too, through e.g., funds to stimulate plantation forestry or to safeguard watersheds with tree cover. But these seem to be so rare and of such small scale in the countries considered that they make only marginal difference at most to the overall picture. So all forestry subsidies treated above are considered perverse on grounds of their deleterious impacts both economic and environmental.

What is the overall scale of these perverse subsides? In the absence of up-to-date data, it is difficult to say in more than exploratory terms. The assessment here postulates some $1 billion per year in those tropical countries reviewed, and $500 million in the United States. The chapter has not presented economic documentation of subsidies in a number of other leading forestry countries such as Canada, Russia, Sweden, Germany, Japan, India, Thailand, Malaysia, Vietnam, Papua New Guinea, Philippines, Ivory Coast, Nigeria, Guyana and Suriname. So far as one can discern, many of the same perverse subsidies occur in these countries too. For the sake of coming up with an overall estimate, however preliminary and approximate, we can reasonably suppose that perverse subsidies worldwide could well be twice the amount above, i.e., $3 billion per year.

To emphasize: this is a very crude estimate—nothing more (and nothing less). It does not reflect, for instance, the costs of reforesting over-logged lands, a cost that would be considerable in the dipterocarp forests of Southeast Asia where loggers often remove one quarter of the woody biomass and injure another half beyond recovery—and a cost that is almost always disregarded in evaluation of tropical forestry. If, as is all too possible, the estimate is off target, it is more likely to be on the low side.

Note too that $3 billion is a small sum in relation to the value of commercial timber worldwide, $400 billion per year. In the case of marine fisheries, perverse subsidies amount to 26 percent of the total commercial value, whereas in forestry they are less than 1 percent. However, and as we shall shortly see, environmental externalities are unusually important in the case of forestry, whereas in fisheries that is far from the case (except for the depletion of major fish stocks). So extensive and significant are forestry externalities that it is worthwhile to look at these implicit subsidies in some detail. Plainly, as forests disappear, so do their environmental goods and services. The external costs of deforestation are borne by present communities and future generations who are thus deprived of forests' benefits—meaning that the external costs are effectively subsidies to deforestation.

Environmental Externalities

Forests supply many goods and services apart from commercial timber and potential agricultural lands. The decline of forests entrains a decline of these goods and services. Herewith an illustrative selection of forestry values at stake in order to demonstrate the scope and scale of the externalities of deforestation.

I. Material goods

Tropical forests provide fuelwood for the 3 billion people in developing countries who use the wood as their main if not sole source of household energy. A proxy indication of how they evaluate their fuelwood may be gained by noting that at least 500 million of them spend between 1.5 and 5 hours a day in roaming far and wide to find adequate supplies *(ASTRA, 1982; Crews and Stauffer, 1997; Kumar and Hotchkiss, 1988; Tinker, 1990)*. Suppose the average length of time spent is 3 hours per day or 1200 hours per year. Suppose too that their time opportunity cost is $1 per day or 10 cents per hour, reflecting what they could gain by spending the same time on cultivating farm fields. So the "shadow" cost per person per year is $120. This means that the total value of forests as sources of fuelwood is $60 billion per year. This is to be compared with the cost of establishing enough plantations to take care of all fuelwood needs, $10-20 billion as a once-and-for-all outlay, plus perhaps $1 billion per year to maintain them.

Then there is a host of non-wood products from tropical forests, including wild fruits, latexes, essential oils, exudates, waxes, tannins, dyes and medicinals *(Lampietti and Dixon, 1995)*. In India, non-wood products are worth $4.3 billion per year, equivalent to 26 percent of wood products *(Chopra, 1993)*. All in all, the value of non-wood products worldwide may now have reached as much as $90 billion a year, including subsistence and non-marketed items *(Pimentel et al., 1996)*.

Even more abundant are wild species and other forms of biodiversity. While covering only 6 percent of Earth's land surface, tropical forests are estimated to contain at least 50 percent, possibly 70 percent and conceivably 90 percent of Earth's species *(Erwin, 1988)*. Half a square kilometer of Malaysia's forests can feature as many tree and shrub species as the whole of the United States and Canada, while a single bush in Peruvian Amazonia has revealed more ant species than in the British Isles *(Wilson 1992)*. As the forests disappear, so do their species, at a rate of some 50-150 per day or 18,000-55,000 per year *(Wilson, 1992)*.

Apart from scientific, aesthetic and ethical values of biodiversity, these losses affect the immediate material welfare of people throughout the world. When we visit our neighbourhood chemist, there is one chance in four that our purchase, whether a drug, medicinal or pharmaceutical, owes its manufacture to materials derived from tropical-forest plants *(Balick et al., 1996)*. These products include antibiotics, antivirals, analgesics, tranquillizers, diuretics, laxatives, and contraceptive pills among many other items. Commercial sales are worth $40 billion a year in the developed world, while their economic value is several times larger *(Principe, 1996)*. The forests are reckoned to contain at least one dozen plant species with capacity to generate superstar drugs against cancer, provided the plants can be identified before they rank among the five species eliminated each day *(Suffness, 1987)*. Three promising leads against AIDS come from tropical forest plants. Potential future drugs awaiting discovery in tropical forests could have a theoretical value ranging from $147 billion *(Mendelsohn and Balick, 1995)* to $420 billion *(Pearce and Puroshothaman, 1993)* to $900 billion *(Gentry, 1993)*.

There are material benefits too from subspecies and populations of wild plants. In the early 1970s Asia's rice crop was hit by a grassy stunt virus that threatened to devastate 300,000 square kilometers of rice fields. Fortunately a single gene from a wild rice in an Indian forest offered resistance against the virus. Then in 1976 another virus, known as ragged stunt disease, emerged; and again, the most potent source of resistance proved to be a wild forest rice. In India alone, the introduction of wild rice strains (plus primitive cultivars) has increased yields by at least $75 million a year *(Evanson, 1991)*.

II. Environmental services

Environmental services are still more bountiful and valuable. Forests stabilize landscapes *(Woodwell, 1993)*. They protect soils, helping them to retain their moisture and to store and cycle nutrients *(Jordan, 1985)*. They serve as buffers against the spread of pests and diseases *(Woodwell, 1995)*. By preserving watershed functions, they regulate water flows in terms of both quantity and quality *(Bruijnzeel, 1990)*, thereby helping to prevent flood-and-drought regimes in downstream territories *(Sfeir-Younis, 1986)*. They are critical to Earth's energy balance *(Woodwell, 1993)*. They modulate climate at local and regional levels through regulation of rainfall regimes and the albedo effect *(Salati and Nobre, 1992)*. They help to reduce global warming through their carbon stocks

(Woodwell and Mackenzie, 1995). Let us take a quick look at certain of these services.

1. Watershed functions

While tropical forests cover only one seventeenth of Earth's land surface, they receive almost half of Earth's rainfall on land, often in heavy downpours. Deforestation of upland catchments, with loss of the forests' "sponge" effect, often leads to disruption of watershed systems, causing year-round water flows in downstream areas to give way to flood-and-drought regimes. As many as 40 percent of developing-world farmers depend upon regular water flows from forested watersheds to irrigate their croplands *(World Bank, 1987)*. In several parts of the humid tropics, the greatest limitation on increased food production does not stem from lack of agricultural land but from shortages of irrigation water during dry seasons. This is especially the case in Southern-Southeast Asia, where many forests are located above rich alluvial valleylands, several of which support some of the highest-density agricultural communities on Earth, farming primarily through irrigation. Indeed two-thirds of Southern-Southeast Asia farmers live in such valleylands, and this is the region where deforestation is more advanced than in virtually any other sector of the tropical forest biome. Decline of watershed services is already affecting the valleylands of the Ganges, Brahmaputra, Irrawaddy, Salween, Chao Phraya and Mekong Rivers *(Durning, 1993; Myers, 1989)*. In India, the value of forest services in regulating river flows and containing floods are roughly assessed at $72 billion a year *(Panayotou and Ashton, 1992; see also Chopra, 1993; Murty, 1994)*.

Deforestation of watersheds also leads to wash-off of topsoil. Siltation of hydropower and irrigation-system reservoirs worldwide, derived in major measure from watershed deforestation, is estimated to levy a cost of at least $6 billion a year *(Mahmood, 1987)*. In just the island of Java, the size of New York state, deforestation-derived siltation of reservoirs, irrigation systems and harbors levied damage costs worth $58 million in 1987, plus additional damages to coastal fisheries and water supplies for urban communities *(Magrath and Arens, 1989)*. Conversely, consider the value of an intact watershed: the Canaima National Park in Venezuela with its 30,000 square kilometers of undisturbed forest supplies hydroelectricity equivalent to 144 million barrels of oil per year *(Garcia, 1984)*, worth about $2.5 billion at today's prices.

2. Regulation of rainfall regimes

Deforestation in the tropics can result in reduced rainfall *(Salati and Nobre, 1992; Myers, 1988; Shukla et al., 1990)*. This is specially significant for agriculture. In the Penang and Kedah States of northwestern Peninsular Malaysia, which have lost almost all their forests, it was found ten years ago that disruption of rainfall regimes lead to 20,000 hectares of paddy ricefields being abandoned and another 72,000 hectares registering a marked production drop-off in this "rice bowl" of the Peninsula *(Chan, 1986).* Similar deforestation-associated changes in rainfall have been documented in Philippines, southwestern India, montane Tanzania, southwestern Ivory Coast, northwestern Costa Rica and the Panama Canal Zone *(Meher-Homji, 1992).* Deforestation can also affect rainfall regimes at much wider levels, e.g., in the entire Amazonia basin *(Salati et al., 1992).*

3. Climate regulation and global warming

Still more important is the climate linkage at the global level, through the carbon sinks of forests worldwide and hence their capacity to mitigate global warming *(Apps and Price, 1996; Ciais et al., 1995; Woodwell and Mackenzie, 1995).* Forests account for two-thirds of net plant growth and carbon fixation on land *(Zak, 1995).* Their plants and soils currently hold 1200 gigatonnes (billion tonnes) of carbon, out of 2000 gigatonnes in all terrestrial plants and soils (by contrast with 750 gigatonnes in the atmosphere) *(Houghton et al., 1990; Woodwell, 1993).* Around half of the forest carbon is located in boreal forests, more than one third in tropical forests, and one seventh in temperate forests *(Dixon et al., 1994; see also Apps et al., 1993).* Boreal forests, being Earth's largest terrestrial biome, probably contain more carbon than all proven fossil fuel reserves. They thus possess the scope for both the greatest change in the global carbon cycle and the greatest potential feedbacks on climate systems *(Nilsson, 1995; Shugart et al., 1992).*

When forests are burned—as is the case with cattle ranching and smallscale agriculture in the humid tropics, and with fires both wild and human-made in the boreal zone—they release their carbon. Of the roughly 7.6 gigatonnes of carbon emitted per year into the global atmosphere and contributing around half of greenhouse-effect processes, 1.6 gigatonnes (plus or minus 0.4 of a gigatonne) come from forest burning in the tropics *(Houghton, 1993),* almost all the rest stemming from combustion of fossil fuels *(Dixon et al., 1994).* Allowing for some sequestration of carbon by temperate and boreal forests, there was a net flux to the atmosphere of 0.9 of a gigatonne (plus or minus 0.4 of a gigatonne) of carbon in 1992 *(Dixon et al., 1994).* This amount has increased markedly in 1997, when more forests were burned worldwide than in any single year of the recorded past.

Furthermore, global warming itself will cause increased die-off and decomposition of forest biomass, in turn triggering a further release of carbon dioxide *(Apps and Price, 1996; Hulme and Viner, 1995).* As much as one third of the world's forests could be threatened in this manner *(Houghton et al., 1995).* This will likely apply especially to boreal forests, which, being located in northern high latitudes where temperatures will rise most in a greenhouse-affected world, could soon start to undergo marked desiccation and die-off *(Apps, 1995; Dixon et al., 1994)*. Were there to be progressive depletion of boreal forests along these lines, their expanse could decline by at least 40 percent and conceivably 60 percent within the next three to five decades. This would release between 1.5 and 3.0 gigatonnes of carbon per year over the period, probably more than is being emitted annually from tropical deforestation today, and equivalent to 20-40 percent of all current anthropogenic emissions of carbon dioxide *(Jardine, 1994; Houghton et al., 1995)*.

We can use a central value of $20 of eventual global-warming damage for every tonne of carbon released *(Brown and Pearce, 1994; Fankhauser, 1994)*. Converting open forests in the tropics to agriculture or pasture would result in a cost of roughly $600-1000 per hectare; conversion of closed secondary forest, $2000-3000 per hectare; and conversion of primary forest, $4000-4400 per hectare *(Brown and Pearce, 1994)*. The carbon-sink attribute offers a far higher rate of return than any alternative form of current land use in tropical forests. Alternatively reckoned, to replace the carbon storage function of tropical forests (never mind temperate and boreal forests) could cost $3.7 trillion *(Panayotou and Ashton, 1992; see also Brown and Adger, 1994; Price and Willis, 1993)*.

4. Overall economic values

Remarkably in light of what is at stake overall, there have been scant attempts to come up with aggregate evaluations of forest outputs. Fortunately there have been some exploratory efforts for a few tropical-forest countries. The analytic methodology spans direct-use values such as timber, non-wood forest products, medicinal plants, hunting and fishing, recreation and tourism, and education; while indirect-use values include soil conservation, nutrient cycling, watershed protection, flood control, microclimatic effects and carbon sequestration. In addition, there is existence value, being the value conferred by assuring the survival of a resource. On top of all these, and perhaps the most important in the indefinitely long run, are option values, including potential values of future use. Using this conceptual construct, the environmental values of Mexico's forests are worth some $4 billion per year *(Adger et al., 1995)*. The total economic value of Costa Rica's 13,000 square kilometers of wildlands, the great majority of them being tropical forests, is between $1.7 billion and $3.7 billion annually. Only one third of the value accrues to Costa Rica, the rest going to the global community *(Castro, 1994; Constantino and Kishor, 1993; see also Pimentel et al., 1997c)*.

An alternative reckoning has recently been provided by Costanza et al., 1997. They look at all benefits derived from forests worldwide, principally raw materials, nutrient cycling, erosion control and climate regulation, plus another 10 categories. They come up with an overall value averaging almost $1000 per hectare per year for the 49 million square kilometers of forests, or a total of $4.7 trillion per year. If we are losing just one 500th of these benefits through loss of 1 percent of forests each year (the true amount is hotly disputed, though most experts agree it is at least 1 percent), that amounts to $9.4 billion.

Still another way to assess the situation is to recall the late 1997 fires that eliminated 20,000 square kilometers (an area larger than Vermont) of forests of Kalimantan (Borneo) and other parts of Indonesia. This gross mismanagement of forests lead to myriad costs: loss of commercial timber and non-wood products, health damages (more than 20 million people suffered smoke-related respiratory troubles), decline in crop yields as haze kept the region in day-long twilight, closure of airports and other communications, grandscale decline of amenity, and many other effects. All in all, the costs surely amounted to $20 billion, possibly much more *(Dudley, 1997; see also Abramowitz, 1998).*

All these calculations are preliminary and exploratory. They need to be firmed up with due despatch. Then, and only then, shall we be in a position to compute what is at stake as forests decline, and thus to calculate the environmental externalities—and hence the implict subsidies—involved in deforestation. As the above demonstrates, the externalities are large indeed, surely in the tens of billions of dollars and possibly in the hundreds of billions of dollars per year. In addition, there are significant social externalities, which remain almost entirely undocumented and quantified economically.

These externalities, were we able to pin them all down, should be counted as additional perverse subsidies. It is not possible to come up with an aggregate reckoning of the economic costs involved, but we can reasonably accept that the annual amount already surpasses (probably by a very long way) the $3 billion postulated for all documented and quantified perverse subsidies in the forestry sector worldwide. In fact, if it does not exceed $3 billion several times over already, it will do so as global warming starts to bite. For the sake of an interim assessment, albeit preliminary if not perfunctory, the amount is crudely estimated here to be at least another $3 billion per year. This brings perverse subsidies in forestry to a total of $6 billion per year. Plainly this is an exceedingly cautious and conservative estimate. The point is not pursued further here because even if we could demonstrate that perverse subsidies amount to as much as, say, $15 billion or even $50 billion today, that would not make much difference to the total in all six sectors combined.